AN ESSAY ON EPIC POETRY

AN ESSAY

ON

EPIC POETRY

(1782)

BY

WILLIAM HAYLEY

A FACSIMILE REPRODUCTION
WITH AN INTRODUCTION
BY

SISTER M. CELESTE WILLIAMSON, SSJ

GAINESVILLE, FLORIDA

SCHOLARS' FACSIMILES & REPRINTS

1968

SCHOLARS' FACSIMILES & REPRINTS
1605 N.W. 14TH AVENUE
GAINESVILLE, FLORIDA, 32601, U.S.A.
HARRY R. WARFEL, GENERAL EDITOR

L. C. CATALOG CARD NUMBER: 68-17013

INTRODUCTION

William Hayley's *An Essay on Epic Poetry* was published June 22, 1782. Ostensibly a commentary in verse on the character and fortunes of the epic, the work goes far beyond the author's expressed intention and as "new" criticism makes some quite respectable contributions to the history of literary theory.

Curiously enough, Hayley wrote this serious and lengthy work at a time when many thoughtful readers were of the opinion that the epic in English was very close to its demise. After having been honored for countless generations as the most exalted and the most virile of all the "kinds," it had sunk by the latter part of the eighteenth century into an anemic languor—hardly able to hold its own against its rival in the narrative form, the sentimental novel. The reasons for this decline were many, but chief of them, Hayley believed, was "System" or the "Rules"—a code of principles by which epic poetry was to be corrected and disciplined by imitation of the ancients. The Rules governed such matters as fable and action, intention of moral instruction, unity, the probable, the marvelous, celestial machinery, appropriate heroes, and the like.

That some of these Rules rested on misinterpretation of the critical dicta of Aristotle, Cicero, Horace, and Longinus we now know; but for about a century the Rules and the critics who appealed to them as absolute authority constituted a force to be reckoned with. Hayley charged that the Rules, by curbing drastically the imagination and freedom of the poet, had drained the epic of its vitality and beauty, and, conversely, that they had drawn into the genre countless and long-since meaningless accretions of literary conventions and ornaments. Measured by the Rules, not even such favorite works as Ariosto's *Orlando Furioso,* Tasso's *Gerusalemme Liberata,* and Spenser's *Faerie Queene* could qualify as true epics, although earlier ages had regarded them as such. Even Homer and Virgil became the subjects of closer scrutiny as the qualities of their epics were examined, compared, and reëxamined from various approaches to ascertain which of them ranked as the greater genius. After Addison's *Spectator* essays on Milton (Nos. 267-309), and under the growing influence of converts to Longinus, Milton was occasionally compared with Homer and Virgil, for an increasing number of critics felt that the sublime character of his *Paradise Lost* placed him without question in their company. No one else was accorded such promotion, however, and time seemed to bear out Bishop Warburton's observation in his *Dissertation on the Sixth Book of the Aeneid,* that with Homer, Virgil, and Milton, "the grand scene was closed, and all farther improvements of the Epic at an end" (see Hayley, p. 120). It can be seen, then, that any modern author ambitious of attempting an epic was soon faced with a dilemma: to write according to the Rules and deliberately produce a bloodless thing, or to write freely according to his wealth of imagination and warmth of passion and risk being refused epic status at all. The modern author, under such conditions, quickly lost his fervor and ordinarily directed his creative genius to less demanding literary forms. It began to appear that the epic impulse, once so magnificent, would die out in England for lack of heroic authors. To rehabilitate the epic, to encourage new poets to resort to it, and to re-focus the image of the true critic, Hayley wrote *An Essay on Epic Poetry*.

At this juncture, it may be well to inquire about the man who presumed to try single-handed to alter the fate of an ancient literary genre which seemed already overwhelmed by mounting critical pressures. Who was Hayley? What preparation had he to warrant attempting such a task?

William Hayley (1745-1820) is today dismissed as a very minor writer who did his best work during the last quarter of the eighteenth century. This is a meager and colorless label for a man who, in Robert Southey's words, was "by grace of the public, king of the bards of Britain" in his day (See "Review of Hayley's Memoirs" in the *Quarterly Review, XXXI* [1825], 289). Although born to wealth and social position, he won fame as a hard-working professional man of letters. He was by turns poet, biographer, translator, playwright, and editor. He was also something of an artist, being particularly capable in miniature painting. He had been educated at Eton and Trinity Hall at Cambridge, but when he decided that Law was not his vocation, he left college without a degree and devoted himself to literature. He achieved his first pronounced success in poetry. His verse, particularly his Horatian epistles (of which *An Essay on Epic Poetry* is a good example), is controlled and carefully polished. Although some modern critics have thought him tamely didactic and without character, his contemporaries deemed him the true successor to Pope, worthy to be offered the Laureateship upon the death of Thomas Warton in 1790. Hayley declined the honor, however, reportedly because of his strong Whig sympathies.

During his long life, he exhibited almost a genius for friendship, attracting to his estate at Eartham in Sussex (an early biographer, Lower, characterized it as another Tusculum), a host of people whose names ranked high in the world of society as well as in that of art and letters. He numbered George Romney, John Flaxman, John Howard, Edward Gibbon, George O'Brien Wyndham, third Earl of Egremont, and William Cowper among his closest friends. Although he himself chose to be remembered as the friend and biographer of Cowper (thus he identified himself in the subtitle of his *Memoirs*), posterity has preferred to link him almost exclusively with William Blake, whose patron and employer he was for about three years. Ironically, Blake himself, through his unkind epigrams, and his biographers, through their zeal to enhance Blake's reputation, have done less than justice to Hayley. Although the fame of many of Hayley's friends now completely overshadows his own, it was the reverse during his life, except for Gibbon and Romney. It is difficult today to realize how much of a power the name "Hayley" was—a power to open exclusive social circles in London and Bath; to incite alert literary reviewers for periodicals to vie with one another in acclaiming his newest work; and to assist young writers and artists to professional success as much by their association with him as by the lavish favors and funds of his old-fashioned patronage. Thus it can be seen that when Hayley took up the cause of the epic in *An Essay on Epic Poetry,* he had a numerous and enthusiastic audience of recognized taste, already won over to grant him a hearing.

It should be understood, however, that Hayley was not merely a fashionable poet; he was a scholar. Of most evident advantage to him was his singularly rich background, due in great part to an unflagging interest in languages. His linguistic studies ranged through Latin, Greek, French, Italian, Spanish, Portuguese, and German, and left their mark on all his mature work, as one can see in *An Essay on Epic Poetry*. He was acutely aware of the treasures of wisdom and art at hand in the languages of other peoples and of other times, and to the end of his life he tried to interest others in them. He pursued his studies by literally shopping around the world for rare books and manuscripts through the good offices of his booksellers, of his friends, and even of members of the diplomatic corps. This penchant for languages and, of course, the resources of his magnificent library gave Hayley some distinct advantages, as he turned his attention to literary history and criticism. One was that his first-hand familiarity with epics of antiquity, and especially with those in medieval Latin and early vernaculars, lent authority to his opinions and comments, particularly in his case against the Rules. Another was that he was able to bring together in one place an assortment of pronouncements on writers, ancient or modern, and demonstrate the validity of his conclusions. This he did with such depth of erudition that it was the hallmark by which even his anonymous works were identified. Finally, his translations attracted considerable support for his epic theories, for his readers could explore new concepts of the epic (new, at least, to English readers) by means of the lengthy sections of Dante's *Inferno* and Ercilla's *La Araucana* which Hayley had inserted into the Notes to Epistle III of the *Epic Poetry*. These translations, together with some short poems and biographical sketches of

Dante, Petrarch, Camoens, and others are especially remarked here because they have a place in the history of the literature of translation which has largely gone unrecognized in eighteenth-century studies. Yet Robert Southey found them so significant in attracting young scholars to the study of romance languages, and so important to the inspiration of English romantic writers, that he did not hesitate to say, "A greater effect was produced upon the rising generation of scholars, by the Notes to his Essay on Epic Poetry, than by any other contemporary work, the Relics of Ancient Poetry alone excepted" (See *Ibid.*, XXXI, 283).

The experience which ultimately proved to be of immediate and practical value to the *Epic Poetry* was that of having, himself, written an epic, "The Charter" (although it was left unfinished), for the insights acquired in coping with the aesthetic and technical problems of the genre he was to explore played a large part in his effectiveness as a critic.

An Essay on Epic Poetry combines several literary traditions, but literary history in verse (here, one of the last and most elaborate of its kind) and literary criticism in Horatian epistles are the most significant. The transitional character of the work is immediately apparent, for even as Hayley proposes to liberate the modern epic poet from "oppressive awe" of the neoclassical Rules and to guide him through the maze of conflicting theories back to the sources of the epic, he is writing in heroic couplets, skillfully wrought. He argues that that epic which is representative of the spirit and ideals of the civilization that gave it birth is a better epic than one constructed according to a set of specifications—specifications which evolved in entirely different conditions of history and literature and have since become outmoded. Yet Hayley is no iconoclast.

He gives the classical writers, Homer, Virgil, Apollonius of Rhodes, and Lucan, their place of honor and affection, even while admitting to their august company writers of both modern times and romantic tendencies. Then, through both verse and notes, he moves the course of the epic out of antiquity, across the no-man's-land of medieval Latin heroic poetry of heterogeneous epic characteristics and national affiliations, into modern times. Not only does he indicate what he believes to be the most noteworthy of the vernacular epics, he also attempts to supply some critical apparatus for discussing them. Through such writers as Dante, Ariosto, Tasso, Boileau, Chaucer, Spenser, and Pope, Hayley widens the scope of the epic and approves as proper epic material history, satire, religion, and romantic love—all of which were deemed unsuitable according to the Rules. He assumes other innovations also: the texture of the verse may change from Milton's to Butler's; there may be double or triple rhyme, or no rhyme at all; form may be anything from blank verse, to couplets, to various stanza patterns. Finally, he admits unity of design to be as valid as unity of action.

The passage from classical to romantic attitudes and interests is smoothly maneuvered. Hayley argues that even within the group of epic writers of acknowledged classical orthodoxy there is more freedom in the matter of fable and action, in the character of the hero, and in the force of passion than the comparatively recent neoclassical critics had been willing to grant. He implies that the old, free-flowing epic impulse, first manifested in ancient times, has been choked off by prevailing conditions of oppression, critical as well as political, and has trickled into literary history. However, through the vernacular epics of other nations, it has broken out afresh and surges with new life, in newer modes, colored by the character of the people among whom it is found. It is only logical, Hayley thinks, that a similar renascence could be brought about in the English epic.

As he turns his regard toward the epic of the future, he has some strong convictions about directions it ought to take. One, for example, is toward more convincing character drawing, and he suggests that the modern epic writer would do well to study Nature—man himself—to probe the complexities of his mind and heart. Another direction, and one linked with character delineation, is toward a more meaningful type of action, and hence toward more closely-knit structure of the epic as a whole. He reasons that shearing away the entire convention of celestial machinery will produce a stronger narrative, for action will be more true to life and more satisfying to the reader when it is motivated by the characters themselves in their reaction to circumstances and to each other, rather than by the interference of supernatural beings. He also recommends another: raising women from minor figures, sometimes allegorical, to participation in the epic action as principal characters; this is allowed even in the ancients, as with Helen and Medea. Still another direction—and this Hayley regards as vital to the new epic—is the expression of the national spirit. The glory of England and proper homage to her heroic sons are the burden of many of his lines in *An Essay on Epic Poetry*. Much of this sentiment, of course, may have been only conformity to the tradition of *domestica facta* so ingrained in contemporary writers, but his emphasis on this point is particularly timely, in view of the war with the American Colonies then in progress.

With this, Hayley concludes his recommendations for improving the modern verse epic. It is ironic that those recommendations appeared beautifully developed, not in the epic, but in the historical novel of the next century, in the Waverley novels of Sir Walter Scott.

An Essay on Epic Poetry reveals Hayley's absorption in another matter, for complexities of a historical nature color his literary purposes. The reader need not proceed very far into the first epistle before he realizes that, in spite of the literary character and message of the work, its controlling idea is freedom. But it is a many-faceted freedom, and the fact that Hayley wrote under the shadow of the war with the American Colonies and of the political and social conflicts at home soon to culminate in the fall of Lord North's ministry, made him, in a sense, vulnerable to suspicion of revolutionary tendencies. Even the man he chose to address as his poem's patron, Rev. Mr. William Mason, was the contemporary poet most involved in problems of freedom, particularly in parliamentary reform, but more deeply and dangerously than Hayley could know.

For Hayley, the cause of the epic and the cause of freedom were allied, as they were in many cultivated minds of the 1770's and 1780's. Through Lucan, the epic had become the symbol of ancient republican ideals and aspirations, and eventually a vehicle of protest against oppression. With *An Essay on Epic Poetry*, Hayley advances the old concept to a new level, and with Parnassian-like perspective views man's continuing struggle for freedom of many kinds as epic in character. As an artist, he puts his work in a larger context than that usually adverted to by revolutionists, by positing freedom as the climate in which alone literature can thrive. He sees the necessity for freedom on various levels of reference: political freedom, the need for which is all around him and to which he can refer only covertly by ancient parallels because of the war hysteria; religious freedom, for the Gordon Riots of June 2-4, 1780, which he witnessed, are still fresh in his mind; freedom from critical tyranny in the form of System or Rules; freedom from poverty; finally, freedom from the evils attendant upon prejudice. Thus it can be seen that Hayley is committing himself to a course of protest—political, religious, aesthetic, and social; and in this he is a true revolutionist, but in a wider connotation than most of his contemporaries were aware of.

Exactly what Hayley's understanding of the term "freedom" was, is difficult to determine, for as the reader pursues his way through *An Essay on Epic Poetry*, he finds the concept varying slightly from epistle to epistle, according to the facet of freedom being explored in each. Certainly there are in it elements of hard, practical Whiggism as well as of transcendent faith in the constitutional liberties gained in the Glorious Revolution; but the ultimate source is an almost impelling desire for freedom (his "passion for freedom") which he found at hand, already fully developed, in his Greek and Latin masters. This in turn he intimately associates with the progress of Italian history; for Hayley, in his far-ranging medieval studies, has come to see the fight of the Italian city-states for freedom from tyranny as similar in principle to the struggles of the republics of Greece and Rome. This spirit of freedom he views as crossing into the literary expression of the peoples involved, and he accepts the major Italian epics as true epics, to be associated with their classical counterparts, and to be judged as representative of their own civilization, although it was a less heroic one.

Hayley regarded *An Essay on Epic Poetry* as undoubtedly his best work; certainly it best represents him as poet, critic, translator, and all-around scholar, for he never excelled the fine workmanship displayed in the quality of the verse, the sustained elevation of tone, or the erudition of the notes. More-over, within the framework of the epic, its development, and its renewal, he attempted some significant advances in literary theory. He made it his paramount aim to secure freedom as a climate in which an author could live and work and receive recognition. He was modern enough to perceive the emergence of a new mode of poetry and to approach it with an open mind, for he maintained that a poem was an artistic entity and that its own aesthetic needs should be considered before the demands of any hard and fast theory it was supposed to follow. He was also classicist enough and antiquarian enough to realize that the critical principles of centuries were basic to literature and learning, and should provide the foundation for any new venture.

The foregoing factors did not, however, make *An Essay on Epic Poetry* in itself "new" criticism. Neither did Hayley's ad-mission of a whole group—Dante, Chaucer, Spenser, Pope, and others to the sacrosanct society of Homer, Virgil, and Milton; nor his acceptance of such unwonted themes as romantic love, humor, and history as the materials of which proper epics are made; nor even the principle of freedom of composition. These were matters of significance to the literary theory of his own time, it is true; but what caused the book to be "new" was the fact that Hayley made of it the medium through which he promulgated attitudes more progressive than those which are usually associated with the epic: a demand for greater freedom of spirit and breadth of vision; a reappraisal of the resources of older cultures, but with a view to applying them to the enrich-ment of future literature; a willingness to experiment with forms and techniques; a sympathy with the very effort of growth and process. Furthermore, he has very definitely associated his book with the critical traditions of Lowth, Hurd, and Thomas Warton for, by his very sizable sections on Italian and Spanish literature in both the text and the notes, he too has extended the boundaries of literary awareness.

The modern reader sees Hayley's achievement with a perspective his contemporaries, however progressive, could not attain to, and it is now apparent that some of the critical principles which are manifested in *An Essay on Epic Poetry* are perhaps seminal, at least significant in the light of later development, and are hence quite respectable contributions to the history of literary theory. In general, the book is a piece of documentary evidence, for it records one aspect of the process of transition by which the age of sensibility passed into the age of romanticism. In particular, it records the elements of change which Hayley found already present in the epics of antiquity and increasingly insistent in later ones—all of which we now recognize as having hastened the demise of the old formal epic as the eighteenth century knew it. At the same time, it is a hopeful work; it looks forward to yet unexplored and inviting prospects of a reborn and more vital narrative genre.

Sister M. Celeste Williamson, SSJ

Mater Dei College
Ogdensburg, New York
July 7, 1967

AN
ESSAY
ON
EPIC POETRY;

IN FIVE EPISTLES

TO THE REV^D. M^R. MASON.

WITH

NOTES.

——

———— Vatibus addere calcar
Ut ſtudio majore petant Helicona virentem. HOR.

——

BY WILLIAM HAYLEY, Esq.

LONDON:

PRINTED FOR J. DODSLEY, IN PALL-MALL.

M.DCC.LXXXII.

EPISTLE

THE FIRST.

A R G U M E N T

OF THE FIRST EPISTLE.

Introduction.—Design of the Poem to remove prejudices which obstruct the cultivation of Epic writing.—Origin of Poetry.—Honors paid to its infancy.—Homer the first Poet remaining.—Difficulty of the question why he had no Successor in Greece.—Remark of a celebrated Writer, that as Criticism flourishes Poetry declines.— Defence of Critics.—Danger of a bigoted acquiescence in critical Systems—and of a Poet's criticising his own works.—Advantages of Friendship and Study of the higher Poets.

EPISTLE I.

PERISH that critic pride, which oft has hurl'd
   Its empty thunders o'er the Epic world;
Which, eager to extend its mimic reign,
Would bind free Fancy in a fervile chain;
With papal rage the eye of Genius blind,   5
And bar the gates of Glory on the mind!
  Such dark decrees have letter'd Bigots penn'd *,
Yet feiz'd that honor'd name, the Poet's Friend.
But Learning from her page their laws will blot;
Scorn'd be their arrogance! their name forgot!   10
Th' indignant Bard, abhorring bafe controul,
Seeks the juft Critic of congenial foul.
Say! MASON, Judge and Mafter of the Lyre!
Harmonious Chief of Britain's living Choir,

* Ver. 7. See NOTE I.

                Say!

Say! wilt Thou liſten to his weaker ſtrains,   15
Who pants to range round Fancy's rich domains;
To vindicate her empire, and diſown
Proud Syſtem, ſeated on her injur'd throne?
Come! while thy Muſe, contented with applauſe,
Gives to her graceful ſong a little pauſe,   20
Enjoying triumphs paſt; at leiſure laid
In thy ſweet Garden's variegated ſhade,
Or fondly hanging on ſome favorite Oak
That Harp, whoſe notes the fate of Mona ſpoke,
Strung by the ſacred Druid's ſocial band,   25
And wiſely truſted to thy kindred hand!
Come! for thy liberal and ingenuous heart
Can aid a Brother in this magic art;
Let us, and Freedom be our guide, explore
The higheſt province of poetic lore,   30
Free the young Bard from that oppreſſive awe,
Which feels Opinion's rule as Reaſon's law,
And from his ſpirit bid vain fears depart,
Of weaken'd Nature and exhauſted Art!
Phantoms! that literary ſpleen conceives!   35
Dullneſs adopts, and Indolence believes!

While

While with advent'rous ftep we wind along
Th' expanfive regions of Heroic fong,
From different fources let our fearch explain
Why few the Chieftains of this wide domain.   40
Haply, infpiriting poetic youth,
Our verfe may prove this animating truth,
That Poefy's fublime, neglected field
May ftill new laurels to Ambition yield ;
Her Epic trumpet, in a modern hand,   45
Still make the fpirit glow, the heart expand.
Be fuch our doctrine! our enlivening aim
The Mufe's honor, and our Country's fame!
    Thou firft and faireft of the focial Arts!
Sovereign of liberal fouls, and feeling hearts,   50
If, in devotion to thy heavenly charms,
I clafp'd thy altar with my infant arms,
For thee neglected the wide field of wealth,
The toils of int'reft, and the fports of health,
Enchanting Poefy! that zeal repay   55
With powers to fing thy univerfal fway!
To trace thy progrefs from thy diftant birth,
Heaven's pure defcendant! dear delight of Earth!
                                        Charm

Charm of all regions ! to no age confin'd !
The prime ennobler of th' afpiring mind !   60
   Nor will thy dignity, fweet Power ! difdain
What Fiction utters in her idle ftrain,
Thy fportive Friend ! who, mocking folemn Truth,
Tells her fond tales of thy untutor'd youth.
As wrong'd Latona (fo her tale begins)   65
To Delphos travell'd with her youthful twins ;
Th' envenom'd Python, with terrific fway,
Crofs'd the fair Goddefs in her deftin'd way :
The heavenly parent, in the wild alarm,
Her little Dian in her anxious arm,   70
High on a ftone, which fhe in terror trod,
Cried to her filial guard, the Archer God,
Bidding with force, that fpoke the Mother's heart,
Her young Apollo launch his ready dart ;
In meafur'd founds her rapid mandate flow'd,   75
The firft foundation of the future Ode !
Thus, at their banquets, fabling Greeks rehearfe *
The fancied origin of facred Verfe :

        * Ver. 77. See NOTE II.

                          And

And though cold Reafon may with fcorn affail,
Or turn contemptuous from their fimple tale,   80
Yet, Poefy! thy fifter Art may ftoop
From this weak fketch to paint th' impaffion'd group.
Though tafte refin'd to modern Verfe deny
The hacknied pageants of the Pagan fky,
Their finking radiance ftill the Canvafs warms,   85
Painting ftill glories in their graceful forms;
Nor canft thou envy, if the world agree
To grant thy Sifter claims denied to thee;
For thee, the happier Art! the elder-born!
Superior rights and dearer charms adorn: 90
Confin'd fhe catches, with obfervance keen,
Her fingle moment of the changeful fcene;
But thou, endu'd with energy fublime,
Unqueftion'd arbiter of fpace and time!
Canft join the diftant, the unknown create,   95
And, while Exiftence yields thee all her ftate,
On the aftonifh'd mind profufely pour
Myriads of forms, that Fancy muft adore.
Yet of thy boundlefs power the deareft part
Is firm poffeffion of the feeling Heart: 100

No progeny of Chance, by Labor taught,
No flow-form'd creature of scholaftic thought,
The child of Paffion thou ! thy lyre she ftrung,
To her parental notes she tun'd thy tongue ;
Gave thee her boldeft fwell, her fofteft tone,   105
And made the compafs of her voice thy own.

    To Admiration, fource of joy refin'd !
Chafte, lovely mover of the fimple mind !
To her, though fceptics, in their pride, declaim,
With many an infult, on her injur'd name ;   110
To her, fweet Poefy ! we owe thy birth,
Thou firft encomiaft of the fruitful Earth !
By her infpir'd, the earlieft mortal found
The ear-delighting charm of meafur'd found ;
He hail'd the Maker of a world fo fair,   115
And the firft accent of his fong was prayer.
O, moft attractive of thofe airy Powers,
Who moft illuminate Man's chequer'd hours !
Is there an Art, in all the group divine,
Whofe dawn of Being muft not yield to thine ?   120
Religion's felf, whofe provident controul
Takes from fierce Man his anarchy of foul,

She

She o'er thy youth with fond affection hung,
And borrow'd music from thy infant tongue.
Law, sterner Law, whose potent voice imprest   125
Severest terror on the human breast,
With thy fresh flow'rs her aweful figure crown'd,
And spoke her mandate in thy softer sound.
E'en cold Philosophy, whom later days
Saw thy mean rival, envious of thy praise;   130
Who clos'd against thee her ungrateful arms,
And urg'd her Plato to defame thy charms;
She from thy childhood gain'd no fruitless aid,
From thee she learnt her talent to persuade.
Gay Nature view'd thee with a smiling glance,   135
The Graces round thee fram'd the frolic dance:
And well might festive Joy thy favor court;
Thy song turn'd strife to peace, and toil to sport.
Exhausted Vigor at thy voice reviv'd,
And Mirth from thee her dearest charm deriv'd.   140
Triumphant Love, in thy alliance blest,
Enlarg'd his empire o'er the gentle breast;
His torch assum'd new lustre from thy breath,
And his clear flame defied the clouds of death.

C   But

But of the splendid train, who felt thy sway,   145
Or drew existence from thy vital ray,
Glory, with fondest zeal, proclaim'd thy might,
And hail'd thee victor of oblivious Night.
Her martial trumpet to thy hand she gave,
At once to quicken, and reward the Brave: 150
It sounds—his blood the kindling Hero pays,
A cheap and ready price for thy eternal praise!
Tho' selfish Fear th' immortal strain deride,
And mock the Warrior's wish as frantic pride!

   Ye gallant, haplefs Dead of distant time,   155
Whose fame has perish'd unembalm'd in rhyme,
As thro' the desert air your ashes fly,
In Fancy's ear the nameless atoms cry,
" To us, unhappy! cruel Fates refuse
" The well-earn'd record of th' applauding Muse." 160
Blest are those Chiefs, who, blazon'd on her roll,
Still waken virtue in each kindred soul;
Their bright existence still on earth prolong,
And shine for ever in the deathless song.
Yet oft Oblivion, in a treacherous shade,   165
Has sunk the tuneful rites to Valor paid;

                                Her

Her palfied lips refufing to rehearfe
The facred, old, traditionary verfe.

As well the curious eye, with keen defire,
Might hope to catch that fpark of vital fire,   170
Which firft thro' Chaos fhot a fudden light,
And quicken'd Nature in its tranfient flight;
As the fond ear to catch the fleeting note,
Which on the ravifh'd air was heard to float,
When firft the Mufe her Epic ftrain began,   175
And every lift'ning Chief grew more than Man.

But, as the Ruler of the new born day
From Chaos rofe, in glory's rich array;
So from deep fhades, impenetrably ftrong,
That fhroud the darken'd world of antient fong,   180
Bright HOMER burfts, magnificently clear,
The folar Lord of that poetic fphere;
Before whofe blaze, in wide luxuriance fpread,
Each Grecian Star hides his diminifh'd head;
Whofe beams departed yet enchant the fight,   185
In Latium's fofter, chafte, reflected light.

Say ye! whofe curious philofophic eye
Searches the depth where Nature's fecrets lie;

Ye, who can tell, how her capricious fit
Directs the flow and ebb of human wit,   190
And why, obedient to her quick command,
Spring-tides of Genius now enrich her fav'rite land,
Now fink, by her to different climes affign'd,
And only leave fome worthlefs weeds behind !
Say ! why in Greece, unrival'd and alone,   195
The Sovereign Poet grac'd his Epic throne ?
Why did the realm that echoed his renown,
Produce no kindred heir to claim his crown ?
If, as the liberal mind delights to think,
Fancy's rich flow'rs their vital effence drink   200
From Liberty's pure ftreams, that largely roll
Their quick'ning virtue thro' the Poet's foul;
Why, in the period when this Friend of Earth
Made Greece the model of heroic worth,
And faw her votaries act, beneath her fway,   205
Scenes more fublime than Fiction can difplay,
Why did the Epic Mufe's filent lyre *
Shrink from thofe feats that fummon'd all her fire ?
Or if, as courtly Theorifts maintain,
The Mufes revel in a Monarch's reign ;   210

* Ver. 207. See NOTE III.

Why,

Why, when young Ammon's soul, athirſt for fame,
Call'd every Art to celebrate his name;
When ready Painting, at his ſovereign nod,
With aweful thunder arm'd this mimic God;
Why did coy Poeſy, tho' fondly woo'd,   215
Refuſe that dearer ſmile for which he ſued,
And ſee him ſhed, in martial Honor's bloom,
The tear of envy on Achilles' tomb?

In vain would Reaſon thoſe nice queſtions ſolve,
Which the fine play of mental powers involve: 220
In Bards of ancient time, with genius fraught,
What mind can trace how thought engender'd thought,
How little hints awak'd the large deſign,
And ſubtle Fancy ſpun her variegated line?
Yet ſober Critics, of no vulgar note,   225
But ſuch as Learning's ſons are proud to quote,
The progreſs of Homeric verſe explain,
As if their ſouls had lodg'd in Homer's brain.
Laughs not the ſpirit of poetic frame,
However ſlightly warm'd by Fancy's flame,   230
When grave Boſſu by Syſtem's ſtudied laws *
The Grecian Bard's ideal picture draws,

* Ver. 231. See NOTE IV.

And

And wifely tells us, that his Song arofe
As the good Parfon's quiet Sermon grows;
Who, while his eafy thoughts no preffure find   235
From hofts of images that croud the mind,
Firft calmly fettles on fome moral text,
Then creeps—from one divifion—to the next?
Nor, if poetic minds more flowly drudge
Thro' the cold comments of this Gallic judge,   240
Will their indignant fpirit lefs deride
That fubtle Pedant's more prefumptive pride,
Whofe bloated page, with arrogance replete,
Imputes to VIRGIL his own dark conceit: *
And from the tortur'd Poet dares to draw   245
That latent fenfe, which HORACE never faw;
Which, if on folid proof more ftrongly built,
Muft brand the injur'd Bard with impious guilt.
     While fuch Dictators their vain efforts wafte
In the dark vifions of diftemper'd Tafte,   250
Let us that pleafing, happier light purfue,
Which beams benignant from the milder few;

* Ver. 244. See NOTE V.

1

Who,

Who, juftly confcious of the doubts that ftart
In all nice queftions on each finer Art,
With modeft doubt affign each likely caufe,   255
But dare to dictate no decifive laws!
'Tis faid by one, who, with this candid claim, *
Has gain'd no fading wreath of Critic fame,
Who, fondly lift'ning to her various rhyme,
Has mark'd the Mufe's ftep thro' many a clime ;   260
That, where the fettled Rules of Writing fpread,
Where Learning's code of Critic Law is read,
Tho' other treafures deck th' enlighten'd fhore,
The germs of Fancy ripen there no more.
Are Critics then, that bold, imperious tribe !   265
The Guards of Genius, who his path prefcribe ;
Are they like Vifirs in an Eaftern court,
Who fap the very power they fhould fupport ?
Whofe fpecious wiles the royal mind unnerve,
And fink the monarch they pretend to ferve.   270
No ! of their value higher far I deem ;
And prize their ufeful toil with fond efteem.

When

When LowTH's firm fpirit leads him to explore
The hallow'd confines of Hebraic lore,
When his free pages, luminous and bold,   275
The glorious end of Poefy unfold,
Affert her powers, her dignity defend,
And fpeak her, as fhe is, fair Freedom's friend;
When thus he fhines his mitred Peers above,
I view his warmth with reverential love;   280
Proud, if my verfe may catch reflected light
From the rich fplendor of a mind fo bright.

  Bleft be the names, to no vain fyftem tied,
Who render Learning's blaze an ufeful guide,
A friendly beacon, rais'd on high to teach   285
The wand'ring bark to fhun the fhallow beach.
But O! ye noble, and afpiring few,
Whofe ardent fouls poetic fame purfue,
Ye, on whom fmiling Heaven, perfection's fource,
Seems to beftow unlimitable force,   290
The inborn vigor of your fouls defend,
Nor lean too fondly on the firmeft friend!
Genius may fink on Criticifm's breaft,
By weak dependance on her truth oppreft,

9   Sleep

Sleep on her lap, and ftretch his lifelefs length,   295
Shorn by her foothing hand of all his ftrength.

Thou wilt not, MASON ! thou, whofe generous heart
Muft feel that Freedom is the foul of Art,
Thou wilt not hold me arrogant or vain,
If I advife the young poetic train   300
To deem infallible no Critic's word ;
Not e'en the dictates of thy Attic HURD :
No ! not the Stagyrite's unqueftion'd page,
The Sire of Critics, fanctified by age !
The nobleft minds, with folid reafon bleft,   305
Who feel that faculty above the reft,
Who argue on thofe arts they never try,
Exalt that Reafon they fo oft apply,
Till in its pride, with tyrannous controul,
It crufh the kindred talents of the foul ;   310
And hence, in every Art, will fyftems rife,
Which Fancy muft furvey with angry eyes ;
And at the lightning of her fcornful fmile,
In frequent ruin finks the labor'd pile.

How oft, my ROMNEY ! have I known thy vein   315
Swell with indignant heat and gen'rous pain,

D   To

To hear, in terms both arrogant and tame,
Some reas'ning Pedant on thy Art declaim:
Its laws and limits when his sovereign taste
With firm precision has minutely trac'd,   320
And in the close of a decisive speech
Pronounc'd some point beyond the Pencil's reach,
How has thy Genius, by one rapid stroke,
Refuted all the sapient things he spoke!
Thy Canvass placing, in the clearest light,   325
His own Impossible before his sight!
O might the Bard who loves thy mental fire,
Who to thy fame attun'd his early lyre,
Learn from thy Genius, when dull Fops decide,
So to refute their systematic pride!   330
Let him, at least, succeeding Poets warn
To view the Pedant's lore with doubt, or scorn,
And e'en to question, with a spirit free,
Establish'd Critics of the first degree!
Among the names that Judgment loves to praise,   335
The pride of ancient, or of modern days;
What Laws of Poesy can Learning shew
Above the Critic song of sage DESPREAUX?

His

His fancy elegant, his judgment nice,
His method eafy, and his ftyle concife;   340
The Bard of Reafon, with her vigor fraught,
Her pureft doctrine he divinely taught;
Nor taught in vain! His precept clear and chafte
Reform'd the errors of corrupted Tafte;
And French Imagination, who was bit   345
By that Tarantula, diftorted Wit,
Ceafing her antie gambols to rehearfe,
Bleft the pure magic of his healing verfe:
With his loud fame applauding Europe rung,
And his juft praife a rival Poet fung.   350
Yet, had this Friend of Verfe-devoted Youth,
This tuneful Teacher of Poetic truth,
Had he but chanc'd his doctrine to diffufe
Ere Milton commun'd with his facred Mufe;
And could that Englifh, felf-dependant foul,   355
Born with fuch energy as mocks controul,
Could his high fpirit, with fubmiffive awe,
Have ftoop'd to liften to a Gallic Law;

D 2   His

His hallow'd fubject, by that Law forbid *,
Might ftill have laid in filent darknefs hid,   360
And, this bright Sun not rifing in our fphere,
Homer had wanted ftill his true compeer.

From hence let Genius to himfelf be juft,
Hence learn, ye Bards, a liberal diftruft;
Whene'er 'tis faid, by Syftem's haughty Son,   365
That what He cannot do, can ne'er be done,
'Tis Fancy's right th' exalted throne to prefs,
Whofe height proud Syftem can but blindly guefs,
Springs, whofe exiftence fhe denies, unlock,
And call rich torrents from the flinty rock.   370
Let the true Poet, who would build a name
In noble rivalfhip of antient fame,
When he would plan, to triumph over Time,
The fplendid fabric of his lofty rhyme,
Let him the pride of Conftantine affume,   375
Th' imperial Founder of the fecond Rome,
Who fcorn'd all limits to his work affign'd, †
Save by th' infpiring God who rul'd his mind;

* Ver. 359. See NOTE VII.
† Ver. 377. See NOTE VIII.

5   Or,

Or, like the fabled * Jove, to afcertain
The doubtful confines of his wide domain,   380
Two Eagles let him fend of equal wing,
Whofe different flight may form a perfect ring,
And, at the point where Senfe and Fancy meet,
There fafely bold, and though fublime difcreet,
His fame's foundation let him firmly lay,   385
Nor dread the danger of difputed fway !

   Yet, if the Bard to glory muft afpire
By free exertion of unborrow'd fire,
Nor, like the Claffic Bigot, vainly deem
No modern Mufe can challenge juft efteem,   390
Unlefs her robe in every fold be preft
To fall precifely like the Grecian veft ;
If the blind notion he muft boldly fhun,
That Beauty's countlefs forms are only one,
And not, when Fancy, from her magic hoard,   395
Would blindly bring him treafures unexplor'd,

* Jupiter, ut perhibent, fpatium quum difcere vellet
    Naturæ, regni nefcius ipfe fui,
Armigeros utrimque duos æqualibus alis
    Mifit ab Eois Occiduifque plagis.
Parnaffus geminos fertur junxiffe volatus ;
    Contulit alternas Pythius axis aves.   CLAUDIAN.

Snap

Snap her light wand, and force her hand to bear
The heavier Compass, and the formal Square;
Let him no less their dangerous pride decline,
Who singly criticise their own design.   400
In that nice toil what various perils lurk !
Not Pride alone may mar the needful work;
But foes more common to the feeling nerve,
Where Taste and Genius dwell with coy Reserve,
The sickly Doubt, with modest weakness fraught,   405
The languid Tedium of o'erlabour'd thought,
The Pain to feel the growing work behind
The finish'd model in the forming mind;
These foes, that oft the Poet's bosom pierce,
These ! that condemn'd to fire Virgilian Verse,   410
Prove that the Bard, a bold, yet trembling elf,
Should find a Critic firmer than himself.
But what fine Spirit will assume the Judge,
Patient thro' all this irksome toil to drudge?
'Tis here, O Friendship ! here thy glories shine;   415
The hard, th' important task is only thine;
For thou alone canst all the powers unite,
That justly make it thy peculiar right:

9   Thine

Thine the fixt eye, which at no foible winks;
Thine the warm zeal, which utters all it thinks,   420
In thofe fweet tones, that hafty Spleen difarm,
That give to painful Truth a winning charm,
And the quick hand of lift'ning Genius teach,
To grafp that excellence he burns to reach:
Thou fweet Subduer of all mental ftrife!   425
Thou Source of vigor! thou Support of life!
Nor Art nor Science could delight or live,
Without that energy thy counfels give:
Genius himfelf muft fink in dumb defpair,
Unbleft, uncherifh'd by thy cheering care.   430

   Nor let the Bard, elate with youthful fire,
When Fancy to his hand prefents the lyre,
When her ftrong plumes his foaring fpirit lift,
When Friendfhip, Heaven's more high and holy gift,
With zeal angelic prompts his daring flight,   435
And round him darts her doubt-difpelling light,
Let him not then, by Vanity betray'd,
Look with unjuft contempt on Learning's aid!
But, as th' advent'rous Seaman, to attain
That bright renown which great Difcoverers gain,   440

Confults

Confults the conduct of each gallant name,
Who fail'd before him in that chace of Fame,
Reviews, with frequent glance, their ufeful chart,
Marks all their aims, and fathoms all their art,
So let the Poet trace *their* happy courfe,   445
So bravely emulate *their* mental force,
Whofe daring fouls, from many a different clime,
Have nobly ventur'd on the fea of Rhyme !
Led by no fear, his fwelling fail to flack,
Let him, with eager eyes, purfue the track ;   450
Not like a Pirate, with infidious views
To plunder every veffel he purfues,
But with juft hope to find yet farther fhores,
And pafs each rival he almoft adores !

END OF THE FIRST EPISTLE.

EPISTLE

EPISTLE

THE SECOND.

A R G U M E N T

OF THE SECOND EPISTLE.

Character of Ancient Poets—Homer—Apollonius Rhodius
—Virgil—Lucan.

EPISTLE II.

HAIL, mighty Father of the Epic line,
Thou vaſt, prolific, intellectual Mine,
Where veins of ancient and of modern gold,
The wealth of each poetic world, have roll'd !
Great Bard of Greece, whoſe ever-during Verſe   5
All ages venerate, all tongues rehearſe ;
Could blind idolatry be juſtly paid,
To aught of mental power by man diſplay'd,
To thee, thou Sire of ſoul-exalting Song,
That boundleſs worſhip might to thee belong ;   10
For, as thy Jove, on his Olympian throne,
In his unrivall'd ſway exults alone,
Commanding Nature by his awful nod,
In high ſecluſion from each humbler God ;
So ſhines thy Genius thro' the cloud of years,   15
Exalted far above thy Pagan peers

By

By the rich ſplendor of creative fire,

And the deep thunder of thy martial lyre;

The conſcious world confeſſes thy controul,

And hails thee Sovereign of the kindling ſoul.   20

    Yet, could thy mortal ſhape reviſit earth,

How would it move, great Bard! thy ſcornful mirth,

To hear vain Pedants to thy Verſe aſſign

Scholaſtic thoughts that never could be thine;

To hear the quaint conceits of modern Pride   25

Blaſpheme thy Fancy and thy Taſte deride?

When thus in Vanity's capricious fit,

We ſee thy fame traduc'd by Gallic wit, *

We ſee a Dwarf, who dares his foot to reſt

On a recumbent Giant's ample cheſt,   30

And, lifting his pert form to public ſight,

Boaſts, like a child, his own ſuperior height.

But neither envious Wit's malignant craft,

Tho' arm'd with Ridicule's envenom'd ſhaft,

Nor fickle Faſhion's more tyrannic ſway,   35

Whoſe varying voice the ſons of Earth obey,

* Ver. 28. See NOTE I.

Can

Can fhake the folid bafe of thy renown,
Or blaft the verdure of thy Laurel crown.
Tho' Time, who from his many-colour'd wings,
Scatters ten thoufand fhades o'er human things,   40
Has wrought unnumber'd changes fince thy birth,
And given new features to the face of earth;
Tho' all thy Gods who fhook the ftarry pole,
Unqueftion'd Rulers of the Pagan foul,
Are fallen with their fanes, in ruin hurl'd,   45
Their worfhip vanifh'd from th' enlighten'd world;
Still its immortal force thy Song retains,
Still rules obedient man and fires his glowing veins;
For Nature's felf, that great and conftant power,
One and the fame thro' every changing hour,   50
Gave thee each fecret of her reign to pierce,
And ftampt her fignet on thy facred Verfe;
That aweful fignet, whofe imperial fway
No age difputes, no regions difobey;
For at its fight the fubject paffions ftart,   55
And open all the paffes of the heart.

   'Twas Nature taught thy Genius to difplay
That hoft of Characters who grace thy lay;

So

So richly varied and fo vaft the ftore,

Her plaftic hand can hardly model more: 60

'Twas Nature, nobleft of poetic Guides,

Gave thee thy flowing Verfe, whofe copious tides

Gufhing luxuriant from high Fancy's fource,

By no vain art diverted in their courfe,

With fplendid eafe, with fimple grandeur roll,   65

Spread their free wealth, and fertilize the foul.

   There are, whom blind and erring zeal betrays

To wound thy Genius with ill-judging praife;

Who rafhly deem thee of all Arts the fire,

Who draw dull fmoke from thy refplendent fire,   70

Pretend thy fancied Miracles to pierce,

And form quaint riddles of thy cleareft Verfe;

Blind to thofe brighter charms and purer worth,

Which make thy Lays the lafting joy of earth.

For why has every age with fond acclaim   75

Swell'd the loud note of thy increafing fame?

Not that cold Study may from thee deduce

Vain codes of myftic lore and laws abftrufe;

But that thy Song prefents, like folar light,

A world in action to th' enraptur'd fight;   80

That,

That, with a force beyond th' enervate rules
Of tame Philofophy's pedantic Schools,
Thy living Images inftruct mankind,
Mould the juft heart, and fire th' heroic mind.
E'en SOCRATES himfelf, that pureft Sage, *   85
Imbib'd his Wifdom from thy moral page ;
And haply Greece, the Wonder of the Earth
For feats of martial fire and civic worth,
That glorious Land, of nobleft minds the nurfe,
Owes her unrivall'd race to thy infpiring Verfe ;   90
For O, what Greek, who in his youthful vein
Had felt thy foul-invigorating ftrain,
Who that had caught, amid the feftive throng,
The public leffon of thy patriot Song,
Could ever ceafe to feel his bofom fwell   95
With zeal to dare, and paffion to excel.
In thee thy grateful country juftly prais'd
The nobleft Teacher of the tribes fhe rais'd ;
Thy voice, which doubly gave her fame to laft,
Form'd future Heroes, while it fung the paft.   100
    What deep regret thy fond admirers feel,
That mythologic clouds thy life conceal ;

* Ver. 85. See NOTE II.

That,

That, like a diftant God, thou'rt darkly fhewn,
Felt in thy Works, but in Thyfelf unknown!
Perchance the fhades that hide thy mortal days   105
From keen Affection's difappointed gaze,
And that Idolatry, fo fondly proud,
With which thy Country to thy genius bow'd,
Might form the caufe why, kindling with thy fire,
No Grecian rival ftruck thy Epic lyre;   110
Perchance, not feeing how thy fteps were train'd,
How they the fummit of Parnaffus gain'd,
On thy oppreffive Glory's flaming pride
Young Emulation gaz'd, and gazing died.

 The Mufes of the Attic Stage impart   115
To many a Votary their kindred art;
And fhe who bids the Theban Eagle bear
Her lyric thunder thro' the ftormy air,
How high foe'er fhe leads his daring flight, *
Guides his bold rivals to an equal height.   120
Of all the Grecian Bards in Glory's race,
'Tis thine alone, by thy unequall'd pace,

* Ver. 119. See NOTE III.

To

To reach the goal with loud applaufe, and hear
No ftep approaching thine, no rival near.
Yet may not Judgment, with fevere difdain,   125
Slight the young RHODIAN's variegated ftrain; *
Tho' with lefs force he ftrike an humbler fhell,
Beneath his hand the notes of Paffion fwell.
His tender Genius, with alluring art,
Difplays the tumult of the Virgin's heart,   130
When Love, like quivering rays that never reft,
Darts thro' each vein, and vibrates in her breaft.
Tho' Nature feel his Verfe, tho' fhe declare
Medea's magic is ftill potent there,
Yet Fancy fees the flighted Poet rove   135
In penfive anger thro' th' Elyfian Grove.
From Critic fhades, whofe fupercilious priae
His Song neglected, or his Powers decried,
He turns indignant—unoppreft by fears,
Behold, he feeks the fentence of his Peers.   140
See their juft band his honeft claim allow,
See pleafure lighten on his laurell'd brow;

* Ver. 126. See NOTE IV.

F   He

He foars the Critic's cold contempt above,
For VIRGIL greets him with fraternal love !

Hail, thou rich Column, on whofe high-wrought frame
The Roman Mufe fupports her Epic fame !   146
Hail, great Magician, whofe illufive charms
Gave pleafing luftre to a Tyrant's arms,
To Jove's pure fceptre turn'd his iron rod,
And made the Homicide a Guardian God !   150
Hail, wond'rous Bard, to Glory's temple led
Thro' paths that Genius rarely deigns to tread ;
For Imitation, fhe whofe fyren fong
Betrays the fkillful and unnerves the ftrong,
Preferving thee on her perfidious fhore,   155
Where many a Poet had been wreck'd before,
Led thee to heights that charm th' aftonifh'd eye,
And with Invention's heaven in fplendor vie.
As Rome herfelf, by long unwearied toil,
Glean'd the fair produce of each foreign foil ;   160
From all her wide Dominion's various parts
Borrow'd their laws, their ufages, their arts ;
Imported knowledge from each adverfe zone,
And made the wifdom of the world her own :

         Thy

Thy patient fpirit thus, from every Bard   165
Whofe mental riches won thy juft regard,
Drew various treafure ; which thy fkill refin'd,
And in the fabric of thy Verfe combin'd.
It was thy glory, as thy fond defire,
To echo the fweet notes of HOMER's lyre ;   170
But with an art thy hand alone can reach,
An art that has endear'd the ftrain of each.
So the young Nymph, whofe tender arms embrace
An elder Sifter of enchanting grace,
Though form'd herfelf with every power to pleafe,   175
By genuine character and native eafe,
Yet fondly copies from her favourite Fair
Her mien, her motion, her attractive air,
Her robe's nice fhape, her riband's pleafing hue,
And every ornament that ftrikes the view ;   180
But fhe difplays, by imitative art,
So quick a fpirit, and fo foft a heart,
The graceful mimic while our eyes adore,
We think the model cannot charm us more :
Tho' feen together, each more lovely fhews,   185
And by comparifon their beauty grows.

Some Critics, to decide which Bard prevails,
Weigh them like Jove, but not in golden scales;
In their false balance th' injur'd GREEK they raise,
VIRGIL sinks loaded with their heavy praise. *   190
Ingenuous Bard, whose mental rays divine
Shaded by modest doubts more sweetly shine;
Thou whose last breath, unconscious of the wrong,.
Doom'd to destruction thy sublimest Song;
How dull their incense in thy sight must burn,   195
How must thy spirit with abhorrence turn
From their disgusting rites, who at thy shrine
Blaspheme thy Master's name, to honor thine!
More equal tribute, in their simpler flowers,
The Poets offer to your separate powers;   200
For all poetic eyes delight to view
Your different forms, and with devotion due
In each the radiant Delphic God they own,
By beauteous majesty distinctly shewn:
But they behold the lofty HOMER stand   205
The bright Colossus of the Rhodian land,

* Ver. 190. See NOTE V.

Beneath

Beneath whofe feet the waves fubmiffive roll,
Whofe towering head appears to prop the pole ;
Stupendous Image ! grand in every part,
And feeming far above the reach of mortal art.   210
In thee, thou lovely Mantuan Bard, appear
The fofter features of the Belvidere ;
That finifh'd grace which fafcinates all eyes,
Yet from the copying hand elufive flies :
Charms fo complete, by fuch pure fpirit warm'd,   215
They make lefs perfect beauty feem deform'd.

  O had thy Mufe, whofe decorating fkill
Could fpread rich foliage o'er the leaflefs hill ;
Had fhe, who knew with nicest hand to frame
The fweet unperifhable wreaths of Fame ;   220
Had fhe, exalted by a happier fate,
Virtue's free Herald, and no Slave of State,
Deck'd worthier fhrines with her unfading flower,
And given to Freedom what fhe gave to Power ;
Then with more keen delight and warmer praife   225
The world had liften'd to thy bolder lays ;
Perchance had ow'd to thee (a mighty debt)
Verfe where Perfection her bright feal had fet,
Where Art could nothing blame and Nature nought regret.

Of

Of coarfer form, with lefs pathetic charms,   230
Hating with Stoic pride a Tyrant's arms,
In the keen fervor of that florid time
When youthful Fancy pours her hafty rhyme,
When all the mind's luxuriant fhoots appear,
Untrimm'd by Art, by Intereft, or Fear,   235
See daring LUCAN for that wreath contend,
Which Freedom twines for her poetic friend.
'Tis thine, thou bold but injur'd Bard, 'tis thine!
Tho' Critic fpleen infult thy rougher line;
Tho' wrong'd thy Genius, and thy Name mifplac'd   240
By vain diftinctions of faftidious Tafte;
Indignant Freedom, with juft anger fir'd,
Shall guard the Poet whom herfelf infpir'd.
What tho' thy early, uncorrected page
Betrays fome marks of a degenerate age;   245
Tho' many a tumid point thy verfe contains,
Like warts projecting from Herculean veins;
Tho' like thy CATO thy ftern Mufe appear,
Her manners rigid, and her frown auftere;
Like him, ftill breathing Freedom's genuine flame,   250
Juftice her idol, Public Good her aim,

Well

Well she supplies her want of softer art
By all the sterling treasures of the heart;
By Energy, from Independance caught,
And the free Vigor of unborrow'd Thought.   255
Thou Bard most injur'd by malicious fate,
Could not thy Blood appease a Tyrant's hate?
Must He, still gall'd by thy poetic claim,
With falshood persecute thy moral fame?
Shall History's pen, to aid his vengeance won, *   260
Brand thee, brave Spirit, as an impious Son,
Who meanly fear'd to yield his vital flood,
And sought his safety by a Parent's blood?
Base calumny, at which Belief must halt,
And blind Credulity herself revolt.   265
Could that firm Youth become so vile a slave,
Whose voice new energy to virtue gave;
Whose Stoic soul all abject thoughts abhorr'd,
And own'd no sordid passion as its lord;
Who in the trying hour of mortal pain,   270
While life was ebbing from his open vein,
Alike unconscious of Remorse and Fear,
His heart unshaken, and his senses clear,

* Ver. 260. See NOTE VI.

Smil'd

Smil'd on his doom, and, like the fabled bird
Whose music on Meander's bank was heard,   275
Form'd into tuneful notes his parting breath,
And sung th' approaches of undreaded death?
Rise, thou wrong'd Bard, above Detraction's reach,
Whose arts in vain thy various worth impeach;
Enjoy that fame thy spirit knew to prize,   280
And view'd so fondly with prophetic eyes.
Tho' the nice Critics of fastidious France
Survey thy Song with many a scornful glance,
And as a Goth the kinder judge accuse,
Who with their great CORNEILLE commends thy Muse,
Let Britain, eager as the Lesbian State   286
To shield thy Pompey from the wrongs of Fate,
To thee with pride a fond attachment shew,
Thou Bard of Freedom, tho' the world's thy foe.
As keenly sensible of Beauty's sway,   290
Let our just isle such generous honor pay
To the fair partner of thy hapless life,
As Lesbos paid to Pompey's lovely Wife. *
Ye feeling Painters, who with genius warm
Delineate Virtue in her softest form,   295

* Ver. 293. See NOTE VII.

2

Let

Let ARGENTARIA on your canvaſs ſhine, *
A graceful mourner at her Poet's ſhrine;
For, nobly fearleſs of the Tyrant's hate,
She mourns her murder'd Bard in ſolemn ſtate;
With pious care ſhe decks his ſplendid tomb,   300
Where the dark Cypreſs ſheds its ſoothing gloom,
There frequent takes her ſolitary ſtand,
His dear Pharſalia in her faithful hand;
That hand, whoſe toil the Muſes ſtill rehearſe,
Which fondly copied his unfiniſh'd Verſe.   305
See, as ſhe bends before his recent urn,
See tender Grief to Adoration turn.
O lovely Mourner, could my Song beſtow
Unfading glory on thy generous woe,
Age after age thy virtue ſhould record,   310
And thou ſhould'ſt live immortal as thy Lord.
Him Liberty ſhall crown with endleſs praiſe,
True to her cauſe in Rome's degenerate days;
Him, like his Brutus, her fond eye regards,
And hails him as the laſt of Roman Bards.   315

* Ver. 296. See NOTE VIII.

END OF THE SECOND EPISTLE.

G   EPISTLE

EPISTLE

THE THIRD.

ARGUMENT

OF THE THIRD EPISTLE.

Sketch of the Northern and the Provençal Poetry.—The most distinguished Epic Poets of Italy, Spain, Portugal, France, and England.

EPISTLE III.

BLEST be the hand that with a generous care,
To the bright Crown which Learning loves to wear,
Reftores the Gem, whofe luftre, faint and pale,
Died in the fold of dark Oblivion's veil.
Such praife, O Mason! to the Bard is due,   5
In whofe fraternal guard thy Genius grew;
O'er whofe untimely grave thy Lyre has paid
Its juft devotion to a Brother's fhade:
And thus hereafter fhall the Britifh Mufe,
In Memory's fane the faireft tablet chufe,   10
To bid her fons your blended names admire,
The pride of Friendfhip's as of Fancy's choir.
  Thy modeft Gray, folicitous to pierce
The dark and diftant fource of modern Verfe,
By ftrings untried firft taught his Englifh Lyre   15
To reach the Gothic Harp's terrific fire:

The

The North's wild fpectres own his potent hand,
And Hell's nine portals at his voice expand ;
With new exiftence by his Verfe endued,
See Gothic Fable wakes her fhadowy brood,   20
Which, in the Runic rhymes of many a *Scald*,
With pleafing dread our Northern fires appall'd.

   Ye brave Progenitors, ye vigorous Source
Of modern Freedom and of Europe's force,
While your rude minds, athirft for martial ftrife,   25
Mock'd all the meaner arts of polifh'd life,
The Mufe ftill led you by her magic clue,
And from your favage ftrength new vigor drew.
In War's dire field your dauntlefs Bards appear'd,
Aloft their animating harps they rear'd,   30
Pour'd through the charging hoft their potent ftrain,
And fwell'd the fiery flood in Valor's vein.

   Souls thus infpir'd, in every fcene elate,
Defied the utmoft rage of adverfe fate ;
In tort'ring death the Royal Captive fang,   35
And fmiles of triumph hid his mortal pang. *

      * Ver. 36. See NOTE I.

Thus

Thus to brave ODIN's Songs, our Northern fire,
Rude, early framer of the modern Lyre,
Fierce Freedom gave an energy fublime,
Parent and Guardian of the Gothic Rhyme.   40
    While nurtur'd in the North's protecting arms,
The modern Mufe difplay'd her infant charms,
Like Jove's undaunted Child her fpirit glow'd,
And force Herculean in her cradle fhew'd;
Her native fcene in roughnefs fhe furpaft,   45
Her breath tempeftuous as the Northern blaft:
But, when to fofter climes the vagrant flew,
And bafk'd beneath a fky of azure hue;
When for her throne the flowery South fhe chofe,
And form'd her crown of the Provençal Rofe;   50
Warm'd by a brighter Sun's relaxing beams,
She tun'd her alter'd voice to tender themes:
Here her gay form a gaudier drefs affumes,
And fhines in Chivalry's imperial plumes;
Her votaries wear proud Honor's myftic glove,   55
And every lyre refounds Romantic Love;
Save when, to burft Oppreffion's mental chain,
Keen Satire mingles with this gallant train,

Strikes Priestly pride with Wit's vindictive flash,
And galls the ghostly Tyrant with her lash. *   60
Afraid of Poesy's expansive flood,
These early Bards along the shallows feud
In some light skiff; for on the depths untried
No full-trimm'd vessel floats in Epic pride.

As infants, eager for regard, abound   65
In sportive efforts of uncertain sound,
Before their little artless lips can reach
The harder elements of perfect speech;
So the young language of each modern clime
Rose by prelusive lays to lofty rhyme.   70
Thro' many an age, while, in the Convent bred,
O'er the chill'd mind scholastic darkness spread,
Those keener Spirits, who from Nature caught
The warmth that kindles to Poetic thought,
Betray'd, Ambition! by thy blind desire,   75
Struck with ill-fated zeal the Latian lyre, †
Tho' Discord's hand the jarring strings had crost,
And all the sweetness of their tone was lost.

* Ver. 60. See NOTE II.
† Ver. 76. See NOTE III.

At

At length, fair Italy, luxuriant land,

Where Art's rich flowers in earlieſt bloom expand, 80

Thy daring DANTE his wild Viſion ſung, *

And rais'd to Epic pomp his native Tongue.

Down Arno's ſtream his new-form'd muſic floats,

The proud vale echoing with his Tuſcan notes.

See the bold Bard now ſink and now aſcend, 85

Wherever Thought can pierce or Life extend;

In his wide circuit from Hell's drear abyſs,

Thro' purifying ſcenes to realms of perfect bliſs,

He ſeems begirt with all that airy throng,

Who brighten or debaſe the Poet's ſong. 90

Sublimeſt Fancy now directs his march

To opening worlds, through that infernal arch

O'er whoſe rough ſummit aweful words are read,

That freeze each entering ſoul with hopeleſs dread.

Now at her bidding his ſtrong numbers flow, 95

And rend the heart at Ugolino's woe;

While Nature's glory-giving tear bedews

A tale unrivall'd by the Grecian Muſe.

Now to thoſe notes that milder grief inſpire,

Pathetic Tenderneſs attunes his lyre, 100

* Ver. 81. See NOTE IV.

H   Which,

Which, foft as murmurs of the plaintive dove,
Tells the fad iffue of illicit love.
But all the worfe companions of his way
Soon into different founds his ductile voice betray :
Satiric Fury now appears his guide,   105
Thro' thorny paths of Enmity and Pride ;
Now quaint Conceit his wand'ring fteps mifleads
Thro' all the hideous forms that Folly breeds ;
Now Prieftly Dullnefs the loft Bard enfhrouds
In cold confufion and fcholaftic clouds.   110
Unequal Spirit ! in thy various ftrain,
With all their influence Light and Darknefs reign ;
In thy ftrange Verfe and wayward Theme alike
New forms of Beauty and Diforder ftrike ;
Extremes of Harmony and Difcord dwell,   115
The Seraph's mufic and the Demon's yell !
The patient Reader, to thy merit juft,
With tranfport glows, and fhudders with difguft.
Thy Failings fprung from thy difaftrous time ;
Thy ftronger Beauties from a foul fublime,   120
Whofe vigor burft, like the volcano's flame,
From central darknefs to the fphere of fame.

3

Of gentler mind, and with a heart to feel
The fondeſt warmth of emulative zeal,
Thy feſtive Scholar, who ador'd thy Lays,   125
And grac'd thy Genius with no ſcanty praiſe,
The gay Boccacio, tempts th' Italian Muſe *
More varied notes and different themes to chuſe;
Themes which her voice had dar'd not yet to found,
Valour's heroic feats by Beauty crown'd.   130
Sweet was the glowing Song; but, ſtrange to tell,
On his bold lyre Oblivion's ſhadows fell;
His richer Tales engroſs'd the World's regard,
And the bright Noveliſt eclips'd the Bard.

In following ages, when Italia's ſhore   135
Blaz'd with the riſing light of Claſſic lore,
Stern Syſtem led, from her new-founded ſchool,
A Poet faſhion'd by her rigid rule:
Behold my Son! (his ſapient Tut'reſs cried)
Who throws the bonds of Gothic rhyme aſide;   140
For whom theſe hands the Grecian Lyre new ſtrung:
She ſpoke exulting, and Trissino ſung. †

* Ver. 127. See NOTE V.
† Ver. 142. See NOTE VI.

In his cold Verfe he kept her Critic laws,
While Pedants own'd their pow'r, and yawn'd applaufe.

Indignant Fancy, who with fcorn furvey'd   145
The fleepy honors to proud Syftem paid,
Smiling to fee that on her rival's brow
The Poppy lurk'd beneath the Laurel bough,
Refolv'd in fportive triumph to difplay
The rich extent of her fuperior fway :   150
From Necromancy's hand, in happieft hour,
She caught the rod of vifionary power ;
And as aloft the magic wand fhe rais'd,
A peerlefs Bard with new effulgence blaz'd,
Born every law of Syftem to difown,   155
And rule by Fancy's boundlefs power alone.
High in mid air, between the Moon and Earth,
The Bard of Pathos now, and now of Mirth,
Pois'd with his lyre between a Griffin's wings,
Her fportive darling, Ariosto, fings.   160
As the light cloud, whofe varying vapors fly,
Driven by the zephyr of the evening fky,
Fixes and charms the never-wearied view,
By taking every fhape and every hue ;

So,

So, by Variety's supreme controul,   165
His changeful numbers seize the willing soul.
Enchanted by his Song, Attention sits,
With features catching every cast by fits,
Like the fond infant, in whose tender brain
Young Sensibility delights to reign;   170
While rapid Joy and Pain each other chase
Thro' the soft muscles of its April face.
In vain the slaves of System would discard
From Glory's classic train this airy Bard;
Delighted Nature her gay fav'rite crown'd,   175
And Envy's clamour in her plaudit drown'd.
Severe Morality, to censure mov'd,
His wanton Lyre with juster blame reprov'd;
But his sweet Song her anger so beguil'd,
That, ere she finish'd her reproof, she smil'd.   180
    Of chaster fire, a rival name succeeds,
Whose bold and glowing hand Religion leads:
In solemn accent, and in sacred state,
With classic lore and Christian zeal elate,
Sweetly pathetic, and sublimely strong,   185
Tasso begins his more majestic song;

H 3

The

The Muſe of Sion, not implor'd in vain,
Guides to th' impaſſion'd ſoul his heavenly ſtrain.
Bluſh, Boileau, bluſh, and for that pride atone,
Which ſlander'd Genius far above thy own;   190
And thou, great injur'd Bard, thy ſtation claim
Amid the Demi-gods of Epic name;
Heir to a mantle by the Muſes ſpun,
Of a poetic Sire the more poetic Son. *

   Nor, tho' juſt Fame her richer palm devote   195
To the high-ſounding lyre of ſerious note,
Shall gay Tassoni want his feſtive crown, †
Who baniſh'd from the Muſe her aweful frown,
And, tuning to light themes her lofty ſtyle,
O'er her grave features ſpread a comic ſmile.   200
   Such various Sons, of Epic fire poſſeſt,
Italia foſter'd on her feeling breaſt.
   Spain, whoſe bold genius with misjudging pride
O'erſteps true glory by too large a ſtride,
Claims higher merit from one Poet's birth,   205
Who rivals all the different Bards of earth:

    * Ver. 194. See NOTE VII.
    † Ver. 197. See NOTE VIII.

                               With

With more than Niobe's parental boaſt,
She calls her ſingle Son himſelf an Hoſt,
And raſhly judges that her VEGA's lyre *
Is equal to the whole Aonian quire.   210

Impetuous Poet! whoſe full brain ſupplied
Such floods of Verſe, and in ſo quick a tide,
Their rapid ſwell, by its unrivall'd height,
Pleas'd, yet produc'd more wonder than delight:
Tho' thy free rhyme from Fancy's fountain guſh,   215
And with the grandeur of the torrent ruſh,
Its troubled ſtreams in dark diſorder roam,
With all the torrent's noiſe and all its foam.

To Emulation fir'd by TASSO's ſtrain,
Thy ſpirit quitted the dramatic plain   220
To ſeek thoſe Epic heights, ſublimely calm,
Whence he had pluck'd his Idumean palm;
But, vainly ſtruggling in a taſk too hard,
Sunk at the feet of that ſuperior Bard.
Brave Spaniard! ſtill thy wounded pride conſole;   225
Time ſhall not ſtrike thy name from Glory's roll,

* Ver. 209. See NOTE IX.

On

On which thy generous and fraternal hand
Emblaz'd each brother of thy tuneful band;
Thy Muse shall share the praise she joy'd to give,
And while thy language lasts thy fame shall live.   230
Perchance, tho' strange the paradox may seem,
That fame had risen with a brighter beam,
Had radiant Fancy less enrich'd thy mind:
Her lavish wealth, for wiser use design'd,
Ruin'd the Poet by its splendid lure,   235
As India's mines have made his country poor.

    With warmth more temperate, and in notes more clear,
That with Homeric richness fill the ear,
The brave ERCILLA sounds, with potent breath, *
His Epic trumpet in the fields of death.   240
In scenes of savage war when Spain unfurl'd
Her bloody banners o'er the western world,
With all his Country's virtues in his frame,
Without the base alloy that stain'd her name,
In Danger's camp this military Bard,   245
Whom Cynthia saw on his nocturnal guard,

* Ver. 239. See NOTE X.

9   Recorded,

Recorded, in his bold defcriptive lay,

The various fortune of the finifh'd day;

Seizing the pen while Night's calm hours afford

A tranfient flumber to his fatiate fword,   250

With noble juftice his warm hand beftows

The meed of Honor on his valiant foes.

Howe'er precluded, by his generous aim,

From high pretenfions to inventive fame,

His ftrongly-colour'd fcenes of fanguine ftrife,   255

His fofter pictures caught from Indian life,

Above the vifionary forms of art,

Fire the awaken'd mind and melt the heart.

 Tho' fierceft tribes her galling fetters drag,

Proud Spain muft ftrike to Lufitania's flag,   260

Whofe ampler folds, in confcious triumph fpread,

Wave o'er her NAVAL POET's laureate head.

Ye Nymphs of Tagus, from your golden cell,

That caught the echo of his tuneful fhell,

Rife, and to deck your darling's fhrine provide   265

The richeft treafures that the deep may hide:

From every land let grateful Commerce fhower

Her tribute to the Bard who fung her power;

I   As

As thofe rich gales, from whence his GAMA caught
A pleafing earneft of the prize he fought,   270
The balmy fragrance of the Eaft difpenfe,
So fteals his Song on the delighted fenfe,
Aftonifhing, with fweets unknown before,
Thofe who ne'er tafted but of claffic lore.
Immortal Bard, thy name with GAMA vies,   275
Thou, like thy Hero, with propitious fkies
The fail of bold adventure haft unfurl'd,
And in the Epic ocean found a world.
'Twas thine to blend the Eagle and the Dove,
At once the Bard of Glory and of Love : *   280
Thy thanklefs Country heard thy varying lyre
To PETRARCH's Softnefs melt, and fwell to HOMER's Fire!
Boaft and lament, ungrateful land, a Name,
In life, in death, thy honor and thy fhame.

Thou nobler realm, whom vanity betrays   285
To load thy letter'd fons with lavifh praife;
Where Eulogy, with one eternal fmile, †
Heaps her faint rofes in a withering pile :

* Ver. 280. See NOTE XI.
† Ver. 287. See NOTE XII.

A City

A City milk-maid, on the firſt of May,

Who, pertly civil, and abſurdly gay, 290

Forms her dull garland in fantaſtic ſtate,

With ill-adjuſted flow'rs and borrow'd plate.

Canſt thou, ſelf-flattering France, with juſtice vaunt

One Epic laurel as thy native plant?

How oft a Gallic hand, with childiſh fire, 295

Has rattled Diſcord on th' heroic lyre,

While their dull aid aſſociate Critics bring,

And vainly teach the uſe of every ſtring!

In Morals, as, with many an empty boaſt,

They practiſe virtue leaſt who preach it moſt; 300

So, haughty Gallia, in thy Epic ſchool,

No great Examples riſe, but many a Rule.*

   Yet, tho' unjuſt to Tasso's nobler lays,

Keen Boileau ſhall not want his proper praiſe; †

He, archly waving his ſatiric rod 305

Thro' the new path which firſt Tassoni trod,

Purſued his ſportive march in happy hour,

And pluck'd from Satire's thorn a feſtive flower.

    * Ver. 302. See NOTE XIII.

    † Ver. 304. See NOTE XIV.

                              His

His facerdotal War fhall wake delight,
And fmiles in Gravity herfelf excite,　　　　　　310
While Canons live to quarrel or to feaft,
And gall can tinge the fpirit of a Prieft.

　Nor, gentle GRESSET, fhall thy fprightly rhyme *
Ceafe to enchant the lift'ning ear of Time:
In thee the Graces all their powers inftill,　　　315
To touch the Epic chords with playful fkill.
The haplefs Parrot whom thy lays endear,
In piety and woe the Trojan's peer;
His heart as tender, and his love more pure,
Shall, like Æneas, live of fame fecure;　　　　320
While female hands, with many a tender word,
Stroke the foft feathers of their fav'rite bird.

　Yet not in childifh fport, or trifling joy,
Do Gallic Fair-ones all their hours employ:
See lovely BOCCAGE, in ambition ftrong, †　　　325
Build, with afpiring aim, her Epic Song!
By Glory fir'd, her rofy lips rehearfe
Thy feats, Columbus, in unborrow'd Verfe.

* Ver. 313. See NOTE XV.
† Ver. 325. See NOTE XVI.

If

If this new Muſe in War's dire field diſplays
No Grecian ſplendor, no Homeric blaze,   330
Attractive ſtill, tho' not in pomp array'd,
She charms like Zama, in her Verſe portray'd;
Whoſe form from dreſs no gorgeous pride aſſumes,
Clad in a ſimple zone of azure plumes.

England's dear gueſt! this Muſe of Gallia caught   335
From our inſpiring Iſle her ardent thought;
Here firſt ſhe ſtrove to reach, with vent'rous hope,
MILTON's chaſte grandeur, and the grace of POPE;
And ſweetly taught, in her mimetic ſtrain,
The Songs of Britain to the Banks of Seine.   340

But ſee! with wounded Pride's indignant glance,
The angry Genius of preſuming France
From ancient ſhrines their Epic wreaths would tear,
To ſwell the glory of her great VOLTAIRE. *

O, form'd in Learning's various paths to ſhine,   345
Encircled from thy birth by all the Nine,
On thee, bleſt Bard, theſe rivals ſeem'd to ſhower
Their various attributes and blended power!

* Ver. 344. See NOTE XVII.

9   But,

But, when their lofty leader bade thee frame
The rich Heroic fong on Henry's fame,   350
Sarcaftic Humour, trifling with her lyre,
Took from th' infpiring Mufe her folemn fire.
No more her fpirit like the Eagle fprings,
Or rides the buoyant air with balanc'd wings:
Tho' rapid ftill, to narrow circuits bound,   355
She, like the darting Swallow, fkims the ground.
Thy Verfe difplays, beneath an Epic name,
Wit's flinty Spark, for Fancy's folar Flame.
While yet thy hand the Epic chords embrac'd,
With playful fpirit, and with frolic hafte,   360
Such lively founds thy rapid fingers drew,
And thro' the feftive notes fo lightly flew,
Nature and Fancy join'd their charms to fwell,
And laughing Humour crown'd thy new Pucelle:
But the chafte Mufes, ftartled at the found,   365
Amid thy fprightly numbers blufh'd and frown'd;
With decent anger, and becoming pride,
Severer Virtue threw the Song afide;
While Juftice own'd it, with a kinder glance,
The wittieft Levity of wanton France.   370

Now,

Now, graver Britain, amiably fevere,
To thee, with native zeal, to thee I fteer;
My vent'rous bark, its foreign circuit o'er,
Exulting fprings to thy parental fhore.

Thou gorgeous Queen, who on thy filvery coaft,   375
Sitteft encircled by a filial hoft,
And feeft thy fons, the jewels of thy crown,
Blaze with each varying ray of rich renown;
If with juft love I hold their Genius dear,
Lament their hardfhips, and their fame revere,   380
O bid thy Epic Mufe, with honor due,
Range her departed Champions in my view!

See, on a party-colour'd fteed of fire,
With Humour at his fide, his trufty Squire,
Gay CHAUCER leads—in form a Knight of old,   385
And his ftrong armour is of fteel and gold;
But o'er it age a cruel ruft has fpread,
And made the brilliant metals dark as lead.

Now gentle SPENSER, Fancy's fav'rite Bard,
Awakes my wonder and my fond regard;   390
Encircling Fairies bear, in fportive dance,
His adamantine fhield and magic lance;

3   While

While Allegory, dreſt with myſtic art,
Appears his Guide ; but, promiſing to dart
A lambent glory round her liſt'ning Son,   395
She hides him in the web herſelf has ſpun.

    Ingenuous COWLEY, the fond dupe of Wit,
Seems like a vapour o'er the field to flit ;
In David's praiſe he ſtrikes ſome Epic notes,
But ſoon down Lethe's ſtream their dying murmur floats.

    While COWLEY vaniſh'd in an amorous riddle,   401
Up roſe the frolic Bard of Bear and Fiddle :
His ſmile exhilarates the ſullen earth,
Adorning Satire in the maſk of Mirth :
Taught by his Song, Fanatics ceaſe their jars,   405
And wiſe Aſtrologers renounce the Stars.
Unrivall'd BUTLER ! bleſt with happy ſkill
To heal by comic verſe each ſerious ill,
By Wit's ſtrong flaſhes Reaſon's light diſpenſe,
And laugh a frantic nation into ſenſe !   410

    Apart, and on a ſacred hill retir'd,
Beyond all mortal inſpiration fir'd,
The mighty MILTON ſits—an hoſt around
Of liſt'ning Angels guard the holy ground ;

                                         Amaz'd

Amaz'd they fee a human form afpire   415
To grafp with daring hand a Seraph's lyre,
Inly irradiate with celeftial beams,
Attempt thofe high, thofe foul-fubduing themes,
(Which humbler Denizens of Heaven decline)
And celebrate, with fanctity divine,   420
The ftarry field from warring Angels won,
And GOD triumphant in his Victor Son.
Nor lefs the wonder, and the fweet delight,
His milder fcenes and fofter notes excite,
When at his bidding Eden's blooming grove   425
Breathes the rich fweets of Innocence and Love.
With fuch pure joy as our Forefather knew
When Raphael, heavenly gueft, firft met his view,
And our glad Sire, within his blifsful bower,
Drank the pure converfe of th' ætherial Power,   430
Round the bleft Bard his raptur'd audience throng,
And feel their fouls imparadis'd in fong.

   Of humbler mien, but not of mortal race,
Ill-fated DRYDEN, with Imperial grace,
Gives to th' obedient lyre his rapid laws ;   435
Tones yet unheard, with touch divine, he draws,

K

The

The melting fall, the rifing fwell fublime,
And all the magic of melodious rhyme.
See with proud joy Imagination fpread
A wreath of honor round his aged head !　　　　440
But two bafe Spectres, tho' of different hue,
The Bard unhappy in his march purfue;
Two vile difgraceful Fiends, of race accurft,
Conceiv'd by Spleen, by meagre Famine nurft,
Malignant Satire, mercenary Praife,　　　　445
Shed their dark fpots on his immortal bays.

　　Poor DAVENANT march'd before, with nobler aim,
His keen eye fixt upon the palm of Fame,
But cruel Fortune doom'd him to rehearfe
A Theme ill-chofen, in ill-chofen Verfe.　　　　450

　　Next came Sir RICHARD, but in woeful plight,
DRYDEN's Led-horfe firft threw the lucklefs Knight.
He rofe advent'rous ftill—O who may count
How oft he tried a different Steed to mount !
Each angry fteed his awkward rider flung;　　　　455
Undaunted ftill he fell, and falling fung.

　　But Æfculapius, who, with grief diftreft,
Beheld his offspring made a public jeft,

Soon

Soon bade a livelier Son with mirth efface
The ſhame he ſuffer'd from Sir RICHARD's caſe.   460
Swift at the word his ſprightly GARTH began
To make an * helmet of a Cloſe-ſtool Pan ;
An Urinal he for his trumpet takes,
And at each blaſt he blows ſee Laughter ſhakes.

Yet peace—new muſic floats on Æther's wings ; 465
Say, is it Harmony herſelf who ſings ?
No ! while enraptur'd Sylphs the Song inſpire,
'Tis POPE who ſweetly wakes the ſilver lyre
To melting notes, more muſically clear
Than Ariel whiſper'd in Belinda's ear.   470
Too ſoon he quits them for a ſharper tone ;
See him, tho' form'd to fill the Epic throne,
Decline the ſceptre of that wide domain,
To bear a Lictor's rod in Satire's train ;
And, ſhrouded in a miſt of moral ſpleen, †   475
Behold him cloſe the viſionary ſcene !

* And his high helmet was a Cloſe-ſtool Pan. DISPENSARY.
† Ver. 475. See NOTE XVIII.

END OF THE THIRD EPISTLE.

K 2   EPISTLE

EPISTLE

THE FOURTH.

A R G U M E N T

OF THE FOURTH EPISTLE.

Remarks on the supposed Parsimony of Nature in bestowing Poetic Genius.—The Evils and the Advantages of Poetry exemplified in the Fate of different Poets.

E P I S T L E IV.

SAY, generous Power, benignant Nature, say,
Who temp'reſt with thy touch our human clay,
Warming the fields of Thought with genial care,
The various fruits of mental growth to bear;
Shall not thy vot'ries glow with juſt diſdain,   5
When Sloth or Spleen thy bounteous hand arraign?
Art thou the Niggard they pretend thou art,
A grudging Parent with a Stepdame's heart;
And doſt thou ſhed, with rare, reluctant toil,
Bright Fancy's germins in the mental ſoil?   10
Is Genius, thy ſweet Plant of richeſt power,
Whoſe dearly priz'd and long-expected flower
More tardy than the Aloe's bloom appears,
Ordain'd to blow but in a thouſand years?
Periſh the ſickly thought—let thoſe who hold   15
Thy quick'ning influence ſo coy, ſo cold,

                Calmly

Calmly the habitable earth furvey,

From time's firſt æra to the paſſing day ;

In what rude clime, beneath what angry ſkies,

Have plants Poetic never dar'd to riſe ?   20

In torrid regions, where 'tis toil to think,

Where ſouls in ſtupid eaſe ſupinely ſink ;

And where the native of the deſert drear

Yields to blank darkneſs half his icy year ;

In theſe unfriendly ſcenes, where each extreme   25

Of heat and cold forbids the mind to teem,

Poetic bloſſoms into Being ſtart,

Spontaneous produce of the feeling heart.

    Can we then deem that in thoſe happier lands,

Where every vital energy expands ;   30

Where Thought, the golden harveſt of the mind,

Springs into rich luxuriance, unconfin'd ;

That in ſuch ſoils, with mental weeds o'ergrown,

The Seeds of Poeſy were thinly ſown ?

    Shall we deny the labor of the ſwain   35

Who to the cultur'd earth confides the grain,

If all the vagrant harpies of the air

From its new bed the pregnant treaſure tear ;

7

If, when scarce rising, with a stem infirm,
It dies the victim of the mining worm;   40
If mildew, riding in the eastern gust,
Turns all its ripening gold to sable dust?

    These foes combin'd (and with them who may cope?)
Are not more hostile to the Farmer's hope,
Than Life's keen passions to that lighter grain   45
Of Fancy, scatter'd o'er the infant brain.
Pleasure, the rambling Bird! the painted Jay!
May snatch the richest seeds of Verse away;
Or Indolence, the worm that winds with art
Thro' the close texture of the cleanest heart,   50
May, if they haply have begun to shoot,
With partial mischief wound the sick'ning root;
Or Avarice, the mildew of the soul,
May sweep the mental field and blight the whole;
Nay, the meek errors of the modest mind,   55
To its own vigor diffidently blind,
And that cold spleen, which falsely has declar'd
The powers of Nature and of Art impair'd,
The gate that Genius has unclos'd may guard,,
And rivet to the earth the rising Bard: 60

L

For

For who will quit, tho' from mean aims exempt,
The cares that summon, and the joys that tempt,
In many a lonely studious hour to try
Where latent springs of Poesy may lie;
Who will from social ease his mind divorce,   65
To prove in Art's wide field its secret force,
If, blind to Nature's frank parental love,
He deems that Verse, descended from above,
Like Heaven's more sacred signs, whose time is o'er,
A gift miraculous, conferr'd no more ?   70

   O Prejudice! thou bane of Arts, thou pest,
Whose ruffian powers the free-born soul arrest;
Thou who, dethroning Reason, dar'st to frame
And issue thy proud laws beneath her name;
Thou Coaster on the intellectual deep,   75
Ordering each timid bark thy course to keep;
Who, lest some daring mind beyond thee steer,
Hast rais'd, to vouch thy vanity and fear,
Herculean pillars where thy sail was furl'd,
And nam'd thy bounds the Limits of the World.   80
Thou braggart, Prejudice, how oft thy breath
Has doom'd young Genius to the shades of death !

How

How often has thy voice, with brutal fire
Forbidding Female hands to touch the lyre,
Deny'd to Woman, Nature's fav'rite child,   85
The right to enter Fancy's opening wild!
Bleft be this fmiling hour, when Britain fees
Her Fair-ones cancel fuch abfurd decrees,
In one harmonious group, with graceful fcorn,
Spring o'er the Pedant's fence of wither'd thorn,   90
And reach Parnaffian heights, where, laurel-crown'd,
This fofter Quire the notes of triumph found;
Where SEWARD, leader of the lovely train,
Pours o'er heroic tombs her potent ftrain;
Potent to footh the honor'd dead, and dart   95
Congenial virtue thro' each panting heart;
Potent thro' fpirits mafculine to fpread
Poetic jealoufy and envious dread;
If Love and Envy could in union reft,
And rule with blended fway a Poet's breaft;   100
The Bards of Britain, with unjaundic'd eyes,
Will glory to behold fuch rivals rife.
Proceed, ye Sifters of the tuneful Shell, *
Without a fcruple, in that Art excel,

* Ver. 103. See NOTE I.

               Which

Which reigns, by virtuous Pleasure's soft controul,   105
In sweet accordance with the Female soul;
Pure as yourselves, and like your charms design'd
To bless the earth, and humanize mankind.

   Where'er that Parent of engaging thought,
Warm Sensibility, like light, has taught   110
The bright'ning mirror of the mind to shew
Nature's reflected forms in all their glow;
Where in full tides the fine affections roll,
And the warm heart invigorates the soul;
In that rich spot, where winds propitious blow,   115
Culture may teach poetic Fame to grow.
Refin'd Invention and harmonious Rhyme,
Are the slow gifts of Study and of Time;
But to the Bard whom all the Muses court,
His Sports are study, and his Studies sport.   120
E'en at this period, when all tongues declare
Poetic talents are a gift most rare,
Unnumber'd Spirits, in our generous isle,
Are ripening now beneath kind Nature's smile,
Whom happy care might lead to lasting fame,   125
And art ennoble with a Poet's name.

Not

Not that 'tis granted this high prize to gain
By light effusions of a sportive vein,
The idle Ballad of a summer's morn,
The child of Frolic, in a moment born :   130
Who views such trifles with a vain regard,
But ill deserves the mighty name of Bard ;
In diff'rent tints see virtuous GRESSET trace
The genuine spirit of Poetic race :

* Let the true Bard (this pleasing Poet sings)   135
   Bid his fair fame on strong foundations rest ;
His be each honour that from Genius springs,
   Esteem'd by Judgment, and by Love carest ;

His the Ambition, that in climes unknown,
   Where'er his wand'ring volume may extend,   140
Where'er that Picture of his mind is shewn,
   In every Reader he may find a Friend.

                           " Be

* Je veux qu'épris d'un nom plus légitime,
   Que non content de se voir estimé,
Par son Genie un Amant de la rime
   Emporte encor le plaisir d'etre aimé ;

Qu'aux régions à lui meme inconnues
   Ou voleront ses gracieux ecrits,
A ce tableau de ses mœurs ingénues,
   Tous ses Lecteurs deviennent ses Amis :

                              Que

Be it his aim to dart the living ray
 Of pureſt pleaſure o'er th' enlighten'd earth ;
And in ſweet union let his works diſplay   145
 The Poet's fancy and the Patriot's worth.

Thus far, O GRESSET, on theſe points agreed,
My ſoul profeſſes thy Poetic Creed ;
Tho' the ſoft languor of thy ſong I blame,
Which preſent eaſe prefers to future fame,   150
Thy nobler maxims I with pride embrace,
That Verſe ſhou'd ever riſe on Virtue's baſe,
And every maſter of this matchleſs art
Exalt the Spirit, and improve the Heart ;
And many a Youth, now riſing into Man,   155
Might build his glory on this noble plan,
With latent powers to make the ſtructure laſt
Till Nature dies, and Time itſelf be paſt :
But O, how intricate the chances lurk,
Whoſe power may drive him from the doubtful work ! 160
Of the ſtrong minds by chaſte Ambition nurſt,
Who burn to rank in Honor's line the firſt,

    Que diſſipant le préjugé vulgaire,
    Il montre enfin que ſans crime on peut plaire,
    Et reunir, par un heureux lien,
    L' Auteur charmant et le vrai Citoyen.

               One

One leaves the Lyre to feize the martial crown,
And one may drop it at a Parent's frown ;
For ftill with fcorn, which anxious fear inflames,   165
Parental care 'gainft Poefy declaims !

    " Fly, fly, my fon, (the fond advifer cries)
" That thorny path, where every peril lies ;
" Oh ! be not thou by that vain Art betray'd,
" Whofe pains are Subftance, and whofe joys are Shade !
" Mark, in the Mufes' miferable throng,   171
" What air-built vifions cheat the Sons of Song !
" This is a leffon taught in every ftreet,
" And Bards may read it at each Stall they meet :
" Take the firft book, behold in many a page   175
" What promifes of life from age to age ;
" The Poet fwears himfelf he ne'er fhall die,
" A troop of rhyming friends fupport the lie :
" Yet fee how foon in Lethe's ftream expire
" This leading Bard and his attendant Quire,   180
" And round thefe boards, their unexpected bier,
" Their ghofts breathe wifdom in the paffing ear :
" For Stalls, like Church-yards, moral truth fupply,
" And teach the vifionary Bard to die.

                              " If

" If prefent fame, thy airy hope, be gain'd,   185

" By vigils purchas'd, and by toil maintain'd,

" What bafe alloy muft fink the doubtful prize,

" Which Envy poifons, and which Spleen denies!

" Obferve what ills the living Bard attend,

" Neglect his lot, and Penury his end!   190

" Behold the world unequally requite.

" Two Arts that minifter to chafte delight,

" Twin-fifters, who with kindred beauty ftrike

" In fortune different, as in charms alike:

" PAINTING, fair Danae! has her Golden fhower,   195

" But Want is POESY's proverbial dower.

  " See, while with brilliant genius, ill applied,

" The noble RUBENS flatters Royal pride,

" Makes all the Virtues, who abjur'd him, wait

" On abject JAMES, in allegoric ftate;   200

" O'er the bafe Pedant his rich radiance flings,

" And deifies the meaneft of our Kings;

" His Son rewards, and Honor owns the deed,

" The fplendid Artift with a princely meed.

" Now turn to MILTON's latter days, and fee   205

" How Bards and Painters in their fate agree;

7

" Behold

" Behold him fell his heaven-illumin'd page,

" Mirac'lous child of his deferted age,

" For fuch a pittance, fo ignobly flight,

" As wounded Learning blufhes to recite ! *   210

   " If changing times fuggeft the pleafing hope,

" That Bards no more with adverfe fortune cope ;

" That in this alter'd clime, where Arts increafe,

" And make our polifh'd Ifle a fecond Greece ;

" That now, if Poefy proclaims her Son,   215

" And challenges the wreath by Fancy won ;

" Both Fame and Wealth adopt him as their heir,

" And liberal Grandeur makes his life her care ;

" From fuch vain thoughts thy erring mind defend,

" And look on CHATTERTON's difaftrous end.   220

" Oh, ill-ftarr'd Youth, whom Nature form'd, in vain,

" With powers on Pindus' fplendid height to reign !

" O dread example of what pangs await

" Young Genius ftruggling with malignant fate !

" What could the Mufe, who fir'd thy infant frame   225

" With the rich promife of Poetic fame ;

<hr>

* Ver. 210. See NOTE II.

M   " Who

" Who taught thy hand its magic art to hide,
" And mock the infolence of Critic pride ;
" What cou'd her unavailing cares oppofe,
" To fave her darling from his defperate foes ;   230
" From preffing Want's calamitous controul,
" And Pride, the fever of the ardent foul ?
" Ah, fee, too confcious of her failing power,
" She quits her Nurfling in his deathful hour !
" In a chill room, within whofe wretched wall   235
" No cheering voice replies to Mifery's call ;
" Near a vile bed, too crazy to fuftain
" Misfortune's wafted limbs, convuls'd with pain,
" On the bare floor, with heaven-directed eyes,
" The haplefs Youth in fpeechlefs horror lies !   240
" The pois'nous vial, by diftraction drain'd,
" Rolls from his hand, in wild contortion ftrain'd :
" Pale with life-wafting pangs, it's dire effect,
' And ftung to madnefs by the world's neglect,
" He, in abhorrence of the dangerous Art,   245
" Once the dear idol of his glowing heart,
" Tears from his Harp the vain detefted wires,.
" And in the frenzy of Defpair expires !

1.   " Pernicious

" Pernicious Poesy! thy baleful sway

" Exalts to weaken, flatters to betray;   250

" When thy fond Votary has to thee resign'd

" The captive powers of his deluded mind,

" Fantastic hopes his swelling breast inflame,

" Tempestous passions tear his shatter'd frame,

" Which sinks; for round it seas of trouble roar,   255

" Admitting agony at every pore;

" While Dullness, whom no tender feelings check,

" Grins at his ruin, and enjoys the wreck ,

" Seen thro' the mist which clouds her heavy eyes,

" The faults of Genius swell to double size,   260

" His generous faults, which her base pride makes known,

" Insulting errors so unlike her own.

   " Far then, my Son, far from this Syren steer;

" Or, if her dulcet song must charm thy ear,

" Let Reason bind thee, like the Greek of yore,   265

" To catch her music, but escape her shore;

" For never shall the wretch her power can seize,

" Regain the port of Fortune, or of Ease."

   Parental Fear thus warns the filial heart,

From this alluring, this insidious Art;   270

But,

But, wounded thus by keen Invective's edge,
Say, can the Muse no juft defence alledge?
In ftriking contraft has fhe not to paint
Her profp'rous Hero, as her murder'd Saint?
'Tis true, fhe oft has fruitlefs vigils kept,   275
And oft, with unavailing forrow, wept
Her injur'd Vot'ries, doom'd to quit the earth
In the fharp pangs of ill-requited worth.
Ye noble Martyrs of poetic name,
" Blifs to your Spirits, to your Mem'ries Fame!"   280
By gen'rous Honor be your toils rever'd,
To grateful Nature be your names endear'd!
To all who Pity's feeling nerve poffefs,
Doubly endear'd by undeferv'd diftrefs.

But, to relieve the pain your wrongs awake,   285
O let the Muse her brighter records take,
Review the crown by living Merit won,
And fhare the triumph of each happier Son.

If the young Bard who ftarts for Glory's goal,
Can fate with prefent fame his ardent foul,   290
Poetic ftory can with truth atteft
This rareft, richeft prize in life poffeft.

See

See the GAY POET of Italia's fhore,
Whom with fond zeal her feeling fons adore,
Pafs, while his heart with exultation beats,   295
Poetic Mantua's applauding ftreets !
See him, while Juftice fmiles, and Envy fnarls,
Receive the Laurel from Imperial Charles ! *
And lo, th' unfading Gift ftill fhines above
Each perifhable mark of Royal Love.   300

   If humbler views the tuneful mind inflame,
If to be rich can be a Poet's aim,
The Mufe may fhew, but in a different clime,
Wealth, the fair produce of applauded Rhyme.
Behold the fav'rite Bard of lib'ral Spain,   305
Her wond'rous VEGA, of exhauftlefs vein ;
From honeft Poverty, his early lot,
With honor fullied by no vicious blot,
Behold him rife on Fortune's glittering wings,
And almoft reach the opulence of Kings ;   310
The high-foul'd Nobles of his native land,
Enrich their Poet with fo frank a hand !

* Ver. 298. See NOTE III.

9   For

For him Pieria's rock with treasure teems,
For him her fountains gush with golden streams ; *
And ne'er did Fortune, with a love more just,   315
Her splendid stores to worthier hands entrust ;
For with the purest current, wide and strong,
His Charity surpast his copious Song.

   If the Enthusiast higher hope pursues,
If from his commerce with th' inspiring Muse   320
He seeks to gain, by no mean aims confin'd,
Freedom of thought and energy of mind ;
To raise his spirit, with ætherial fire,
Above each little want and low desire ;
O turn where MILTON flames with Epic rage,   325
Unhurt by poverty, unchill'd by age :
Tho' danger threaten his declining day,
Tho' clouds of darkness quench his visual ray,
The heavenly Muse his hallow'd spirit fills
With raptures that surmount his matchless ills ;   330
From earth she bears him to bright Fancy's goal,
And distant fame illuminates his soul !

   Too oft the wealthy, to proud follies born,
Have turn'd from letter'd Poverty with scorn.

     * Ver. 314. See NOTE IV.

                        Dull

Dull Opulence! thy narrow joys enlarge ;   335
To ſhield weak Merit is thy nobleſt charge :
Search the dark ſcenes where drooping Genius lies,
And keep from ſorrieſt ſights a nation's eyes,
That, from expiring Want's reproaches free,
Our generous country may ne'er weep to ſee   340
A future CHATTERTON by poiſon dead,
An OTWAY fainting for a little bread.

   If deaths like theſe deform'd our native iſle,
Some Engliſh Bards have baſk'd in Fortune's ſmile.
Alike in Station and in Genius bleſt,   345
By Knowledge prais'd, by Dignity careſt,
POPE's happy Freedom, all baſe wants above,
Flow'd from the golden ſtream of Public Love ;
That richeſt antidote the Bard can ſeize,
To ſave his ſpirit from its worſt diſeaſe,   350
From mean Dependance, bright Ambition's bane,
Which bluſhing Fancy ſtrives to hide in vain.
To POPE the titled Patron joy'd to bend,
Still more ennobled when proclaim'd his friend ;
For him the hands of jarring Faction join   355
To heap their tribute on his HOMER's ſhrine.

                                Proud

Proud of the frank reward his talents find,
And nobly confcious of no venal mind,
With the juft world his fair account he clears,
And owns no debt to Princes or to Peers.   360

    Yet, while our nation feels new thirft arife
For that pure joy which Poefy fupplies,
Bards, whom the tempting Mufe enlifts by ftealth,
Perceive their path is not the road to wealth,
To honorable wealth, young Labor's fpoil,   365
The due reward of no inglorious toil ;
Whofe well-earn'd comforts nobleft minds engage,
The juft afylum of declining age ;
Elfe had we feen a warm Poetic Youth
Change Fiction's rofes for the thorns of Truth,   370
From Fancy's realm, his native field, withdraw,
To pay hard homage to feverer Law?

    O thou bright Spirit, whom the Afian Mufe
Had fondly fteep'd in all her fragrant dews,
And o'er whofe early Song, that mental feaft,   375
She breath'd the fweetnefs of the rifled Eaft ;
Since independant Honor's high controul
Detach'd from Poefy thy ardent foul,

To

To feek with better hopes Perfuafion's feat,
Bleft be thofe hopes, and happy that retreat !   380
Which with regret all Britifh Bards muft fee,
And mourn a Brother loft in lofing thee.

 Nor leads the Poet's path to that throng d gate
Where crouching Priefts on proud Preferment wait ;
Where, while in vain a thoufand vot'ries fawn,   385
She robes her fav'rite few in hallow'd Lawn :
Elfe, liberal MASON, had thy fpotlefs name,
The Ward of Virtue as the Heir of Fame,
In lifts of mitred Lords been ftill unread,
While Mitres drop on many a Critic's head ?   390
Peace to all fuch, whofe decent brows may bear
Thofe facred honors plac'd by Learning there ;
May juft refpect from brutal infult guard
Their Crown, unenvied by the genuine Bard !
Let Poefy, embellifh'd by thy care,   395
Pathetic MASON ! with juft pride declare,
Thy breaft muft feel a more exulting fire,
Than Pomp can give, or Dignity infpire,
When Nature tells thee that thy Verfe imparts
The thrill of pleafure to ten thoufand hearts ;   400

N

And

And often has fhe heard ingenuous Youth,
Accomplifh'd Beauty, and unbiafs'd Truth,
Thofe faithful harbingers of future fame,
With tender intereft pronounce thy name
With lively gratitude for joy refin'd,   405
Gift of thy Genius to the feeling mind.
Thefe are the honors which the Mufe confers,
The radiant Crown of living light is her's ;
And on thy brow fhe gave thofe gems to blaze,
That far outfhine the Mitre's tranfient rays ; 410
Gems that fhall mock malignant Envy's breath,
And fhine ftill brighter thro' the fhades of death.

 For me, who feel, whene'er I touch the lyre,
My talents fink below my proud defire ;
Who often doubt, and fometimes credit give, 415
When Friends affure me that my Verfe will live ;
Whom health too tender for the buftling throng
Led into penfive fhade and foothing fong ;
Whatever fortune my unpolifh'd rhymes
May meet, in prefent or in future times, 420
Let the bleft Art my grateful thoughts employ,
Which fooths my forrow and augments my joy ;

         Whence

Whence lonely Peace and focial Pleafure fprings,
And Friendfhip, dearer than the fmile of Kings!
While keener Poets, queruloufly proud,   425
Lament the Ills of Poefy aloud,
And magnify, with Irritation's zeal,
Thofe common evils we too ftrongly feel,
The envious Comment and the fubtle Style
Of fpecious Slander, ftabbing with a fmile;   430
Frankly I wifh to make her Bleffings known,
And think thofe Bleffings for her Ills atone:
Nor wou'd my honeft pride that praife forego,
Which makes Malignity yet more my foe.

　　If heart-felt pain e'er led me to accufe   435
The dangerous gift of the alluring Mufe,
'Twas in the moment when my Verfe impreft
Some anxious feelings on a Mother's breaft.

　　O thou fond Spirit, who with pride haft fmil'd,
And frown'd with fear, on thy poetic child,   440
Pleas'd, yet alarm'd, when in his boyifh time
He figh'd in numbers, or he laugh'd in rhyme;
While thy kind cautions warn'd him to beware
Of Penury, the Bard's perpetual fnare;

Marking the early temper of his foul, 445
Carelefs of wealth, nor fit for bafe controul:
Thou tender Saint, to whom he owes much more
Than ever Child to Parent ow'd before,
In life's firft feafon, when the fever's flame
Shrunk to deformity his fhrivell'd frame, 450
And turn'd each fairer image in his brain
To blank confufion and her crazy train,
'Twas thine, with conftant love, thro' ling'ring years,
To bathe thy Idiot Orphan in thy tears;
Day after day, and night fucceeding night, 455
To turn inceffant to the hideous fight,
And frequent watch, if haply at thy view
Departed Reafon might not dawn anew.
Tho' medicinal art, with pitying care,
Cou'd lend no aid to fave thee from defpair, 460
Thy fond maternal heart adher'd to Hope and Prayer:
Nor pray'd in vain; thy child from Pow'rs above
Receiv'd the fenfe to feel and blefs thy love;
O might he thence receive the happy fkill,
And force proportion'd to his ardent will, 465
With Truth's unfading radiance to emblaze
Thy virtues, worthy of immortal praife!

Nature,

Nature, who deck'd thy form with Beauty's flowers,
Exhaufted on thy foul her finer powers ;
Taught it with all her energy to feel   470
Love's melting foftnefs, Friendfhip's fervid zeal,
The generous purpofe, and the active thought,
With Charity's diffufive fpirit fraught ;
There all the beft of mental gifts fhe plac'd,
Vigor of Judgment, purity of Tafte,   475
Superior parts, without their fpleenful leaven,
Kindnefs to Earth, and confidence in Heaven.

 While my fond thoughts o'er all thy merits roll,
Thy praife thus gufhes from my filial foul ;
Nor will the Public with harfh rigor blame   480
This my juft homage to thy honor'd name ;
To pleafe that Public, if to pleafe be mine,
Thy Virtues train'd me—let the praife be thine.

 Since thou haft reach'd that world where Love alone,
Where Love Parental can exceed thy own ;   485
If in celeftial realms the bleft may know
And aid the objects of their care below,
While in this fublunary fcene of ftrife
Thy Son poffeffes frail and feverifh life,

If

If Heaven allot him many an added hour,   490
Gild it with virtuous thought and mental **power,**
Power to exalt, with every aim refin'd,
The lovelieſt of the Arts that bleſs mankind!

END OF THE FOURTH EPISTLE.

EPISTLE

EPISTLE

THE FIFTH.

A R G U M E N T

OF THE FIFTH EPISTLE.

Examination of the received opinion, that supernatural Agency is essential to the Epic Poem.—The folly and injustice of all arbitrary systems in Poetry.—The Epic province not yet exhausted.—Subjects from English History the most interesting.—A national Epic Poem the great desideratum in English literature.—The Author's wish of seeing it supplied by the genius of Mr. MASON.

E P I S T L E V.

ILL-FATED Poefy! as human worth,
Prais'd, yet unaided, often finks to earth;
So fink thy powers; not doom'd alone to know
Scorn, or neglect, from an unfeeling Foe,
But deftin'd more oppreffive wrong to feel   5
From the mifguided Friend's perplexing zeal.
Such Friends are thofe, who in their proud difplay
Of thy young beauty, and thy early fway,
Pretend thou'rt robb'd of all thy warmth fublime,
By the benumbing touch of modern Time.   10

What! is the Epic Mufe, that lofty Fair,
Who makes the difcipline of Earth her care!
That mighty Minifter, whom Virtue leads
To train the nobleft minds to nobleft deeds!
Is fhe, in office great, in glory rich,   15
Degraded to a poor, pretended Witch,

O   Who

Who rais'd her fpells, and all her magic power,
But on the folly of the favoring hour?
Whofe dark, defpis'd illufions melt away
At the clear dawn of Philofophic day?   20
To fuch they fink her, who lament her fall
From the high Synod of th' Olympian Hall;
Who worfhip Syftem, hid in Fancy's veil,
And think that all her Epic force muft fail,
If fhe no more can borrow or create   25
Celeftial Agents to uphold her ftate.
To prove if this fam'd doctrine may be found
To reft on folid, or on fandy ground,
Let Critic Reafon all her light diffufe
O'er the wide empire of this injur'd Mufe,   30
To guide our fearch to every varied fource
And feparate finew of her vital force.—
To three prime powers within the human frame,
With equal energy fhe points her aim:
By pure exalted Sentiment fhe draws   35
From Judgment's fteady voice no light applaufe;
By Nature's fimple and pathetic ftrains,
The willing homage of the Heart fhe gains;

The

The precious tribute she receives from these,
Shines undebas'd by changing Time's decrees;　　　40
The noble thought, that fir'd a Grecian soul,
Keeps o'er a British mind its firm controul;
The scenes, where Nature seems herself to speak,
Still touch a Briton, as they touch'd a Greek:
To captivate admiring Fancy's eyes,　　　45
She bids celestial decorations rise;
But, as a playful and capricious child
Frowns at the splendid toy on which it smil'd;
So wayward Fancy now with scorn surveys
Those specious Miracles she lov'd to praise;　　　50
Still fond of change, and fickle Fashion's dupe,
Now keen to soar, and eager now to stoop,
Her Gods, Dev'ls, Saints, Magicians, rise and fall,
And now she worships each, now laughs at all.

If then within the rich and wide domain　　　55
O'er which the Epic Muse delights to reign,
One province weaker than the rest be found,
'Tis her Celestial Sphere, or Fairy Ground:
Her realm of Marvels is the distant land,
O'er which she holds a perilous command;　　　60

O 2

For, plac'd beyond the reach of Nature's aid,
Here her worſt foes her tottering force invade :
O'er the wide precinct proud Opinion towers,
And withers with a look its alter'd powers ;
While laviſh Ridicule, pert Child of Taſte !   65
Turns the rich confine to ſo poor a waſte,
That ſome, who deem it but a cumbrous weight,
Would lop this Province from its Parent State.

What mighty voice firſt ſpoke this wond'rous law,
Which ductile Critics ſtill repeat with awe —   70
That man's unkindling ſpirit muſt refuſe
A generous plaudit to th' Heroic Muſe,
Howe'er ſhe paint her ſcenes of manly life,
If no ſuperior Agents aid the ſtrife ?

In days of courtly wit, and wanton mirth,   75
The looſe PETRONIUS gave the maxim birth ; *
Perchance, to ſooth the envious Nero's ear,
And ſink the Bard whoſe fame he ſigh'd to hear ;
To injure LUCAN, whoſe advent'rous mind,
Inflam'd by Freedom, with juſt ſcorn reſign'd   80

* Ver. 76. See NOTE I.

I   Th'

Th' exhausted fables of the starry pole,
And found a nobler theme in CATO's soul:
To wound him, in the mask of Critic art,
The subtle Courtier launch'd this venom'd dart,
And following Critics, fond of Classic lore,　　　　85
Still echo the vain law from shore to shore ;
On Poets still for Deities they call,
And deem mere earthly Bards no Bards at all.
Yet, if by fits the mighty HOMER nods,
Where sinks he more than with his sleepy Gods?　　90
E'en LUCAN proves, by his immortal name,
How weak the dagger levell'd at his fame ;
For in his Song, which Time will ne'er forget,
If Taste, who much may praise, will much regret,
'Tis not the absence of th' Olympian state,　　　　95
Embroil'd by jarring Gods in coarse debate :
'Tis nice arrangement, Nature's easy air,
In scenes unfolded with superior care ;
'Tis softer diction, elegantly terse,
And the fine polish of Virgilian Verse.　　　　　　100
O blind to Nature ! who assert the Muse
Must o'er the human frame her empire lose,

　　　　　　　　　　　　　　　　　　Failing

Failing to fly, in Fancy's wild career,
Above this vifible diurnal fphere!

   Behold yon penfive Fair! who turns with grief   105
The tender Novel's foul-poffeffing leaf!
Why with moift eyes to thofe foft pages glu'd,
Forgetting her fix'd hours of fleep and food;
Why does fhe keenly grafp its precious woes,
Nor quit the volume till the ftory clofe?   110
'Tis not that Fancy plays her revels there,
Cheating the mind with lucid forms of air;
'Tis not that Paffion, in a ftyle impure,
Holds the warm fpirit by a wanton lure:
'Tis fuffering Virtue's fympathetic fway,   115
That all the fibres of her breaft obey;
'Tis Action, where Immortals claim no part;
'Tis Nature, grappled to the human heart.

   If this firm Sov'reign of the feeling breaft
Can thus the fafcinated thought arreft,   120
And thro' the bofom's deep receffes pierce,
Ungrac'd, unaided by enchanting Verfe,
Say! fhall we think, with limited controul,
She wants fufficient force to feize the foul,

When

When Harmony's congenial tones convey   125
Charms to her voice, that aid its magic fway?
If Admiration's hand, with eager grafp,
Her darling HOMER's deathlefs volume clafp,
Say to what fcenes her partial eyes revert!
Say what they firft explore, and laft defert!   130
The fcenes that glitter with no heavenly blaze,
Where human agents human feelings raife,
While Truth, enamor'd of the lovely line,
Cries to their parent Nature, "Thefe are thine."
When Neptune rifes in Homeric ftate,   135
And on their Lord the Powers of Ocean wait;
Tho' pliant Fancy trace the fteps he trod,
And with a tranfient worfhip own the God,
Yet colder readers with indifference view,
The Sovereign of the deep, and all his vaffal crew,   140
Nor feel his watery pomp their mind enlarge,
More than the pageant of my Lord May'r's barge.
But when Achilles' wrongs our eyes engage,
All bofoms burn with fympathetic rage:
And when thy love parental, Chief of Troy!   145
Haftes to relieve the terrors of thy boy,

Our

Our senses in thy fond emotion join,
And every heart's in unison with thine.

    Still in the Muse's ear shall Echo ring,
That heavenly Agents are her vital spring?   150
Those who conclude her winning charms arise
From Beings darting from the distant skies,
Appear to cherish a conceit as vain,
As once was harbour'd in Neanthus' brain,
When he believ'd that harmony must dwell   155
In the cold concave of the Orphic shell:
The ancient Lyre, to which the Thracian sung,
Whose hallow'd chords were in a temple hung,
The shallow Youth with weak ambition sought,
And of the pilfering Priest the relique bought;   160
Viewing his treasure with deluded gaze,
He deem'd himself the heir of Orphic praise;
But when his awkward fingers tried to bring
Expected music from the silent string,
Not e'en the milder brutes his discord bore,   165
But howling dogs the fancied Orpheus tore. *

* Ver. 166. See NOTE II.

When

When the true Poet, in whofe frame are join'd
Softnefs of Heart and Energy of Mind,
His Epic fcene's expanfive limit draws,
Faithful to Nature's univerfal laws;   170
If thro' her various walks he boldly range,
Marking how oft her pliant features change;
If, as fhe teaches, his quick powers fupply
Succeffive pictures to th' aftonifh'd eye,
Where nobleft paffions nobleft deeds infpire,   175
And radiant fouls exhibit all their fire;
Where fofter forms their fweet attractions blend,
And fuffering Beauty makes the world her friend;
If thus he build his Rhyme, with varied art,
On each dear intereft of the human heart,   180
His genius, by no vain conceits betray'd,
May fpurn faint Allegory's feeble aid.

   Th' Heroic Mufe, in earthly virtue ftrong,
May drive the hoft of Angels from her Song,
As her fair Sifter Mufe, the Tragic Queen,   185
Has banifh'd Ghofts from her pathetic fcene,
Tho' her high foul, by SHAKESPEARE's magic fway'd,
Still bends to buried Denmark's aweful Shade.

P

If

If we efteem this Epic Queen fo great,
To fpare her heavenly train, yet keep her ftate,   190
'Tis not our aim, with fyftematic pride,
To fink their glory, or their powers to hide,
Who add, when folded in the Mufe's arms,
Celeftial beauty to her earthly charms.

   Sublimely fafhion'd, by no mortal hands,   195
The dome of mental Pleafure wide expands:
Form'd to prefide o'er its allotted parts,
At different portals ftand the feparate Arts;
But every portal different paths may gain,
Alike uniting in the myftic Fane.   200
Contentious mortals on thefe paths debate;
Some, wrangling on the road, ne'er reach the gate,
While others, arm'd with a defpotic rod,
Allow no pafs but what themfelves have trod.
The nobleft fpirits, to this foible prone,   205
Have flander'd powers congenial with their own:
Hence, on a Brother's genius Milton frown'd,
Scorning the graceful chains of final found,
And to one form confin'd the free fublime,
Infulting Dryden as the Man of Rhyme.   210

Caprice

Caprice ftill gives this lafting ftruggle life;
Rhyme and Blank Verfe maintain their idle ftrife:
The friends of one are ftill the other's foes,
For ftubborn Prejudice no mercy knows.
As in Religion, Zealots, blindly warm,   215
Neglect the Effence, while they grafp the Form;
Poetic Bigots, thus perverfely wrong,
Think Modes of Verfe comprize the Soul of Song.

  If the fine Statuary fill his part
With all the powers of energetic Art;   220
If to the figures, that, with fkill exact,
His genius blends in one impaffion'd act,
If to this Group fuch fpeaking force he give,
That ftartled Nature almoft cries " They live;"
All tongues with zeal th' enchanting work applaud, 225
Nor the great Artift of due praife defraud,
Whether he form'd the rich expreffive mafs
Of Parian marble, or Corinthian brafs;
For each his powers might fafhion to fulfil
The nobleft purpofe of mimetic fkill;   230
Each from his foul might catch Promethean fire,
And fpeak his talents, till the world expire.

'Tis

'Tis thus that MILTON's Verfe, and DRYDEN's Rhyme,
Are proof alike againſt the rage of Time;
Each Maſter modell'd, with a touch ſo bold,   235
The rude materials which he choſe to mould,
That each his portion to perfection brought,
Accompliſhing the glorious end he ſought.

Falſe to themſelves, and to their intereſt blind,
Are thoſe cold judges, of faſtidious mind,   240
Who with vain rules the ſuffering Arts would load,
Who, ere they ſmile, conſult the Critic's code;
Where, puzzled by the different doubts they ſee,
(For who ſo oft as Critics diſagree?)
They loſe that pleaſure by free ſpirits ſeiz'd,   245
In vainly ſettling how they ſhould be pleas'd.

Far wiſer thoſe, who, with a generous joy,
Nor blindly fond, nor petulantly coy,
Follow each movement of the varying Muſe,
Whatever ſtep her airy form may chuſe,   250
Nor to one march her rapid feet confine,
While eaſe and ſpirit in her geſture join;
Thoſe who facilitate her free deſire,
To melt the heart, or ſet the ſoul on fire;

Who,

Who, if her voice to fimple Nature lean,   255
And fill with Human forms her Epic fcene;
Pleas'd with her aim, affift her moral plan,
And feel with manly fympathy for Man:
Or if fhe draw, by Fancy's magic tones,
Ætherial Spirits from their fapphire thrones,   260
Her Heavenly fhapes with willing homage greet,
And aid, with ductile thought, her bright deceit;
For, if the Epic Mufe ftill wifh to tower
Above plain Nature's firm and graceful power,
Tho' Critics think her vital powers are loft   265
In cold Philofophy's petrific froft;
That Magic cannot her funk charms reftore,
That Heaven and Hell can yield her nothing more;
Yet may fhe dive to many a fecret fource
And copious fpring of vifionary force: 270
India yet holds a Mythologic mine,
Her ftrength may open, and her art refine:
Tho' Afian fpoils the realms of Europe fill,
Thofe Eaftern riches are unrifled ftill;
Genius may there his courfe of honor run,   275
And fpotlefs Laurels in that field be won. *

* Ver. 276. See NOTE III.

Yet

Yet nobler aims the Bards of Britain court,
Who fteer by Freedom's ftar to Glory's port;
Our gen'rous Ifle, with far fuperior claim,
Afks for her Chiefs the palm of Epic fame.   280
In every realm where'er th' Heroic Mufe
Has deign'd her glowing fpirit to infufe,
Her tuneful Sons with civic fplendor blaze,
The honour'd Heralds of their country's praife,
Save in our land, the nation of the earth   285
Ordain'd to give the brighteft Heroes birth !—
By fome ftrange fate, which rul'd each Poet's tongue,
Her deareft Worthies yet remain unfung.

Critics there are, who, with a fcornful fmile,
Reject the annals of our martial Ifle,   290
And, dead to patriot Paffion, coldly deem
They yield for lofty Song no touching theme.

What ! can the Britifh heart, humanely brave,
Feel for the Greek who loft his female flave ?
Can it, devoted to a favage **Chief**,   295
Swell with his rage, and foften with his grief ?
And fhall it not with keener zeal embrace
Their brighter caufe, who, born of Britifh race,

5   With

With the ftrong cement of the blood they fpilt,
The fplendid fane of Britifh Freedom built?   300
Bleft Spirits, who, with kindred fire endued,
Thro' different ages this bright work purfued,
May Art and Genius crown your fainted band
With that poetic wreath your Deeds demand!

    While, led by Fancy thro' her wide domain,   305
Our fteps advance around her Epic plain;
While we furvey each laurel that it bore,
And every confine of the realm explore,
See Liberty, array'd in light ferene,
Pours her rich luftre o'er th' expanding fcene!   310
Thee, MASON, thee fhe views with fond regard,
And calls to nobler heights her fav'rite Bard.
Tracing a circle with her blazing fpear,
" Here," cries the Goddefs, " raife thy fabric here,
Build on thefe rocks, that to my reign belong,   315
The nobleft bafis of Heroic Song!
Fix here! and, while thy growing works afcend,
My voice fhall guide thee, and my arm defend."
As thus fhe fpeaks, methinks her high beheft
Imparts pure rapture to thy confcious breaft,   320

                                   Pure

Pure as the joy immortal NEWTON found,
When Nature led him to her utmoſt bound,
And clearly ſhew'd, where unborn ages lie,
The diſtant Comet to his daring eye;
Pure as the joy the Sire of mortals knew,   325
When bliſsful Eden open'd on his view,
When firſt he liſten'd to the voice Divine,
And wond'ring heard, " This Paradiſe is thine."
With ſuch delight may'ſt thou her gift receive!
May thy warm heart with bright ambition heave   330
To raiſe a Temple to her hallow'd name,
Above what Grecian artiſts knew to frame!
Of Engliſh form the ſacred fabric rear,
And bid our Country with juſt rites revere
The Power, who ſheds, in her benignant ſmile,   335
The brighteſt Glory on our boaſted Iſle!

    Juſtly on thee th' inſpiring Goddeſs calls;
Her mighty taſk each weaker Bard appalls:
'Tis thine, O MASON! with unbaffled ſkill,
Each harder duty of our Art to fill;   340
'Tis thine, in robes of beauty to array,
And in bright Order's lucid blaze diſplay,

The

The forms that Fancy, to thy wishes kind,
Stamps on the tablet of thy clearer mind.
How softly sweet thy notes of pathos swell,   345
The tender accents of Elfrida tell;
Caractacus proclaims, with Freedom's fire,
How rich the tone of thy sublimer Lyre;
E'en in this hour, propitious to thy fame,
The rural Deities repeat thy name: 350
With festive joy I hear the sylvan throng
Hail the completion of their favorite Song,
Thy graceful Song! in honor of whose power,
Delighted Flora, in her sweetest bower,
Weaves thy unfading wreath;—with fondest care,   355
Proudly she weaves it, emulously fair,
To match that crown, which in the Mantuan grove
The richer Ceres for her VIRGIL wove!
See! his Euridice herself once more
Revisits earth from the Elysian shore!   360
Behold! she hovers o'er thy echoing glade!
Envy, not love, conducts the pensive Shade,
Who, trembling at thy Lyre's pathetic tone,
Fears lest Nerina's fame surpass her own.

Q   Thou

Thou happy Bard! whofe fweet and potent voice   365
Can reach all notes within the Poet's choice;
Whofe vivid foul has led thee to infufe
Dramatic life in the preceptive Mufe;
Since, bleft alike with Beauty and with Force,
Thou rivall'ft Virgil in his Sylvan courfe,   370
O be it thine the higher palm to gain,
And pafs him in the wide Heroic plain!
To fing, with equal fire, of nobler themes,
To gild Hiftoric Truth with Fancy's beams!
To Patriot Chiefs unfung thy Lyre devote,   375
And fwell to Liberty the lofty note!

With humbler aim, but no ungenerous view,
My fteps, lefs firm, their lower path purfue;
Of different Arts I fearch the ample field,
Mark its paft fruits, and what it yet may yield;   380
With willing voice the praife of Merit found,
And bow to Genius wherefoever found;
O'er my free Verfe bid nobleft names prefide,
Tho' Party's hoftile lines thofe names divide;
Party! whofe murdering fpirit I abhor,   385
More fubtly cruel, and lefs brave than War.

2   Party!

Party! infidious Fiend! whofe vapors blind
The light of Juftice in the brighteft mind;
Whofe feverifh tongue, whence deadly venom flows,
Bafely belies the merit of her foes!   390
O that my Verfe with magic power were bleft,
To drive from Learning's field this baleful peft!
Fond, fruitlefs wifh! the mighty tafk would foil
The firmeft fons of Literary Toil;
In vain a letter'd Hercules might rife   395
To cleanfe the ftable where this Monfter lies:
Yet, if the Imps of her malignant brood,
With all their Parent's acrid gall endu'd;
If Spleen pours forth, to Mockery's apifh tune,
Her gibing Ballad, and her bafe Lampoon,   400
On faireft names, from every blemifh free,
Save what the jaundic'd eyes of Party fee;
My glowing fcorn will execrate the rhyme,
Tho' laughing Humor ftrike its tuneful chime;
Tho' keeneft Wit the glitt'ring lines inveft   405
With all the fplendor of the Adder's creft.
    Sublimer MASON! not to thee belong
The reptile beauties of envenom'd Song.

Q 2

Thou

'Thou chief of living Bards ! O be it ours,
In fame tho' different, as of different powers,   410
Party's dark clouds alike to rife above,
And reach the firmament of Public Love !
May'ft thou afcend Parnaffus' higheft mound,
In triumph there the Epic Trumpet found;
While, with no envious zeal, I thus afpire   415
By juft applaufe to fan thy purer fire ;
And of the Work which Freedom pants to fee,
Which thy firm Genius claims referv'd for thee,
In this frank ftyle my honeft thoughts impart,
If not an Artift yet a friend to Art.   420

NOTES.

NOTES.

N O T E S

F I R S T E P I S T L E.

NOTE I. Ver. 7.

SUCH dark decrees have letter'd Bigots penn'd,
   Yet feiz'd that honor'd name, the Poet's Friend.] ·Of the feveral
authors who have written on Epic Poetry, many of the moft celebrated
are more likely to confound and deprefs, than to enlighten and exalt
the young Poetical Student. The Poetics of Scaliger, which are little
more than a laboured panegyric of Virgil, would lead him to regard the
Æneid as the only ftandard of perfection ; and the more elegant and accomplifhed Vida inculcates the fame pufillanimous leffon, though in
fpirited and harmonious verfe.

> Unus hic ingenio præftanti gentis Achivæ
> Divinos vates longe fuperavit, et arte,
> Aureus immortale fonans. ftupet ipfa pavetque,
> Quamvis ingentem miretur Græcia Homerum.

> Ergo ipfum ante alios animo venerare Maronem,
> Atque unum fequere, utque potes, veftigia ferva !
> VIDA.

See how the Grecian Bards, at diftance thrown,
With reverence bow to this diftinguifh'd fon;
Immortal founds his golden lines impart,
And nought can match his Genius but his Art;

5

E'en

E'en Greece turns pale and trembles at his fame,
Which shades the lustre of her Homer's name.
— — — — — — —

Hence, sacred Virgil from thy soul adore
Above the rest, and to thy utmost power
Pursue the glorious paths he struck before.

PITT's Translation.

A Critic, who lately rose to great eminence in our own country, has endeavoured by a more singular method to damp the ardour of inventive Genius, and to annihilate the hopes of all who would aspire to the praise of originality in this higher species of poetical composition. He has attempted to establish a Triumvirate in the Epic world, with a perpetuity of dominion. Every reader who is conversant with modern criticism will perceive that I allude to the following passage in the famous Dissertation on the sixth Book of Virgil:—" Just as Virgil rivalled Homer, so Milton emulated both of them. He found Homer possessed of the province of Morality; Virgil of Politics; and nothing left for him but that of Religion. This he seized, as aspiring to share with them in the government of the Poetic world: and, by means of the superior dignity of his subject, hath gotten to the head of that Triumvirate, which took so many ages in forming. These are the three species of the Epic Poem; for its largest sphere is *human action*, which can be considered but in a *moral*, political, or religious view: and These the three *Makers*; for each of their Poems was struck out at a heat, and came to perfection from its first essay. Here then the grand scene was closed, and all farther improvements of the Epic at an end."

I apprehend that few critical remarks contain more *absurdity* (to use the favourite expression of the author I have quoted) than the preceding lines. Surely Milton is himself a proof that *human action* is not the largest sphere of the Epic Poem; and as to Virgil, his most passionate admirers must allow, that in subject and design he is much less of an original than Camoens or Lucan. But such a critical statute of limitation, if I may call it so, is not less pernicious than absurd. To disfigure the sphere of Imagination with these capricious and arbitrary zones is an injury to science. Such Criticism, instead of giving spirit

7

and

and energy to the laudable ambition of a youthful Poet, can only lead him to ftart like Macbeth at unreal mockery, and to exclaim, when he is invited by Genius to the banquet, " The Table's full."

NOTE II. Ver. 77.

Thus, at their banquets, fabling Greeks rehearfe
The fancied origin of facred Verfe.] For this fable, fuch as it is, I am indebted to a paffage in Athenæus, which the curious reader may find in the clofe of that fanciful and entertaining compiler, page 701 of Cafaubon's edition.

NOTE III. Ver. 207.

Why did the Epic Mufe's filent lyre
Shrink from thofe feats that fummon'd all her fire?] I have ventured to fuppofe that Greece produced no worthy fucceffor of Homer, and that her exploits againft the Perfians were not celebrated by any Poet in a manner fuitable to fo fublime a fubject;—yet an author named Chærilus is faid to have recorded thofe triumphs of his country in verfe, and to have pleafed the Athenians fo highly as to obtain from them a public and pecuniary reward. He is fuppofed to have been a cotemporary of the hiftorian Herodotus. But from the general filence of the more early Greek writers concerning the merit of this Poet, we may, I think, very fairly conjecture that his compofitions were not many degrees fu-perior to thofe of his unfortunate namefake, who frequented the court of Alexander the Great, and is faid to have fung the exploits of his Sove-reign, on the curious conditions of receiving a piece of gold for every good verfe, and a box on the ear for every bad one. The old Scholiaft on Horace, who has preferved this idle ftory, concludes it by faying, that the miferable Bard was beat to death in confequence of his contract. Some eminent modern Critics have indeed attempted to vindicate the reputation of the more early Chærilus, who is fuppofed to be confounded, both by Horace himfelf, and afterwards by Scaliger, with the Chærilus rewarded by Alexander. Voffius *, in particular, appears a warm advo-cate in his behalf, and appeals to various fragments of the ancient Bard

* De Hiftoricis Græcis.

R   preferved

preferved by Ariftotle, Strabo, and others, and to the teftimony of Plutarch in his favour. But on confulting the fragments he has referred to, they rather fortify than remove my conjecture. The fcrap preferved by Ariftotle in his Rhetoric is only half a verfe, and quoted without any commendation of its author. The two citations in Strabo amount to little more. The curious reader may alfo find in Athenæus an Epitaph on Sardanapalus, attributed to this Poet; who is mentioned by the fame author as peculiarly addicted to the groffer exceffes of the table.——Let us now return to that Chærilus whom Horace has " damn'd to everlafting fame." The judicious and elegant Roman Satirift feems remarkably unjuft, in paying a compliment to the poetical judgment of his patron Auguftus, at the expence of the Macedonian hero. Alexander appears to have poffeffed much more poetical fpirit, and a higher relifh for poetry, than the cold-blooded Octavius. It is peculiarly unfair, to urge his liberality to a poor Poet as a proof that he wanted critical difcernment, when he had himfelf fo thoroughly vindicated the delicacy of his tafte, by the enthufiaftic Bon-mot, that he had rather be the Therfites of Homer than the Achilles of Chærilus.

NOTE IV. VERSE 231.

When grave Boffu by Syftem's ftudied laws
The Grecian Bard's ideal picture draws.] Though Boffu is called " the beft explainer of Ariftotle, and one of the moft learned and judicious of modern critics," by a writer for whofe opinions I have much efteem, I cannot help thinking that his celebrated Effay on Epic Poetry is very ill calculated either to guide or to infpirit a young Poet. The abfurdity of his advice concerning the mode of forming the fable, by chufing a moral, inventing the incidents, and then fearching hiftory for names to fuit them, has been fufficiently expofed : and as to his leading idea, concerning the defign of Homer in the compofition of the Iliad and Odyffey, I apprehend moft poetical readers muft feel that he is probably miftaken ; for it is a conjectural point, and placed beyond the poffibility of decifion. Perhaps few individuals differ more from each other in their modes of thinking, by the force of education and of national manners, than a modern French Critic and an early Poet of Greece ; yet the former will often pretend, with the moft decifive air,

to

to lay open the fenforium of an ancient Bard, and to count every link in the chain of his ideas. Thofe who are moft acquainted with the movements of imagination, will acknowledge the fteps of this airy power to be fo light and evanefcent in their nature, that perhaps a Poet himfelf, in a few years after finifhing his work, might be utterly unable to recollect the exact train of thought, or the various minute occurrences which led him to the general defign, or directed him in the particular parts of his poem. But, in fpite of the interval of many hundred centuries, the decifive magic of criticifm can call up all the fhadows of departed thought that ever exifted in his brain, and difplay, with a moft aftonifhing clearnefs, the precife ftate of his mind in the moment of compofition.

" Homere," fays Boffu, " * voyoit les Grecs pour qui il écrivoit, diviféz en autant d'etats qu'ils avoient de villes confiderables: chacune faifoit un corps a part & avoit fa forme de gouvernement independamment de toutes les autres. Et toute-fois ces etats differens etoient fouvent obligéz de fe reünir comme en un feul corps contre leurs ennemis communs. Voila fans doute deux fortes de gouvernemens bien differens, pour etre commodement reunis en un corps de morale, & en un feul poëme.

" Le poëte en a donc fait deux fables feparées. L'une eft pour toute la Grece reünie en un feul corps, mais compofée de parties independantes les unes des autres, comme elles etoient en effet ; & l'autre eft pour chaque etat particulier, tels qu'ils etoient pendant la paix, fans ce premier rapport & fans la neceffité de fe reünir.

" Homere a donc pris pour le fond de fa fable, cette grande verité, que la Mefintelligence des princes ruine leurs propres etats."

On the Odyffey Boffu remarks, " Que la verité qui fert de fond à cette fiction, & qui avec elle compofe la fable, eft, que l'abfence d'une perfonne hors de chez foi, ou qui n'a point l'œil à ce qui s'y fait, y caufe de grands defordres +."

On the mature confideration of thefe two moral axioms, the Critic fuppofes the fublime Bard to have begun his refpective Poems ; for Homer, continues he, " ‡ n'avoit point d'autre deffein que de former

---

* Livre i. chap. 8.　　　† Livre i. chap. 10.　　　‡ Livre i. chap. 13.

R 2　　　　　　　　　　　　　agreablement

agreablement les mœurs de ſes Citoïens, en leur propoſant, comme dit Horace, ce qui eſt utile ou pernicieux, ce qui eſt honnete ou ce qui ne l'eſt pas : - - - il n'a entrepris de raconter aucune action particuliere d'Achille ou d'Ulyſſe. Il a fait la fable et le deſſein de ſes poemes, ſans penſer à ces princes ; & enſuite il leur a fait l'honneur de donner leurs noms aux heros qu'il avoit feints."

The preceding remarks of this celebrated Critic have been frequently admired as an ingenious conjecture, which moſt happily illuſtrates the real purpoſe of Homer. To me they appear ſo much the reverſe, that if I ventured to adopt any decided opinion on a point ſo much darkened by the clouds of antiquity, I ſhould rather incline to the idea which Boſſu affects to explode, and ſuppoſe the Poems of Homer intended panegyrics on the very princes whom the Critic affirms he never thought of while he was deſigning the works which have made them immortal.

There is a ſtriking paſſage on this ſubject in a dialogue of Plato, which I ſhall enlarge upon, for two reaſons : 1ſt, As it proves that the latter perſuaſion concerning the purpoſe of Homer was enter-tained at Athens ; and 2dly, Becauſe it gives me a pleaſing oppor-tunity of ſupporting the learned Madame Dacier againſt an ill-grounded cenſure of a late Engliſh critic. In her Preface to the Odyſſey, ſhe aſſerts that the judgment of antiquity decided in favor of the Iliad ; and ſhe appeals to part of the ſentence in Plato to which I have alluded, as a proof of her aſſertion. Mr. Wood, in a note to the Introduction of his Eſſay on Homer, endeavours to ſhew the inſufficiency of this proof ; and ſtill farther, to convince us that Madame Dacier was utterly miſ-taken in her ſenſe of the paſſage to which ſhe appealed. If he ventures to contradict this learned lady, he does not however inſult her with that inſolent pertneſs with which ſhe is frequently treated in the notes to Pope's Homer ; and which, for the honour of our Engliſh Poet, I will not ſuppoſe to be his. But though Mr. Wood endeavours to ſup-port his opinion by argument, I apprehend that he is himſelf miſtaken, and that Madame Dacier is perfectly right in underſtanding the words of Socrates in their literal ſenſe, without the leaſt mixture of irony. It is true, indeed, that the aim of Socrates, in the courſe of the dialogue, is to ridicule the preſumption and ignorance of the ſophiſt Hippias, in the

moſt

moſt ironical manner; but the particular ſpeech on which Madame
Dacier founds her opinion, is a plain and ſimple addreſs to Eudicus, before he enters on his debate with the Sophiſt. It turns on the moſt
ſimple circumſtance, the truth of which Eudicus could hardly be ignorant of, namely, the ſentiments of his own father concerning the
Poems of Homer. As theſe ſentiments are ſuch as I believe moſt admirers of the ancient Bard have entertained on the point in queſtion, I
perfectly agree with Madame Dacier in thinking that Socrates means to
be literal and ſerious, when he ſays to Eudicus, Τȣ ϛȣ πατρος Απημαντȣ
ηκȣον οτι η Ιλιας καλλιον ειη ποιημα ῳ Ομηρῳ η η Οδυσσεια τοσȣτῳ δε καλλιον οσῳ αμεινων Αχιλλευς Οδυσσεως ειη. εκατερον γαρ των ποιηματων το μεν εις
Οδυσσεα εφη πεποιησθαι, το δ' εις Αχιλλεα. Plat. Hip. min. edit. Serrani,
tom. i. pag. 363. " I have heard your father Apemantus ſay, that the
Iliad of Homer was a finer poem than his Odyſſey, and as far ſurpaſſed
it in excellence as the virtue of Achilles ſurpaſſed the virtue of Ulyſſes;
for thoſe two poems, he ſaid, were purpoſely compoſed in honour of
thoſe two heroes: the Odyſſey, to ſhew the virtues of Ulyſſes; the
Iliad, thoſe of Achilles." Plato's Leſſer Hippias, tranſlated by Syden-
ham, page 13.

Let us now return to Boſſu; whoſe opinion concerning the purpoſe
of Homer we may venture to oppoſe, ſupported as it is by an ingenious
interpretation of ſome ambiguous paſſages in the Poetics of Ariſtotle;
and this oppoſition may be grounded, not ſo much on the ſentence which
I have quoted from Plato, as on the probable conduct of Epic compoſition in the early ages of poetry. In ſuch periods as produced the
talents of Virgil and of Dryden, when all the arts of refined flattery
were perfectly underſtood, we can eaſily conceive that they might both
be tempted to compliment the reigning monarch under the maſk of ſuch
heroic names as hiſtory could ſupply, and their genius accommodate to
their purpoſe. We find accordingly, that the Roman Bard is ſuppoſed
to have drawn a flattering portrait of his Emperor in the character of
Æneas, and that the Engliſh Poet has, with equal ingenuity, enwrapt
the diſſolute Charles the Second in the Jewiſh robes of King David.
But in ſo rude an age as we muſt admit that of Homer to have been;
when the Poet was certainly more the child of Nature than of Art; when
he had no hiſtory to conſult, perhaps no patron to flatter, and no critics

to

to elude or obey ; in fuch an age, may we not more naturally conjecture, that poetical compofition was neither laboured in its form, nor deep in its defign ? that, inftead of being the flow and fyftematic product of political reafoning, it was the quick and artlefs offspring of a ftrong and vivifying fancy, which, brooding over the tales of tradition, foon raifed them into fuch life and beauty, as muft fatisfy and enchant a warlike and popular audience, ever ready to liften with delight to the heroic feats of their anceftors.

If the learned Boffu appears unfortunate in his fyftem concerning the purpofe of Homer, he may be thought ftill more fo in his attempt to analyze the Divinities of Virgil ; for, to throw new light on the convention of the Gods, in the opening of the tenth Æneid, he very ferioufly informs us, that " * Venus is divine mercy, or the love of God towards virtuous men ; and Juno his juftice."

I cannot conclude thefe very free ftrictures on a celebrated author, without bearing a pleafing teftimony to the virtues of the man.—Boffu is allowed by the biographers of his country to have been remarkable for the mildeft manners and moft amiable difpofition ; totally free from that imperious and bigotted attachment to fpeculative opinions, which the fcience he cultivated is fo apt to produce. He endeared himfelf to Boileau by a generous act of friendfhip, that led to an intimacy between them, which was diffolved only by the death of the former, in 1680.

N O T E V. VERSE 244.

Imputes to Virgil his own dark conceit.] As it requires much leifure to examine, and more fkill to unravel an intricate hypothefis, twifted into a long and laboured chain of quotation and argument, the Differtation on the fixth Book of Virgil remained for fome time unrefuted. The public very quietly acquiefced in the ftrange pofition of its author, " That Æneas's adventure to the infernal fhades, is no other than a figurative defcription of his initiation into the Myfteries ; and particularly a very exact one of the fpectacles of the Eleufinian." At length a fuperior but anonymous Critic arofe, who, in one of the moft judicious

---

* Book v. chap. 1.

and

and spirited essays that our nation has produced on a point of classical literature, completely overturned this ill-founded edifice, and exposed the arrogance and futility of its assuming architect. The Essay I allude to is entitled " Critical Observations on the Sixth Book of the Æneid ;" printed for Elmsly, 1770 : and as this little publication is, I believe, no longer to be purchased, the curious reader may thank me for transcribing a few of its most striking passages.

Having ridiculed, with great spirit and propriety, Warburton's general idea of the Æneid as a political institute, and his ill-supported assertion, that both the ancient and modern poets afforded Virgil a pattern for introducing the Mysteries into this famous episode, the author proceeds to examine how far the Critic's hypothesis of initiation may be supported or overthrown by the text of the Poet. " It is," says he, " from extrinsical circumstances that we may expect the discovery of Virgil's allegory. Every one of these circumstances persuades me, that Virgil described a real, not a mimic world, and that the scene lay in the Infernal Shades, and not in the Temple of Ceres.

" The singularity of the Cumæan shores must be present to every traveller who has once seen them. To a superstitious mind, the thin crust, vast cavities, sulphureous steams, poisonous exhalations, and fiery torrents, may seem to trace out the narrow confine of the two worlds. The lake Avernus was the chief object of religious horror ; the black woods which surrounded it, when Virgil first came to Naples, were perfectly suited to feed the superstition of the people *. It was generally believed, that this deadly flood was the entrance of Hell † ; and an oracle was once established on its banks, which pretended, by magic rites, to call up the departed spirits ‡. Æneas, who revolved a more daring enterprize, addresses himself to the priestess of those dark regions. Their conversation may perhaps inform us whether an initiation, or a descent to the Shades, was the object of this enterprize. She endeavours to deter the hero, by setting before him all the dangers of his rash undertaking.

* Strabo, l. v. p. 168.   † Sil. Ital. l. xii.   ‡ Diod. Siculus, l. iv. p. 267. edit. Wesseling.

———Facilis

——— Facilis defcenfus Averni ;
Noctes atque dies patet atri janua Ditis :
Sed revocare gradum, fuperafque evadere ad auras,
Hoc opus, hic labor eft *.

" Thefe particulars are abfolutely irreconcileable with the idea of
initiation, but perfectly agreeable to that of a real defcent.   That every
ftep and every inftant may lead us to the grave, is a melancholy truth.
The Myfteries were only open at ftated times, a few days at moft in the
courfe of a year.   The mimic defcent of the Myfteries was laborious and
dangerous, the return to light eafy and certain.   In real death this order
is inverted.

——— Pauci quos æquus amavit
Jupiter, aut ardens evexit ad æthera virtus,
Diis geniti, potuere †.

Thefe heroes, as we learn from the Speech of Æneas, were Hercules, Orpheus, Caftor and Pollux, Thefeus, and Pirithous.   Of all
thefe antiquity believed, that, before their death, they had feen the
habitations of the dead ; nor indeed will any of the circumftances tally
with a fuppofed initiation.   The adventure of Eurydice, the alternate
life of the Brothers, and the forcible intrufion of Alcides, Thefeus,
and Pirithous, would mock the endeavours of the moft fubtle critic,
who fhould try to melt them down into his favourite Myfteries.   The
exploits of Hercules, who triumphed over the King of Terrors,

Tartareum ille manu cuftodem in vincla petivit
Ipfius a folio regis, traxitque trementem ‡.

was a wild imagination of the Greeks § ; but it was the duty of ancient
Poets to adopt and embellifh thefe popular traditions ; and it is the
intereft of every man of tafte to acquiefce in *their poetical fictions.*"
    " Virgil has borrowed, as ufual, from Homer his epifode of the

* Æneid vi. 126.   † Ibid. vi. 129.   ‡ Ibid. vi. 395.
§ Homer Odyff. l. xi. ver. 623. Apoll. Bib. l. ii. c. 5.

Infernal Shades, and, as ufual, has infinitely improved what the Grecian had invented.   If among a profufion of beauties I durft venture to point out the moft ftriking beauties of the fixth Book, I fhould perhaps obferve, 1. That after accompanying the hero through the filent realms of Night and Chaos, we fee, with aftonifhment and pleafure, a new creation burfting upon us. 2. That we examine, with a delight which fprings from the love of virtue, the juft empire of Minos, in which the apparent irregularities of the prefent fyftem are corrected; where the patriot who died for his country is happy, and the tyrant who oppreffed it is miferable.   3. As we intereft ourfelves in the hero's fortunes, we fhare his feelings :—the melancholy Palinurus, the wretched Deiphobus, the indignant Dido, the Græcian kings, who tremble at his prefence, and the venerable Anchifes, who embraces his pious fon, and difplays to his fight the future glories of his race : all thefe objects affect us with a variety of pleafing fenfations.

   " Let us for a moment obey the mandate of our great Critic, and confider thefe aweful fcenes as a mimic fhew, exhibited in the Temple of Ceres, by the contrivance of the prieft, or, if he pleafes, of the legiflator.   Whatever was animated (I appeal to every reader of tafte) whatever was terrible, or whatever was pathetic, evaporates into lifelefs allegory.

——— Tenuem fine viribus umbram.
——————————— Dat inania verba,
Dat fine mente fonum, greffufque effingit euntis.

The end of philofophy is truth ; the end of poetry is pleafure.   I willingly adopt any interpretation which adds new beauties to the original ; I affift in perfuading myfelf that it is juft, and could almoft fhew the fame indulgence to the Critic's as to the Poet's fiction.   But fhould a grave Doctor lay out fourfcore pages in explaining away the fenfe and fpirit of Virgil, I fhould have every inducement to believe that Virgil's foul was very different from the Doctor's."

   Having fhewn, in this fpirited manner, how far the hypothefis of the Critic is inconfiftent with particular paffages, and with the general character of the Poet, the Effayift proceeds to alledge " two fimple

S   reafons,

reasons, which perfuade him that Virgil has not revealed the fecret of the Eleufinian myfteries : the firft is *his ignorance,* and the fecond *his difcretion.*" The author then proves, by very ingenious hiftorical arguments, 1ft, That it is probable the Poet was never initiated himfelf ; and, 2dly, That if he were fo, it is more probable that he would not have violated the laws both of religion and of honour, in betraying the fecret of the Myfteries ; particularly, as that fpecies of profanation is mentioned with abhorrence by a cotemporary Poet.

> —————Vetabo, qui Cereris facrum
> Vulgârit arcanæ, fub iifdem
> Sit trabibus, fragilemque mecum
> Solvat phafelum.
> Hor. l. iii. od. 2.

When Horace compofed the Ode which contains the preceding paffage, " the Æneid (continues my author) and particularly the fixth Book, were already known to the public *. The deteftation of the wretch who reveals the Myfteries of Ceres, though expreffed in general terms, muft be applied by all Rome to the author of the fixth Book of the Æneid. Can we ferioufly fuppofe that Horace would have branded with fuch wanton infamy one of the men in the world, whom he loved and honoured the moft † ?

" Nothing remains to fay, except that Horace was himfelf ignorant of his friend's allegorical meaning ; which the Bifhop of Gloucefter has fince revealed to the world. It may be fo ; yet, for my own part, I fhould be very well fatisfied with underftanding Virgil no better than Horace did."

Such is the forcible reafoning of this ingenious and fpirited writer. I have been tempted to tranfcribe thefe confiderable portions of his Work, by an idea (perhaps an ill-founded one) that the circulation of his little Pamphlet has not been equal to its merit. But if it has been in any degree neglected by our country, it has not efcaped

* Donat. in Virgil. Propert. l: ii. el. xxv. v. 66.
† Hor, l. i. od. 3. l. i. ferm. v. ver. 39, &c.

the

the researches, or wanted the applause, of a learned and judicious foreigner. Professor Heyne, the late accurate and accomplished Editor of Virgil, has mentioned it, in his Comments to the sixth Book of the Æneid, with the honour it deserves. He remarks, indeed, that the Author has censured the learned Prelate with some little acrimony; " Paullo acrius quam velis." But what lover of poetry, unbiassed by personal connection, can speak of Warburton without some marks of indignation ? If I have also alluded to this famous Commentator with a contemptuous asperity, it arises from the persuasion that he has sullied the page of every Poet whom he pretended to illustrate ; and that he frequently degraded the useful and generous profession of Criticism into a mean instrument of personal malignity : or (to use the more forcible language of his greatest antagonist) that he " invested himself in the high office of Inquisitor General and Supreme Judge of the Opinions of the Learned ; which he assumed and exercised with a ferocity and despotism without example in the Republic of Letters, and hardly to be paralleled among the disciples of Dominic *." It is the just lot of tyrants to be detested ; and of all usurpers, the literary despot is the least excusable, as he has not the common tyrannical plea of necessity or interest to alledge in his behalf; for the prevalence of *his edicts* will be found to sink in proportion to the arbitrary tone with which they are pronounced. The fate of Warburton is a striking instance of this important truth. What havock has the course of very few years produced in that pile of imperious criticism which he had heaped together ! Many of his notes on Shakespeare have already resigned their place to the superior comments of more accomplished Critics ; and perhaps the day is not far distant, when the volumes of Pope himself will cease to be a repository for the lumber of his friend. The severest enemies of Warburton must indeed allow, that several of his remarks on his Poetical Patron are entitled to preservation, by their use or beauty ; but the greater part, I apprehend, are equally destitute of both : and how far the Critic was capable of disgracing the Poet, must be evident to every reader who recollects that the nonsense in the Essay on Criticism, where

* Letter to Warburton by a late Professor, &c. page 9. 2d edition.

Pegasus

Pegasus is made to *snatch a grace*, which is justly censured by Dr. Warton, was first introduced into the poem by an arbitrary transposition of the editor.

Though arrogance is perhaps the most striking and characteristical defect in the composition of this assuming Commentator, he had certainly other critical failings of considerable importance; and it may possibly be rendering some little service to the art which he professed, to investigate the peculiarities in this singular writer, which conspire to plunge him in the crowd of those *evanescent critics* (if I may use such an expression) whom his friend Pope beheld in so clear a vision, that he seems to have given us a prophetical portrait of his own Commentator.

> Critics I saw, that others' names efface,
> And fix their own, with labour, in the place;
> Their own, like others', soon their place resign'd,
> Or disappear'd, and left the first behind.

I shall therefore hazard a few farther observations, not only on this famous Critic of our age and country, but on the two greater names of antiquity, to each of whom he has been declared superior by the partial voice of enthusiastic friendship. I wish not to offend his most zealous adherents; and, though I cannot but consider him as a literary usurper, I speak of him as a great Historian said of more exalted tyrants, sine ira et studio, quorum causas procul habeo.——There seem to be three natural endowments requisite in the formation of an accomplished critic;—strong understanding, lively imagination, and refined sensibility. The first was the characteristic of Aristotle, and by the consent of all ages he is allowed to have possessed it in a superlative degree. May I be pardoned for the opinion, that he enjoyed but a very moderate portion of the *other two*? I would not absolutely say that he had neither Fancy nor Feeling; but that his imagination was *not brilliant*, and that his sensibility was not exquisite, may I think be fairly presumed from the general tenor of his prose; nor does the little relique of his poetry contradict the idea. The two qualities in which Aristotle may be supposed defective, were the very two which peculiarly distinguish Longinus; who certainly wanted not understanding, though he might not possess the philosophi-

cal

cal fagacity of the Stagyrite.   When confidered in every point of view,
he appears the moft confummate character among the Critics of antiquity.   If Warburton bore any refemblance to either of thefe mighty
names, I apprehend it muft be to the former, and perhaps in imagination he was fuperior to Ariftotle ; but, of the three qualities which I
have ventured to confider as requifite in the perfect Critic, I conceive
him to have been miferably deficient in the laft, and certainly the moft
effential of the three ; for, as the great Commentator of Horace has phi-
lofophically and truly remarked, in a note to that Poet, " Feeling, or
Sentiment, is not only the fureft, but the fole ultimate arbiter of works
of genius *."   A man may poffefs an acute underftanding and a lively
imagination, without being a found Critic ; and this truth perhaps cannot be more clearly fhewn than in the writings of Warburton.   His
underftanding was undoubtedly acute, his imagination was lively ; but
Imagination and Sentiment are by no means fynonymous ; and he certainly wanted thofe finer feelings which conftitute accuracy of difcernment, and a perfect perception of literary excellence.   In confequence
of this defect, inftead of feizing the real fenfe and intended beauties of
an author, he frequently followed the caprices of his own active fancy,
which led him in queft of fecret meanings and myfterious allufions ;
thefe he readily found, and his powers of underftanding enabled him to
drefs them up in a plaufible and fpecious form, and to perfuade many
readers that he was (what he believed himfelf to be) the reftorer of genuine Criticifm.   As a farther proof that he was deftitute of refined fen-
fibility, I might alledge the peculiarity of his diction, which, as Dr.
Johnfon has very juftly remarked, is coarfe and impure.   Perhaps it
may be found, that in proportion as authors have enjoyed the quality
which I fuppofe him to have wanted, they have been more or lefs diftinguifhed by the eafe, the elegance, and the beauty of their language :
were I required to fortify this conjecture by examples, I fhould produce
the names of Virgil and Racine, of Fenelon and Addifon—that Addi-
fon, who, though infulted by the Commentator of Pope with the names
of an indifferent Poet and a worfe Critic, was, I think, as much fuperior
to his infulter in critical tafte, and in folidity of judgment, as he con-

* Notes on the Epiftle to Auguftus. ver. 210.

feffedly

feſſedly was in the harmony of his ſtyle, and in all the finer graces of beautiful compoſition.

NOTE VI. Verse 257.

'Tis ſaid by one, who, with this candid claim,
Has gain'd no fading wreath of critic fame.] Theſe, and the ſix ſubſequent lines, allude to the following paſſage in Dr. Warton's Eſſay on Pope. "I conclude theſe reflections with a remarkable fact. In no poliſhed nation, after Criticiſm has been much ſtudied, and the rules of writing eſtabliſhed, has any very extraordinary work ever appeared. This has viſibly been the caſe in Greece, in Rome, and in France, after Ariſtotle, Horace, and Boileau had written their Arts of Poetry. In our own country, the rules of the Drama, for inſtance, were never more completely underſtood than at preſent; yet what unintereſting, though faultleſs, Tragedies have we lately ſeen? ſo much better is our judgment than our execution. How to account for the fact here mentioned, adequately and juſtly, would be attended with all thoſe difficulties that await diſcuſſions relative to the productions of the human mind, and to the delicate and ſecret cauſes that influence them; whether or no the natural powers be not confined and debilitated by that timidity and caution which is occaſioned by a rigid regard to the dictates of art; or whether that philoſophical, that geometrical, and ſyſtematical ſpirit ſo much in vogue, which has ſpread itſelf from the ſciences even into polite literature, by conſulting only *reaſon*, has not diminiſhed and deſtroyed *ſentiment*, and made our poets write from and to the *head*, rather than the heart, or whether, laſtly, when juſt models, from which the rules have neceſſarily been drawn, have once appeared, ſucceeding writers, by vainly and ambitiouſly ſtriving to ſurpaſs thoſe juſt models, and to ſhine and ſurpriſe, do not become ſtiff and forced, and affected in their thoughts and diction." Warton's Eſſay, page 209, 3d edition.——I admire this ingenious and modeſt reaſoning; but, for the honour of that ſeverer art, which this pleaſing writer has the happy talent to enliven and embelliſh, I will venture to ſtart ſome doubts concerning the fact itſelf for which he endeavours to account. Perhaps our acquaintance with thoſe writings of Greece and Rome, which were ſubſequent to Ariſtotle and Horace, is not ſufficiently perfect to decide the point either way in reſpect

to thofe countries. But with regard to France, may we not affert, that her poetical productions, which arofe after the publication of Boileau's Didactic Effay, are at leaft equal, if not fuperior, to thofe which preceded that period ? If the Henriade of Voltaire is not a fine Epic poem, it is allowed to be the beft which the French have to boaft; not to mention the dramatic works of that extraordinary and univerfal author. If this remarkable fact may indeed be found true, I fhould rather fuppofe it to arife from the irritable nature of the poetic fpirit, fo peculiarly averfe to reftraint and controul. The Bard who could gallop his Pegafus over a free and open plain, might be eager to engage in fo pleafing an exercife; but he who obferved the direction-pofts fo thickly and fo perverfely planted, that, inftead of affifting his career, they muft probably occafion his fall, would eafily be tempted to defcend from his fteed, and to decline the courfe. Let me illuftrate this conjecture by a ftriking fact, in the very words of the Poet juft mentioned, who was by no means deficient in poetical confidence, and who has left us the following anecdote of himfelf, in that pleafing little anonymous work entitled, Commentaire Hiftorique fur les Oeuvres de l'Auteur de la Henriade. " Il lut un jour plufieurs chants de ce poeme chez le jeune Préfident de Maifons, fon intime ami. On l'impatienta par des objections; il jetta fon manufcrit dans le feu. Le Préfident Hénaut l'en retira avec peine. " Souvenez vous (lui dit Mr. Hénaut) dans une de fes lettres, que c'eft moi qui ai fauvé la Henriade, et qu'il m'en a couté une belle paire de manchettes."

To return to the Effay on Pope.—I rejoice that the amiable Critic has at length obliged the public with the conclufion of his moft engaging and ingenious work: he has the fingular talent to inftruct and to pleafe even thofe readers who are moft ready to revolt from the opinion which he endeavours to eftablifh; and he has in fome degree atoned for that excefs of feverity which his firft volume difcovered, and which funk the reputation of Pope in the eyes of many, who judge not for themfelves, even far below that mortifying level to which he meant to reduce it. Had Pope been alive, to add this fpirited effay to the bundle of writings againft himfelf which he is faid to have collected, he muft have felt, that, like the dagger of Brutus, it gave the moft painful blow, from the character of the affailant:

" All

" All the confpirators, fave only he,
Did that they did in envy of great Cæfar ;
He, only, in a general honeft thought,
And common good to all, made one of them."

Yet Pope afcended not the throne of Poetry by ufurpation, but was
feated there by a legal title ; of which I fhall fpeak farther in a fubfequent note.

NOTE VII.   VERSE 359.

His hallow'd fubject, by that Law forbid,
Might ftill have laid in filent darknefs hid.]   Boileau's Art of Poetry
made its firft appearance in 1673, fix years after the publication of Paradife Loft.   The verfes of the French Poet to which I have particularly
alluded are thefe :

C'eft donc bien vainement que nos auteurs décus,
Banniffant de leurs vers ces ornemens reçus,
Penfent faire agir Dieu, fes faints, et fes prophetes,
Comme ces dieux éclos du cerveau des Poëtes :
Mettent à chaque pas le lecteur en enfer ;
N'offrent rien qu' Aftaroth, Belzebuth, Lucifer.
De la foi d'un Chrétien les myfteres terribles
D'ornemens egayés, ne font point fufceptibles.
L'Evangile à l'efprit n'offre de tous côtés
Que penitence à faire, et tourmens merités :
Et de vos fictions le mélange coupable,
Même à fes vérités donne l'air de la fable.
Et quel objet enfin à prefenter aux yeux
Que le Diable toujours hurlant contre les cieux,
Qui de votre héros veut rabaiffer la gloire,
Et fouvent avec Dieu balance la victoire.

> Poetique de DESPREAUX, chant iii. ver. 193, &c.

The preceding lines, which are faid to have been levelled at the Clovis
of Defmaretz, appear fo pointed againft the fubject of Milton, that we
might almoft believe them intended as a fatire on our divine Bard.
There

There is nothing in Boileau's admirable Didactic Essay so liable to objection as the whole passage concerning Epic poetry. His patronage of
the old Pagan divinities, and his oblique recommendation of Classical
heroes, are alike exceptionable. Even a higher name than Boileau has
failed in framing precepts for the Epic Muse. The maxims delivered by
Tasso himself, in his Discourse on Epic poetry, are so far from perfect,
that an agreeable and judicious French critic has very justly said of him,
" S'il eût mis sa theorie en pratique, son poeme n'auroit pas tant de
charmes *." I am not so vain as to think of succeeding in the point
where these immortal authors have failed; and I must beg my reader to
remember, that the present work is by no means intended as a code of
laws for the Epic poet; it is not my design

> To write receipts how poems may be made.

For I think the writer who would condescend to frame this higher species of composition according to the exact letter of any directions whatever, may be most properly referred to that admirable receipt for an Epic
poem with which Martinus Scriblerus will happily supply him. My
serious desire is to examine and refute the prejudices which have produced, as I apprehend, the neglect of the Heroic Muse: I wish to kindle
in our Poets a warmer sense of national honour, with ambition to excel
in the noblest province of poesy. If my essay should excite that generous enthusiasm in the breast of any young poetic genius, so far from
wishing to confine him by any arbitrary dictates of my own imagination,
I should rather say to him, in the words of Dante's Virgil,

> Non aspettar mio dir più, nè mio cenno
> Libero, dritto, sano è tuo arbitrio,
> E fallo fora non fare a suo senno.

NOTE VIII. VERSE 377.

Who scorn'd all limits to his work assign'd,
Save by th' inspiring God who rul'd his mind.] " On foot, with a lance
in his hand, the Emperor himself led the solemn procession, and directed

* Marmontel Poetique Françoise.

T the

the line, which was traced as the boundary of the deftined capital;
till the growing circumference was obferved with aftonifhment by the
affiftants, who at length ventured to obferve, that he had already ex-
ceeded the moft ample meafure of a great city. "I fhall ftill advance,"
replied Conftantine, " till he, the invifible guide who marches before me, thinks proper to ftop."

GIBBON, Vol. II. page 11.

END OF THE NOTES TO THE FIRST EPISTLE.

NOTES

N O T E S

TO THE

SECOND EPISTLE.

NOTE I.   VERSE 28.

WE see thy fame traduc'd by Gallic wit.] Homer, like moſt tranſcendent characters, has found detractors in every age. We learn from a paſſage in the life of Socrates by Diogenes Laertius, that the great Poet had, in his life-time, an adverſary named Sagaris, or Syagrus; and his calumniator Zoilus is proverbially diſtinguiſhed. In the Greek Anthologia, there is a ſepulchral inſcription on a ſlanderer of the ſovereign Bard, which, for its enthuſiaſtic ſingularity, I ſhall preſent to the reader.

Εις Παρθενιον Φωκαεα εις Ομηρον παροινησαντα.

Ει και υπο χθονι κειται, ομως ετι και κατα πισσαν
    Τε μιαρογλωσσε χευατε Παρθενιε,
Ουνεκα Πιεριδεσσιν ενημεσε μυρια κεινα
    Φλεγματα, και μυσαραν απλυσιην ελεγων.
Ηλασε και μανιης επι δη τοσον, ωστ' αγορευσαι
    Πηλον Οδυσσειην και βατον Ιλιαδα.
Τοιγαρ υπεζοφιαισιν Ερινυσιν αμμεσον ηπται
    Κωκυτε, κλοιω λαιμον απαγχομενος.

Anthologia, p. 70. Edit. Oxon. 1766.

On

On Parthenius the Phocenſian, who calumniated **Homer**.

> Here, though deep buried he can rail no more,
> Pour burning pitch, on baſe Parthenius pour;
> Who on the ſacred Muſes dar'd to ſpirt
> His frothy venom and poetic dirt:
> Who ſaid of Homer, in his frantic ſcorn,
> The Odyſſey was mud, the Iliad thorn:
> For this, dark Furies, in your ſnakes enroll,
> And through Cocytus drag the ſland'rous ſoul.

Parthenius, ſay the Commentators, was a diſciple of Dionyſius of Alexandria, who flouriſhed under Nero and Trajan. Erycius, the author of the inſcription, is ſuppoſed to have lived in the ſame age. Among the modern adverſaries of Homer, the French are moſt remarkable for their ſeverity and injuſtice: nor is it ſurpriſing, that the nation which has diſplayed the fainteſt ſparks of Epic fire, ſhould be the moſt ſolicitous to reduce the oppreſſive ſplendor of this exalted luminary. The moſt depreciating remarks on genius, in every walk, are generally made by thoſe who are the leaſt able to prove its rivals; and often, perhaps, not ſo much from the prevalence of envious malignity, as from the want of vivid and delicate perception. The merits and the failings of Homer were agitated in France with all the heat and acrimony of a theological diſpute. Madame Dacier diſtinguiſhed herſelf in the conteſt by her uncommon talents and erudition: ſhe combated for the Grecian Bard with the ſpirit of Minerva defending the Father of the Gods. It muſt however be confeſt, that ſhe ſometimes overſtepped the modeſty of wiſdom, and caught, unwarily, the ſcolding tone of Juno. It is indeed amuſing, to obſerve a people, who pique themſelves on their extreme politeneſs, and cenſure Homer for the groſs behaviour of his Gods, engaging among themſelves in a ſquabble concerning this very Poet, with all the unrefined animoſity of his Olympian Synod. In the whole controverſy there is nothing more worthy of remembrance and of praiſe, than the lively elegance and the pleaſing good-humour of Mr. de la Motte, who, though not one of the moſt exalted, was certainly one of the moſt amiable, characters in the literary world; and made a generous return to the ſeverity of his female antagoniſt, by writing an ode in her praiſe.

Voltaire

Voltaire has pointed out, with his usual spirit, the failings of La Motte in his Abridgement of the Iliad; but he has frequently fallen himself into similar defects, and is equally unjust to Homer, against whom he has levelled the most bitter sarcasms, both in prose and verse. Voltaire attacking Homer, is like Paris shooting his arrow at the heel of Achilles: the two Poets are as unequal as the two ancient Warriors; yet Homer, like Achilles, may have his vulnerable spot; but with this happy difference, that although the shaft of ridicule, which is pointed against him, may be tinged with venom, its wound cannot be mortal. Perhaps no better answer can be made to all those who amuse themselves with writing against Homer, than the following reply of Madame Dacier to the Abbé Terrasson, who had attacked her favourite Bard in two abusive volumes :—" Que Monsieur l'Abbé Terrasson trouve Homere sot, ridicule, extravagant, ennuyeux, c'est son affaire, le public jugera si c'est un defaut à Homere de deplaire à M. l'Abbé Terrasson, ou à M. l'Abbé Terrasson de ne pas gouter Homere."

NOTE II.   VERSE 85.

E'en Socrates himself, that purest Sage,
Imbib'd his Wisdom from thy moral page.] Dio Chrysostom, in one of his orations, has called Socrates the disciple of Homer, and drawn a short parallel of their respective merits; observing in honour of both, " Ουη.ες Ποιητης γεγονεν οιος ηδεις αλλος, Σωκρατης δε Φιλοσοφος."

DION. CHRYS. p. 559.

NOTE III.   VERSE 119.

How high soe'er she leads his daring flight, &c.] I mean not to injure the dignity of Pindar by this assertion. Though Quinctilian, in drawing the character of the Grecian Lyric Poets, has given him high pre-eminence in that choir, we may, I think, very fairly conjecture that some odes of Alcæus and Stesichorus were not inferior to those of the Theban Bard, who is said to have been repeatedly vanquished in a poetical contest by his female antagonist Corinna. The absurd jealousy of our sex concerning literary talents, has led some eminent writers to question the merits of Corinna, as Olearius has observed, in his Dissertation on the female Poets of Greece. But her glory seems to have been fully established

by

by the public memorial of her picture, exhibited in her native city, and adorned with a symbol of her victory. Pausanias, who saw it, supposes her to have been one of the handsomest women of her time; and the ingenuity of some Critics imputes her success in the poetical contest to the influence of her beauty. They have taken some liberties less pardonable with her literary reputation, and, by their curious comments on a single Greek syllable, made the sublime Pindar call his fair rival *a Sow*, though the unfortunate word συνεκαλει, which may be twisted into that meaning, signifies, in its more obvious construction, that the Poet challenged his successful antagonist to a new trial of skill. — For a more minute account of this singular piece of criticism, I must refer the reader to the notes on Corinna, in the Fragmenta Poetriarum, by Wolfius. Time has left us only a few diminutive scraps of Corinna's Poetry; but Plutarch, in his Treatise on the Glory of the Athenians, has preserved one of her critical Bon-mots, which may deserve to be repeated. That author asserts, that Corinna instructed Pindar in his youth, and advised him to adorn his composition with the embellishments of fable. The obedient Poet soon brought her some verses, in which he had followed her advice rather too freely; when his Tutress, smiling at his profusion, τη χειρι δειν εφη σπειρειν, αλλα μη ολω τω θυλακω.

N O T E IV. Verse 126.

Yet may not Judgment, with severe disdain,
Slight the young Rhodian's variegated strain.] Apollonius, surnamed the Rhodian from the place of his residence, is supposed to have been a native of Alexandria; where he is said to have recited some portion of his Poem, while he was yet a youth. Finding it ill received by his countrymen, he retired to Rhodes, where he is conjectured to have polished and completed his Work, supporting himself by the profession of Rhetoric, and receiving from the Rhodians the freedom of their city. He at length returned, with considerable honour, to the place of his birth, succeeding Eratosthenes in the care of the Alexandrian Library, in the reign of Ptolemy Euergetes, who ascended the throne of Egypt in the year before Christ 246. That prince had been

educated

educated by the famous Ariſtarchus, and rivalled the preceding ſove-
reigns of his liberal family in the munificent encouragement of
learning. Apollonius was a diſciple of the poet Callimachus; but their
connection ended in the moſt violent enmity, which was probably
owing to ſome degree of contempt expreſſed by Apollonius for the
light compoſitions of his maſter. The learned have vainly endeavoured
to diſcover the particulars of their quarrel. — The only Work of Apollonius which has deſcended to modern times, is his Poem, in four
Books, on the Argonautic expedition. Both Longinus and Quintilian
have aſſigned to this Work the mortifying character of Mediocrity; but
there lies an appeal from the ſentence of the moſt candid and enlightened Critics to the voice of Nature; and the merit of Apollonius
has little to apprehend from the deciſion of this ultimate judge. His
Poem abounds in animated deſcription, and in paſſages of the moſt tender and pathetic beauty. How finely painted is the firſt ſetting forth
of the Argo! and how beautifully is the wife of Chiron introduced,
holding up the little Achilles in her arms, and ſhewing him to his
father Peleus as he ſailed along the ſhore! But the chief excellence in
our Poet, is the ſpirit and delicacy with which he has delineated the
paſſion of love in his Medea. That Virgil thought very highly of his
merit in this particular is ſufficiently evident from the minute exactneſs
with which he has copied many tender touches of the Grecian Poet.
Thoſe who compare the third Book of Apollonius with the fourth of
Virgil, may, I think, perceive not only that Dido has ſome features of
Medea, but that the two Bards, however different in their reputation,
reſembled each other in their genius; and that they both excel in delicacy and pathos.

NOTE V. Verse 190.

Virgil ſinks loaded with their heavy praiſe.] Scaliger appears to be the
moſt extravagant of all the Critics who have laviſhed their undiſtinguiſh-
ing encomiums on Virgil, by aſſerting that he alone is entitled to the
name of Poet. Poetices, lib. iii. c. 2. — Though the opinion of
Spence, and other modern Critics, concerning the character of Æneas,
conſidered as an allegorical portrait of Auguſtus, ſeems to gain ground,
yet it might perhaps be eaſy to overturn the ingenious conjectures
and

and the fanciful reasoning by which that idea has been supported.
This attempt would have the sanction of one of the most judicious
Commentators of Virgil; for the learned Heyne expresly rejects all
allegorical interpretation, and thinks it improbable that a Poet of so
correct a judgment could have adopted a plan which must necessarily
contract and cramp his powers. He even ventures to assert, that if the
character of Æneas was delineated as an allegorical portrait of Augustus,
the execution of it is unhappy. The strongest argument which has
been adduced to support this conjecture, is founded on the ingenious
interpretation of the following passage in the opening of the third
Georgic :

> Primus ego in patriam mecum, modo vita supersit,
> Aonio rediens deducam vertice Musas :
> Primus Idumæas referam tibi, Mantua, palmas ;
> Et viridi in campo templum de marmore ponam
> Propter aquam, tardis ingens ubi flexibus errat
> Mincius, et tenerâ prætexit arundine ripas.
> In medio mihi Cæsar erit, templumque tenebit, &c.

These lines, in which Virgil expresses his intention of dedicating a
temple to Augustus, have been considered as the *noblest allegory of ancient
Poetry* * ; and the great Critic who first started the idea, has expatiated,
in the triumph of his discovery, on the *mysterious* beauties they contain :
but the whole of this hypothesis is unfortunately built upon the rejec-
tion of three verses, which are pronounced unworthy of the Poet, and
which, though found in every MS. the Critic claims a right of re-
moving. A licence so extraordinary cannot even be justified by the
talents of this accomplished writer ; for if the less elegant passages of
the ancient Poets might be removed at pleasure, their compositions
would be exposed to the caprice of every fantastic commentator. The
obvious and literal interpretation not only renders this violence unne-
cessary, but is more agreeable to the judgment of the Poet and the man-

---

* Hurd's Horace, vol. ii. page 44.

ners

ners of his age. The cuftom of erecting real temples was fo familiar to antiquity, that a Roman would never have fufpected the edifice was to be raifed only with poetical materials. We may even conjecture, from a line of Statius, that the Poet himfelf had a temple erected to his memory; and, without any breach of probability, we may admit his intention of giving his living Emperor fuch a teftimony of his gratitude. This adulation, though fhocking to us, was too generally juftified by example to oblige the Poet to palliate it by a fiction. He had before acquiefced in the divinity of his Imperial Patron, and had expreffed the idea in its full fenfe.

> Namque erit ille mihi femper *Deus*, illius aram
> Sæpe tener noftris ab ovilibus imbuet agnus.
> > Eclog. I.

> Ingredere et votis jam *nunc* affuefce vocari.
> > Georg. I.

Having made fuch an invocation in the beginning of his Work, was his *delicacy* afterwards to be fhocked, and oblige him to pay a compliment under the difguife of an obfcure conceit? for that allegory muft be allowed to be obfcure, which had remained through fo many ages unexplained. The unfortunate rejected lines, for whofe elegance we do not contend, may at leaft be refcued from impropriety by a literal interpretation of the preceding paffage; for, difmifs the conjectured allegory, and the chief objections againft them remain no longer. If the phrafeology be peculiar, it is at leaft fupported by concurring MSS. The adjective *ardens* is fometimes undoubtedly joined to a word that does not denote a fubftance of heat or flame, as the Critic himfelf admits in the cafe of *ardentes hoftes*, to which we may add the *verbum ardens* of Cicero. As to the line which is faid to contain the moft glaring note of illegitimacy,

> Tithoni primâ quot abeft ab origine Cæfar,

many reafons might induce the Poet to ufe the name of Tithonus, which at this diftance of time it is not eafy for us to conjecture. Per-

U   haps

haps he chofe it to vary the expreffion of *Affaraci Proles*, which he had
adopted in the preceding lines. The abfurdity of the fubject-matter,
and the place in which it is introduced, that are infifted on as the principal objections, arife folely from the allegorical hypothefis : without it
the conftruction will be plain and natural. The Poet expreffes his
intention of erecting a temple to Auguftus, and expatiates on the mag-
nificence with which it was to be adorned : he then returns to his prefent poetical fubject ;

Interea Dryadum fylvas faltufque fequamur :

and, having dwelt a little on that, to avoid too long a digreffion, very
naturally refumes the praifes of the Emperor, by alluding to the
fublimer fong which he intended to devote to him *hereafter*.

Mox tamen ardentes accingar dicere pugnas
Cæfaris. ——————

Perhaps the important pofition that gave rife to this conjecture, and to
others of a fimilar complexion, " that the propriety of allegorical compofition made the diftinguifhed pride of ancient poetry," is as queftion-
able as the conjecture itfelf ; and a diligent and judicious perufal of the
ancient Poets might convince us, that fimplicity was their genuine
character, and that many of their allegorical beauties have originated in
the fertile imagination of their commentators. Ariftarchus, indeed, the
celebrated model of ancient criticifm, rejected with great fpirit the allegorical interpretations of Homer, as we are informed by Eufthathius ;
but the good Archbifhop of Theffalonica, who, like fome modern pre-
lates, had a paffion for allegory, cenfures the great Critic of Alexandria
for his more fimple mode of conftruction, and fuppofes it an injury to
the refined beauties and profound wifdom of the Poet. Ἀρισταρχος μεντοι
μηδεν τι των Ομηρ... αλληγορειν αξιων, ȣ μονον υπερβολικον τι λεγει αλλα και
σοφιας μεγαλης αφαιρειται τον ποιητην. Eusth. vol. iii. page 1300.

NOTE VI. Verse 260.

Shall Hiftory's pen, to aid his vengeance won.] There is hardly any eminent perfonage of antiquity who has fuffered more from detraction, both

in

in his literary and moral character, than the poet Lucan. His fate, indeed, feems in all points to have been peculiarly fevere. His early death, at an age when few Poets have even laid the foundation of their capital work, is itfelf fufficient to excite our compaffion and regret; but to perifh by the envious tyranny of Nero, may be confidered as a bleffing, when compared with the more cruel misfortune of being branded with infamy in the immortal pages of Tacitus. As I am per-fuaded that the great Hiftorian has inadvertently adopted the groffeft calumny againft our Poet, I fhall moft readily affign my reafons for thinking fo. It may firft be proper to give a fhort fketch of Lucan's life.—He was the fon of Annæus Mela, the youngeft brother of Seneca; and though born at Corduba, was conveyed to Rome at the age of eight months : a circumftance, as his more indulgent critics obferve, which fufficiently refutes the cenfure of thofe who confider his language as provincial. At Rome he was educated under the Stoic Cornutus, fo warmly celebrated by his difciple Perfius the Satirift, who was the in-timate friend of our Poet. In the clofe of his education Lucan is faid to have paffed fome time at Athens. On his return to Rome he rofe to the office of Quæftor, before he had attained the legal age. He was afterwards inrolled among the Augurs; and married a lady of noble birth, of whofe amiable character I fhall fpeak more at large in a fubfe-quent note. Lucan had for fome time been admitted to familiarity with Nero, when the Emperor chofe to contend for poetical honours by the public recital of a poem he had compofed on Niobe; and fome verfes of this imperial production are fuppofed to be preferved in the firft Satire of Perfius. Lucan had the hardinefs to repeat a poem on Orpheus, in competition with that of Nero; and, what is more remark-able, the judges of the conteft were juft and bold enough to decide againft the Emperor. From hence Nero became the perfecutor of his fuccefs-ful rival, and forbade him to produce any poetry in public. The well-known confpiracy of Pifo againft the tyrant foon followed; and Taci-tus, with his ufual farcaftic feverity, concludes that Lucan engaged in the enterprize from the poetical injuries he had received : a remark which does little credit to the candour of the Hiftorian; who might have found a much nobler, and, I will add, a more probable motive for his conduct, in the generous ardor of his character, and his paffionate adora-

tion

tion of freedom. In the sequel of his narration, Tacitus alledges a charge against our Poet, which, if it were true, must lead us to detest him as the most abject of mankind. The Historian asserts, that Lucan, when accused of the conspiracy, for some time denied the charge; but, corrupted at last by a promise of impunity, and desirous to atone for the tardiness of his confession, accused his mother Atilla as his accomplice. This circumstance is so improbable in itself, and so little consonant to the general character of Lucan, that some writers have treated it with contempt, as a calumny invented by Nero to vilify the object of his envious abhorrence. But the name of Tacitus has given such an air of authority to the story, that it may seem to deserve a more serious dis-cussion, particularly as there are two subsequent events related by the same Historian, which have a tendency to invalidate the accusation so injurious to our Poet. The events I mean are, the fate of Annæus, and the escape of Atilla, the two parents of Lucan. The former died in consequence of an accusation brought against him, after the death of his son, by Fabius Romanus, who had been intimate with Lucan and forged some letters in his name, with the design of proving his father concerned in the conspiracy. These letters were produced to Nero, who sent them to Annæus, from an eager desire, says Tacitus, to get possession of his wealth. From this fact two inferences may be drawn, according to the different lights in which it may be considered:—If the accusation against Annæus was just, it is clear that Lucan had not betrayed his fa-ther, and he appears the less likely to have endangered by his confession the life of a parent, to whom he owed a still tenderer regard:—If Annæus was not involved in the conspiracy, and merely put to death by Nero for the sake of his treasure, we may the more readily believe, that the tyrant who murdered the father from avarice, might calumniate the son from envy. But the escape of Atilla affords us the strongest reason to conclude that Lucan was perfectly innocent of the abject and unnatural treachery, of which Tacitus has supposed him guilty. Had the Poet really named his mother as his accomplice, would the vindic-tive and sanguinary Nero have spared the life of a woman, whose family he detested, particularly when other females were put to death for their share in the conspiracy? That Atilla was not in that number, the Historian himself informs us in the following remarkable sentence,

Atilla

Atilla mater Annæi Lucani, fine abfolutione, fine fupplicio, diffimulata; thus tranflated by Gordon : " The information againft Atilla, the mother of Lucan, was diffembled; and, without being cleared, fhe efcaped unpunifhed."

The preceding remarks will, I hope, vindicate to every candid mind the honour of our Poet; whofe firmnefs and intrepidity of charaĉter are indeed very forcibly difplayed in that piĉture of his death which Tacitus himfelf has given us. I fhall prefent it to the Englifh reader in the words of Gordon : — Lucan, " while his blood iffued in ftreams, perceiving his feet and hands to grow cold and ftiffen, and life to retire by little and little to the extremities, while his heart was ftill beating with vital warmth, and his faculties no wife impaired, recolleĉted fome lines of his own, which defcribed a wounded foldier expiring in a manner that refembled this. The lines themfelves he rehearfed; and they were the laft words he ever uttered." The Annals of Tacitus, Book xv. — The critics differ concerning the verfes of the Pharfalia which the author quoted in fo memorable a manner. I fhall tranfcribe the two paffages he is fuppofed to have repeated, and only add that Lipfius contends for the latter.

> Sanguis erant lacrymæ : quæcunque foramina novit
> Humor, ab his largus manat cruor : ora redundant,
> Et patulæ nares : fudor rubet : omnia plenis
> Membra fluunt venis : totum eft pro vulnere corpus.
>
> Lib. ix. 814.

> Now the warm blood at once, from every part,
> Ran purple poifon down, and drain'd the fainting heart.
> Blood falls for tears ; and o'er his mournful face
> The ruddy drops their tainted paffage trace.
> Where'er the liquid juices find a way,
> There ftreams of blood, there crimfon rivers ftray.
> His mouth and gufhing noftrils pour a flood,
> And e'en the pores ouze out the trickling blood ;
> In the red deluge all the parts lie drown'd,
> And the whole body feems one bleeding wound.
>
> Rowe.

5

Scinditur

Scinditur avulfus; nec ficut vulnere fanguis
Emicuit lentus; ruptis cadit undique venis,
Difcurfufque animæ, diverfa in membra meantis,
Interceptus aquis.

Lib. iii. v. 638.

No fingle wound the gaping rupture feems,
Where trickling crimfon wells in flender ftreams;
But, from an op'ning horrible and wide,
A thoufand veffels pour the burfting tide:
At once the winding channel's courfe was broke,
Where wand'ring life her mazy journey took;
At once the currents all forgot their way,
And loft their purple in the azure fea.

Rowe.

Such was the death of Lucan, before he had completed his twenty-
feventh year. If his character as a man has been injured by the Hiftorian, his poetical reputation has been treated not lefs injurioufly by the
Critics. Quintilian, by a frivolous diftinction, difputes his title to be
clafied among the Poets; and Scaliger fays, with a brutality of language
difgraceful only to himfelf, that he feems rather to *bark* than to *fing*.
But thefe infults may appear amply compenfated, when we remember,
that in the moft polifhed nations of modern Europe the moft elevated
and poetic fpirits have been his warmeft admirers; that in France he
was idolized by Corneille, and in England tranflated by Rowe.—The
fevereft cenfures on Lucan have proceeded from thofe who have
unfairly compared his language to that of Virgil: but how unjuft and
abfurd is fuch a comparifon! it is comparing an uneven block of
porphyry, taken rough from the quarry, to the moft beautiful fuper-
ficies of polifhed marble. How differently fhould we think of Virgil
as a poet, if we poffeffed only the verfes which he wrote at that period
of life when Lucan compofed his Pharfalia! In the difpofition of his
fubject, in the propriety and elegance of diction, he is undoubtedly far
inferior to Virgil: but if we attend to the bold originality of his defign,
and to the vigour of his fentiments; if we confider the Pharfalia as the

rapid

rapid and uncorrected sketch of a young poet, executed in an age when the spirit of his countrymen was broken, and their taste in literature corrupted, it may justly be esteemed as one of the most noble and most wonderful productions of the human mind.

NOTE VII. VERSE 293.

As Lesbos paid to Pompey's lovely Wife.] Pompey, after his defeat at Pharsalia, proceeded to Lesbos, as he had left his wife Cornelia to the protection of that island; which received the unfortunate hero with a sublime generosity. The Lesbians entreated him to remain amongst them, and promised to defend him. Pompey expressed his gratitude for their fidelity, but declined the offer, and embarked with Cornelia. The concern of this gallant people on the departure of their amiable guest is thus described by Lucan:

> ————— dixit; moestamque carinae
> Imposuit comitem. Cunctos mutare putares
> Tellurem patriaeque solum : sic litore toto
> Plangitur, infestae tenduntur in aethera dextrae ;
> Pompeiumque minus, cujus fortuna dolorem
> Moverat, ast illam, quam toto tempore belli
> Ut civem videre suam, discedere cernens
> Ingemuit populus; quam vix, si castra mariti
> Victoris peteret, siccis dimittere matres
> Jam poterant oculis : tanto devinxit amore
> Hos pudor, hos probitas, castique modestia vultus.
>
> Lib. viii. v. 146.

> He ceas'd; and to the ship his partner bore,
> While loud complainings fill the sounding shore ;
> It seem'd as if the nation with her pass'd,
> And banishment had laid their island waste.
> Their second sorrows they to Pompey give ;
> For her as for their citizen they grieve :
> E'en though glad victory had call'd her thence,
> And her Lord's bidding been the just pretence,

The

The Lesbian matrons had in tears been drown'd,
And brought her weeping to their wat'ry bound:
So was she lov'd, so winning was her grace,
Such lowly sweetness dwelt upon her face.   ROWE.

NOTE VIII.   VERSE 296.

Let Argentaria on your canvass shine.] Polla Argentaria was the daughter of a Roman Senator, and the wife of Lucan. She is said to have transcribed and corrected the three first books of the Pharsalia, after the death of her husband. It is much to be regretted that we possess not the poem which he wrote on the merits of this amiable and accomplished woman; but her name is immortalized by two surviving Poets of that age. The veneration which she paid to the memory of her husband, is recorded by Martial; and more poetically described in that pleasing and elegant little production of Statius, *Genethliacon Lucani*, a poem which I the more readily commend, as I may be thought by some readers unjust towards its author, in omitting to celebrate his Thebaid. I confess, indeed, the miscellaneous poems of Statius appear to me his most valuable work: in most of these there is much imagination and sentiment, in harmonious and spirited verse. The little poem which I have mentioned, on the anniversary of Lucan's birth, is said to have been written at the request of Argentaria. The Author, after invoking the poetical deities to attend the ceremony, touches with great delicacy and spirit on the compositions of Lucan's childhood, which are lost, and the Pharsalia, the production of his early youth; he then pays a short compliment to the beauty and talents of Argentaria, laments the cruel fate which deprived her so immaturely of domestic happiness; and concludes with the following address to the shade of Lucan:

> At tu, seu rapidum poli per axem
> Famæ curribus arduis levatus,
> Qua surgunt animæ potentiores,
> Terras despicis, et sepulchra rides:
> Seu pacis meritum nemus reclusæ
> Felix Elysiis tenes in oris,
> Quo Pharsalica turba congregatur;

Et

Et te nobile carmen infonantem
Pompeii comitantur et Catones:
Tu magna facer et fuperbus umbra
Nefcis Tartaron, et procul nocentum
Audis verbera, pallidumque vifa
Matris lampade refpicis Neronem.
Adfis lucidus; et vocante Polla
Unum, quæfo, diem deos filentum
Exores; folet hoc patere limen
Ad nuptas redeuntibus maritis.
Hæc te non thiafis procax dolofis
Falfi numinis induit figuras;
Ipfum fed colit, et frequentat ipfum
Imis altius infitum medullis;
Ac folatia vana fubminiftrat
Vultus, qui fimili notatus auro
Stratis prænitet, excubatque fomno
Securæ. Procul hinc abite mortes;
Hæc vitæ genitalis eft origo;
Cedat luctus atrox, genifque manent
Jam dulces lacrymæ, dolorque feftus
Quicquid fleverat ante nunc adoret.

But you, O! whether to the fkies
On Fame's triumphant car you rife,
(Where mightier fouls new life affume)
And mock the confines of the tomb;
Or whether in Elyfium bleft
You grace the groves of facred reft,
Where the Pharfalian heroes dwell;
And, as you ftrike your Epic fhell,
The Pompeys and the Catos throng
To catch the animating fong;
Of Tartarus the dread controul
Binds not your high and hallow'd foul;

Diftant

Diſtant you hear that wailing coaſt,
And ſee the guilty Nero's ghoſt
Grow pale with anguiſh and affright,
His mother flaſhing on his ſight.
   Be preſent to your Polla's vows,
While to your honour'd name ſhe bows!
One day let your intreaties gain
From thoſe who rule the ſhadowy train!
Their gates have op'd to bleſs a wife,
And given a huſband back to life.
In you the tender Fair invites
No fancied god with frantic rites;
You are the objeét of her prayers,
You in her inmoſt heart ſhe bears:
And, ſtampt on mimic gold, your head
Adorns the faithful mourner's bed,
And ſooths her eyes before they cloſe,
The guardian of her chaſte repoſe.
   Away with all funereal ſtate!
From hence his nobler life we date:
Let Mourning change the pang ſevere
To fond Devotion's grateful tear!
And feſtal grief, its anguiſh o'er,
What it lamented, now adore!

I cannot cloſe this note without obſerving, that the preceding verſes have a ſtrong tendency to prove, that Lucan was perfeétly innocent in regard to the accuſation which I have examined before. Had he been really guilty of baſely endangering the life of his mother, it is not probable that his wife would have honoured his memory with ſuch enthuſiaſtic veneration, or that Statius, in verſes deſigned to do him honour, would have alluded to *the mother* of Nero. The Reader will pardon my recurring to this ſubjeét, as it is pleaſing to make uſe of every argument which may remove ſo odious and unjuſt a ſtain from a manly and exalted charaéter.

NOTES

N O T E S

T O   T H E

T H I R D   E P I S T L E.

N O T E   I.   VERSE 36.

AND smiles of triumph hid his mortal pang.] An allusion to *ridens moriar*, the close of the celebrated Northern Ode, by the Danish king Regner Lodbrog ; a translation of which is inserted in the curious little volume of Runic poetry, printed for Dodsley, 1763.

Bartholin, in his admirable Essay on the Causes which inspired the Danes with a Contempt of Death, affirms, that it was customary with the Northern warriors to sing their own exploits in the close of life. He mentions the example of a hero, named Hallmundus, who being mortally wounded, commanded his daughter to attend while he composed a poem, and to inscribe it on a tablet of wood. BARTHOLIN. Lib. i. cap. 10.

N O T E   II.   VERSE 60.

And galls the ghostly Tyrant with her lash.] The poetry of Provence contains many spirited satires against the enormities of the Clergy. The most remarkable, is the bold invective of the Troubadour Guillaume Figueira, in which he execrates the avarice and the cruelty of Rome. The Papal cause found a female Poet to defend it : Germonda of Montpellier composed a poetical reply to the satire of Figueira. See MILLOT's Hist. des Troubadours, vol. ii. p. 455.

NOTE

N O T E III.   VERSE 76.

Struck with ill-fated zeal the Latian lyre.]   There never was a century utterly destitute of ingenious and elegant Poets, says the learned Polycarp Leyser, after having patiently traced the obscure progress of Latin poetry through all the dark ages.   Indeed the merit of some Latin Poets, in a period that we commonly suppose involved in the grossest barbarism, is singularly striking;   many of these are of the Epic kind, and, as they describe the manners and customs of their respective times, a complete review of them might form a curious and entertaining work. I shall briefly mention such as appear most worthy of notice.

Abbo, a Parisian monk, of the Benedictine order, wrote a poem on the siege of Paris by the Normans and the Danes, at which he was present, in the year 886: it is printed in the second volume of Duchesne's Script. Francorum; and, though it has little or no poetical merit, may be regarded as an historical curiosity.   The following lines, addressed to the city of Paris, in the beginning of the work, may serve as a specimen of its language:

> Dic igitur præpulchra polis, quod Danea munus
> Libavit tibimet, soboles Plutonis amica,
> Tempore quo præsul domini et dulcissimus heros
> Gozlinus temet pastorque benignus alebat!
> Hæc inquit, miror, narrare potest aliquisne?
> Nonne tuis idem vidisti oculis? refer ergo:
> Vidi equidem, jussisque tuis parebo libenter.

Leyser has confounded this Poet with another of this name; but Fabricius has corrected the mistake, in his Bibliotheca Latina mediæ et infimæ Ætatis.

Guido, Bishop of Amiens from the year 1058 to 1076, wrote an Heroic poem on the exploits of William the Conqueror, in which, according to Ordericus Vitalis, he imitated both Virgil and Statius. William of Apulia composed, at the request of Pope Urban the IId, a poem, in five books, on the actions of the Normans in Sicily, Apulia, and Calabria, to the death of Robert Guiscard their prince; addressing his

his work to the fon of that hero. It was written between the years 1080 and 1099; firſt printed in 1582, 4to.; and again in Muratori's Script. Ital. Du Cange, in his Notes to the Alexiad of the Princeſs Anna Comnena, has illuſtrated that hiſtory by frequent and long quotations from William of Apulia; but though the learned Critic gives him the title of Scriptor Egregius, his poetry appears to me but a few degrees ſuperior to that of the Monk Abbo, whom I have juſt mentioned. The Reader may judge from the following paſſage, which I ſelect not only as a ſpecimen of the Author's ſtyle, but as it ſhews that the wives of theſe martial Princes ſhared with them in all the perils of war.

> Uxor in hoc bello Roberti forte ſagitta
> Quadam læſa fuit, quæ vulnere territa, nullam
> Dum ſperabat opem, ſe pene ſubegerat hoſti,
> Navigio cujus ſe commendare volebat,
> Inſtantis metuens vicina pericula lethi:
> Hanc deus eripuit, fieri ludibria nolens
> Matronæ tantæ tam nobilis et venerandæ.

The Princeſs Comnena has alſo celebrated the fortitude which this Heroine, whoſe name was Gaita, diſplayed in the battle; and it is remarkable, that the royal female Hiſtorian deſcribes the noble Amazon more poetically than the Latin Poet.

Gualfredo, an Italian, who ſucceeded to the biſhoprick of Siena in the year 1080, and died in 1127, wrote an Heroic poem on the expedition of Godfrey of Boulogne, which is ſaid to be ſtill preſerved in MS. at Siena. I believe Gualfredo is the firſt Poet, in point of time, who treated of the happy ſubject of the Cruſades; which was afterwards embelliſhed by two very elegant writers of Latin verſe, Iſcanus and Gunther, of whom I ſhall preſently ſpeak, and at length received its higheſt honour from the genius of Taſſo. There is alſo an early Latin poem on this ſubject, the joint production of two writers, named Fulco and Ægidius, whom the accurate Fabricius places in the beginning of the 13th century; the title of the work is Hiſtoria Geſtorum Viæ noſtri Temporis Hieroſolymitanæ. It is printed in the fourth volume of Ducheſne's Script. Franc. and with conſiderable additions in the third volume of

Anecdota

Anecdota Edmundi Martene. I transcribe part of the opening of this poem, as the curious reader may have a pleasure in comparing it with that of Tasso.

> Ardor ineft, inquam, fententia fixaque menti
> Verfibus et numeris tranfmittere pofteritati
> Qualiter inftinctu deitatis, et aufpice cultu
> Eft aggreffa via memorando nobilis actu,
> Qua facrofancti violantes jura fepulchri
> Digna receperunt meriti commercia pravi.
> Inque fuis Francis antiqua refurgere Troja
> Cœpit, et edomuit Chrifto contraria regna.

I will only add the portrait of Godfrey:

> Inclytus ille ducum Godefridus culmen honofque,
> Omnibus exemplum bonitatis militiæque,
> Sive hafta jaculans æquaret Parthica tela,
> Cominus aut feriens terebraret ferrea fcuta,
> Seu gladio pugnans carnes refecaret et offa,
> Sive eques atque pedes propelleret agmina denfa,
> Hic inimicitiis cunctis fibi conciliatis
> Cunctis poffeffis pro Chrifti pace relictis
> Arripuit callem Chriftum fectando vocantem.

The poem clofes with the capture of Jerufalem.

Laurentius of Verona, who flourifhed about the year 1120, wrote an Heroic poem, in feven books, entitled, Rerum in Majorica Pifanorum. Edidit Ughellus, tom. 3. Italiæ facræ.

But in merit and reputation, thefe early Latin Poets of modern time are very far inferior to Philip Gualtier de Chatillon, who feems to have been the firft that caught any portion of true poetic fpirit in Latin verfe. He was Provoft of the Canons of Tournay * about the year 1200, according to Mr. Warton, who has given fome fpecimens of his ftyle in the fecond Differtation prefixed to his admirable Hiftory of Englifh Poetry. I fhall therefore only add, that the beft edition of his Alexandreid, an Heroic

---

* Fabricius calls him Epifcopus Magalonenfis. Bib. Lat. tom. ii. p. 255.

poem

poem in ten books on Alexander the Great, was printed at Leyden, 4to, 1558.

The superior merit of Josephus Iscanus, or Joseph of Exeter, has been also displayed by the same judicious Encomiast, in the Dissertation I have mentioned; nor has he failed to commemorate two Latin Epic Poets of the same period, and of considerable merit for the time in which they lived—Gunther, and William of Bretagny; the first was a German monk, who wrote after the year 1108, and has left various historical and poetical works; particularly two of the Epic kind—Solymarium, a poem on the taking of Jerusalem by Godfrey of Bulloign; and another, entitled Ligurinus, on the exploits of the Emperor Frederick Barbarossa, which he completed during the life of that Prince. The first was never printed; of the latter there have been several editions, and one by the celebrated Melancthon, in 1569. That his poetical merit was considerable in many respects, will appear from the following verses, in which he speaks of himself.

> Hoc quoque me famæ, si desint cætera, solum
> Conciliare potest, quod jam per multa latentes
> Sæcula, nec clausis prodire penatibus ausas
> Pierides vulgare paro, priscumque nitorem
> Reddere carminibus, tardosque citare poetas

William of Bretagny was preceptor to Pierre Charlot, natural son of Philip Augustus, King of France, and addressed a poem to his pupil, entitled Karlotis, which is yet unpublished; but his greater work, called Philippis, an Heroic poem in twelve books, is printed in the collections of Duchesne and Pithæus; and in a separate 4to volume, with a copious commentary by Barthius. Notwithstanding the praises bestowed on this Author by his learned Commentator, who prefers him to all his contemporaries, he appears to me inferior in poetic spirit to his three rivals, Gualtier de Chatillon, Iscanus, and Gunther. Yet his work is by no means despicable in its style, and may be considered as a valuable picture of the times in which he lived; for he was himself engaged in many of the scenes which he describes. His professt design is to celebrate the exploits of Philip Augustus; and he closes his poem with the

death

death of that Monarch, which happened in 1223. He addreſſes his work, in two ſeparate poetical dedications, to Lewis, the ſucceſſor of Philip, and to Pierre Charlot his natural ſon, who was Biſhop of Noyon in 1240, and died 1249. He ſeems to have been excited to this compo-ſition by the reputation of Gualtier's Alexandreid; to which he thus alludes, in the verſes addreſſed to Lewis:

Geſta ducis Macedum celebri deſcribere verſu
Si licuit Gualtere tibi, quæ ſola relatu
Multivago docuit te vociferatio famæ.

▬   ▬   ▬   ▬

Cur ego quæ novi, proprio quæ lumine vidi,
Non auſim magni magnalia ſcribere regis,
Qui nec Alexandro minor eſt virtute, nec illo
Urbi Romuleæ totum qui ſubdidit orbem?

He takes occaſion alio, in two other parts of his poem, to pay a liberal compliment to Gualtier, to whom, in poetical ability, he confeſſes himſelf inferior; but this inferiority his admirer Barthius will not allow. Of their reſpective talents the reader may judge, who will compare the paſſage which Mr. Warton has cited from the Alexandreid, with the following lines, in which William of Bretagny uſes the very ſimile of his predeceſſor, comparing his hero Philip to a young lion.

Rex dolet ereptum comitem ſibi, frendit, et iræ
Occultare nequit tectos ſub pectore motus,
Nam rubor in vultu duplicatus prodit aperte
Quam gravis illuſtrem trahit indignatio mentem.
Qualiter in Lybicis ſpumante leunculo rictu
Saltibus ungue ferox, et dentibus aſper aduncis
Fortis et horriſonis anno jam pene ſecundo,
Cui venatoris venabula forte per armos
Deſcendere levi ſtringentia vulnere corpus,
Colla rigens hirſuta jubis deſævit in hoſtem
Jam retrocedentem, nec eum tetigiſſe volentem,
Cum nihil ex facto referat niſi dedecus illo.

Nec

Nec mora nec requies, quin jam deglutiat ipfum,
Ni prudens hoftis prætenta cufpide fcuto
Unguibus objecto, dum dat veftigia retro,
In loca fe retrahat non irrumpenda leoni.
Sic puer in comitem rex debacchatur et ipfum
Subfequitur preffo relegens veftigia greffu.

I will add the following paffage from the eleventh Book, as it contains an animated portrait, and a fimile more original than the preceding.

At lævo in cornu, qui nulli marte fecundus,
Bolonides pugnæ infiftit, cui fraxinus ingens
Nunc implet dextram, vix ulli bajula, qualem
In Bacchi legimus portaffe Capanea cunas,
Quam vix fulmineo dejecit Jupiter ictu:
Nunc culter vitæ impatiens, nunc fanguine pugni
Mucro rubens; gemina e fublimi vertice fulgens
Cornua conus agit, fuperafque eduxit in auras
E coftis affumpta nigris, quas faucis in antro
Branchia balenæ Britici colit incola ponti;
Ut qui magnus erat magnæ fuperaddita moli
Majorem faceret phantaftica pompa videri.
Ac velut in faltus fcopulofa Bieria faltu
Præcipiti mittit ingenti corpore cervum,
Cujus multifidos numerant a cornibus annos,
Menfe fub Octobri nondum Septembre peracto,
Annua quando novis Venus incitat ignibus illum,
Curfitat in cervos ramofa fronte minores,
Omnibus ut pulfis victor fub tegmine fagi
Connubio cervam folus fibi fubdat amatam.
Haud fecus e peditum medio, quibus ipfe rotundo
Ut caftro cauta fe circumfepferat arte,
Profiliens volat in Thomam, Robertigenafque
Drocarum Comitem, Belvacenumque Philippum
Bolonides.———

Y   William

William of Bretagny had an immediate fucceffor in Latin poetry, who appears to have at leaft an equal portion of poetical fpirit; the name of this Author is Nicholas de Brai, who wrote an Heroic poem on the actions of Louis the VIIIth, after the death of that Monarch, and addreffed it to William of Auvergne, who was Bifhop of Paris from the year 1228 to 1248. As a fpecimen of his defcriptive power, I felect the following lines, which form part of a long defcription of a Goblet prefented to the King on his acceffion:

———— Parant intrare palatia regis
Magnifici cives, gratiffima dona ferentes,
Tegmina quos ornant variis infculpta figuris;
Et patrem patriæ jucunda voce falutant,
Et genibus flexis præfentant ditia dona.

Offertur crater, quem fi fit credere dignum
Perditus ingenio fabricavit Mulciber auro;
Margine crateris totus depingitur orbis,
Et feries rerum brevibus diftincta figuris:
Illic pontus erat, tellus et pendulus aer,
Ignis ad alta volans cœli fupereminet illis:
Quatuor in partes orbis diftinguitur, ingens
Circuit oceanus immenfis fluctibus orbem.
Ingenio natura fuo duo lumina fecit
Fixa tenore poli, mundi famulantia rebus.

The Author proceeds to defcribe Thebes and Troy, as they are figured on this fuperb Goblet; and concludes his account of the workmanfhip with the four following lines, of peculiar beauty for the age in which they appeared:

Martis adulterium refupino margine pinxit
Mulciber, et Venerem laqueis cum Marte ligavit;
Pluraque cælaffet fub margine, fed pudor illi
Obftat, et ingentis renovatur caufa doloris.

This

This Poem, which the author feems to have left imperfect, is printed in the fifth volume of Duchefne's Script. Francorum.—England is faid to have produced another Heroic Poet of confiderable merit, who celebrated in Latin verfe the exploits of Richard the Firft, and who was called Gulielmus Peregrinus, from his having attended that Prince to the Holy Land. Leland mentions him by the name of Gulielmus de Canno, and Pits calls him Poetarum fui temporis apud noftrates facile Princeps; but I do not find that his Work was ever printed; nor do the feveral biographical writers who fpeak of him, inform us where it exifts in MS.

In Italy the Latin language is fuppofed to have been cultivated with ftill greater fuccefs, and the reftoration of its purity is in great meafure afcribed to Albertino Muffato, whofe merits were firft difplayed to our country by the learned author of the Effay on Pope.—Muffato was a Paduan, of high rank and great talents, but unfortunate. He died in exile, 1329, and left, befides many fmaller Latin pieces, an Heroic Poem, De Geftis Italorum poft Henricum VII. Cæfarem, feu de Obfidione Domini Canis Grandis de Verona circa mænia Paduanæ civitatis et Conflictu ejus. — Quadrio, from whom I tranfcribe this title, fays it is printed in the tenth volume of Muratori. Voffius, who fpeaks of him as an Hiftorian, afferts that he commanded in the war which is the fubject of his Poem.

In a few years after the death of Muffato, Petrarch received the laurel at Rome, for his Latin Epic poem, entitled Africa; a performance which has funk fo remarkably from the high reputation it once obtained, that the great admirer and encomiaft of Petrarch, who has publifhed three entertaining quarto volumes on his life, calls it " Un ouvrage fans chaleur, fans invention, fans interet, qui n'a pas meme le merite de la verfification & du ftyle, & dont il eft impoffible de foutenir la lecture.— I muft obferve, however, that Taffo, in his Effay on Epic Poetry, beftows a very high encomium on that part of Petrarch's Latin poem in which he celebrates the loves of Sophonifba and Mafiniffa; and indeed the cenfure of this amiable French writer, who in other points has done ample juftice to the merits of Petrarch, appears to me infinitely too fevere. There are many paffages in this neglected Poem conceived with great force and imagination, and expreffed with equal elegance of lan-

Y 2

guage.

guage. I shall select some verses from that part of it which has been honoured by the applause of Tasso. The following lines describe the anguish of the young Numidian Prince, when he is constrained to abandon his lovely bride:

Volvitur inde thoro (quoniam sub pectore pernox
Sævit amor, lacerantque truces præcordia curæ)
Uritur, invigilant mœror, metus, ira, furorque,
Sæpe & absentem lacrymans dum stringit amicam
Sæpe thoro dedit amplexus, et dulcia verba.
Postquam nulla valent violento fræna dolori,
Incipit, et longis solatur damna querelis.
Cura mihi nimium, vita mihi dulcior omni
Sophonisba vale : non te mea cura videbo
Leniter æthereos posthac componere vultus,
Effusofque auro religantem ex more capillos.
Dulcia, non cælum mulcentia verba, Deofque,
Oris odorati, secretaque murmura carpam.
Solus ero gelidoque insternam membra cubili,
Atque utinam socio componat amica sepulchro,
Et simul hic vetitos, illic concorditer annos
Contingat duxisse mihi sors optima busti.
Si cinis amborum commixtis morte medullis
Unus erit, Scipio nostros non scindet amores.
O utinam infernis etiam nunc una latebris
Umbra simus, liceat pariter per clauftra vagari
Myrtea, nec nostros Scipio disjungat amores.
Ibimus una ambo flentes, et passibus iisdem
Ibimus, æterno connexi fœdere, nec nos
Ferreus aut æquos Scipio interrumpet amores.

The well-known catastrophe of the unfortunate Sophonisba is related with much poetical spirit. The close of her life, and her first appearance in the regions of the dead, are peculiarly striking.

Illa manu pateramque tenens, & lumina cælo
Attollens, Sol alme, inquit, superique valete !

Masinissa

Mafiniffa vale, noftri memor : inde malignum
Ceu fitiens haurit non mota fronte venenum,
Tartareafque petit violentus fpiritus umbras.

———

Nulla magis Stygios mirantum obfeffa corona
Umbra lacus fubiit, poftquam divifa triformis
Partibus haud æquis ftetit ingens machina mundi.
Obtuitu attonito ftabant horrentia circum
Agmina Pœnarum, fparfoque rigentia villo
Eumenidum tacitis inhiabant rictibus ora.
Regia vis oculis inerat, pallorque verendus
Et vetus egregia majeftas fronte manebat.
Indignata tamen fuperis, irataque morti
Ibat et exiguo defigens lumina flexu.

With Petrarch I may clofe this curfory review of the neglected authors who wrote Heroic poems in Latin, during the courfe of the dark ages.—A peculiar circumftance induces me to add another name to the preceding lift. John, Abbot of Peterborough, in the reign of Edward the Third, wrote an Heroic poem, entitled Bellum Navarrenfe, 1366 de Petro rege Aragoniæ, & Edwardo Principe. This performance, containing five hundred and fixty verfes, is faid to be preferved in MS. in the Bodleian Library ; and I have thought it worthy of notice, becaufe it treats of the very fubject on which Dryden informs us he had once projected an Epic poem.

Of the many Latin compofitions of the Epic kind, which later times have produced, the Chriftiad of Vida, the Sarcotis of Maffenius, and the Conftantine of Mambrun, appear to me the moft worthy of regard ; but even thefe are feldom perufed : and indeed the Poet, who in a polifhed age prefers the ufe of a dead language to that of a living one, can only expect, and perhaps only deferves, the attention of a few curious fequeftered ftudents.

NOTE

NOTE IV. VERSE 81.

Thy daring Dante his wild Vision sung.] Dante Allighieri was born at
Florence, in May 1265, of an ancient and honourable family. Boccacio,
who lived in the same period, has left a very curious and entertaining
Treatise, on the Life, the Studies, and Manners of this extraordinary
Poet; whom he regarded as his master, and for whose memory he professed the highest veneration. This interesting biographer relates, that
Dante, before he was nine years old, conceived a passion for the lady
whom he has immortalized in his singular Poem. Her age was near his
own; and her name was Beatrice, the daughter of Folco Portinari, a
noble citizen of Florence. Of this fair one the best accounts are obscure. Some refining commentators have even denied her corporeal existence; affirming her to be nothing more or less than Theology. But we
may question if Theology was ever the mistress of so young a lover.
The passion of Dante, however, like that of his successor Petrarch, seems
to have been of the chaste and Platonic kind, according to the account
he has himself given of it, in one of his early productions, entitled
Vita Nuova; a mixture of mysterious poetry and prose, in which he
mentions both the origin of his affection and the death of his mistress,
who, according to Boccacio, died at the age of twenty-four. The same
author asserts, that Dante fell into a deep melancholy in consequence of
this event, from which his friends endeavoured to raise him, by per-
suading him to marriage. After some time he followed their advice,
and repented it; for he unfortunately made choice of a lady who bore
some resemblance to the celebrated Xantippe. The Poet, not possessing
the patience of Socrates, separated himself from her with such vehement
expressions of dislike, that he never afterwards admitted her to his presence, though she had borne him several children.—In the early part of
his life he gained some credit in a military character; distinguishing
himself by his bravery in an action where the Florentines obtained a
signal victory over the citizens of Arezzo. He became still more eminent by the acquisition of civil honours; and at the age of thirty-five
he rose to be one of the chief magistrates of Florence, when that
dignity was conferred by the suffrages of the people. From this ex-
altation

altation the Poet himſelf dated his principal misfortunes, as appears from the fragment of a letter quoted by Lionardo Bruni, one of his early biographers, where Dante ſpeaks of his political failure with that liberal franknefs which integrity infpires.—Italy was at that time diſtracted by the contending factions of the Ghibellins and the Guelphs: the latter, among whom Dante took an active part, were again divided into the Blacks and the Whites. Dante, ſays Gravina, exerted all his influence to unite theſe inferior parties; but his efforts were ineffectual, and he had the misfortune to be unjuſtly perſecuted by thoſe of his own faction. A powerful citizen of Florence, named Corſo Donati, had taken meaſures to terminate theſe inteſtine broils, by introducing Charles of Valois, brother to Philip the Fair, King of France. Dante, with great vehemence, oppoſed this diſgraceful project, and obtained the baniſhment of Donati and his partizans. The exiles applied to the Pope (Boniface the VIIIth) and by his aſſiſtance ſucceeded in their deſign. Charles of Valois entered Florence in triumph, and thoſe who had oppoſed his admiſſion were baniſhed in their turn. Dante had been diſpatched to Rome as the ambaſſador of his party, and was returning, when he received intelligence of the revolution in his native city. His enemies, availing themſelves of his abſence, had procured an iniquitous ſentence againſt him, by which he was condemned to baniſhment, and his poſſeſſions were confiſcated. His two enthuſiaſtic biographers, Boccacio and Manetti, expreſs the warmeſt indignation againſt this injuſtice of his country. Dante, on receiving the intelligence, took refuge in Siena, and afterwards in Arezzo, where many of his party were aſſembled. An attempt was made to ſurprize the city of Florence, by a ſmall army which Dante is ſuppoſed to have attended: the deſign miſcarried, and our Poet is conjectured to have wandered to various parts of Italy, till he found a patron in the great Can della Scala, Prince of Verona, whom he has celebrated in his Poem. The high ſpirit of Dante was ill ſuited to courtly dependence; and he is ſaid to have loſt the favour of his Veroneze patron by the rough franknefs of his behaviour. From Verona he retired to France, according to Manetti; and Boccacio affirms that he diſputed in the Theological Schools of Paris with great reputation. Bayle queſtions his viſiting Paris at this period of his life, and thinks it improbable, that a man, who had been one of

6   the

the chief magistrates of Florence, should condescend to engage in the public squabbles of the Parisian Theologists; but the spirit both of Dante, and the times in which he lived, sufficiently account for this exercise of his talents; and his residence in France at this season is confirmed by Boccacio, in his life of our Poet, which Bayle seems to have had no opportunity of consulting.

The election of Henry Count of Luxemburgh to the empire, in November 1308, afforded Dante a prospect of being restored to his native city, as he attached himself to the interest of the new Emperor, in whose service he is supposed to have written his Latin treatise De Monarchia, in which he asserted the rights of the Empire against the encroachments of the Papacy. In the year 1311, he instigated Henry to lay siege to Florence; in which enterprize, says one of his Biographers, he did not appear in person, from motives of respect towards his native city. The Emperor was repulsed by the Florentines; and his death, which happened in the succeeding year, deprived Dante of all hopes concerning his re-establishment in Florence.

After this disappointment, he is supposed to have passed some years in roving about Italy in a state of poverty and distress, till he found an honourable establishment at Ravenna, under the protection of Guido Novello da Polenta, the lord of that city, who received this illustrious exile with the most endearing liberality, continued to protect him through the few remaining years of his life, and extended his munificence to the ashes of the Poet.

Eloquence was one of the many talents which Dante possessed in an eminent degree. On this account he is said to have been employed on fourteen different embassies in the course of his life, and to have succeeded in most of them. His patron Guido had occasion to try his abilities in a service of this nature, and dispatched him as his ambassador to negociate a peace with the Venetians, who were preparing for hostilities against Ravenna. Manetti asserts that he was unable to procure a public audience at Venice, and returned to Ravenna by land, from his apprehensions of the Venetian fleet; when the fatigue of his journey, and the mortification of failing in his attempt to preserve his generous patron from the impending danger, threw him into a fever, which terminated in death on the 14th of September 1321. He died, however,

in

in the palace of his friend, and the affectionate Guido paid the moft tender regard to his memory. This magnificent patron, fays Boccacio,
commanded the body to be adorned with poetical ornaments, and, after
being carried on a bier through the ftreets of Ravenna by the moft illuf-
trious citizens, to be depofited in a marble coffin. He pronounced himfelf the funeral oration, and expreffed his defign of erecting a fplendid
monument in honour of the deceafed: a defign which his fubfequent
misfortunes rendered him unable to accomplifh. At his requeft, many
epitaphs were written on the Poet: the beft of them, fays Boccacio,
by Giovanni del Virgilio of Bologna, a famous author of that time, and
the intimate friend of Dante. Boccacio then cites a few Latin verfes,
not worth tranfcribing, fix of which are quoted by Bayle as the compofition of Dante himfelf, on the authority of Paul Jovius. In 1483
Bernardo Bembo, the father of the celebrated Cardinal, raifed a hand-
fome monument over the neglected afhes of the Poet, with the following
infcription:

> Exigua tumuli Danthes hic forte jacebas
>   Squallenti nulli cognita pæne fitu;
> At nunc marmoreo fubnixus conderis arcu,
>   Omnibus et cultu fplendidiore nites:
> Nimirum Bembus, Mufis incenfus Etrufcis,
>   Hoc tibi, quem in primis hæ coluere, dedit.

Before this period the Florentines had vainly endeavoured to obtain the
bones of their great Poet from the city of Ravenna. In the age of
Leo the Xth they made a fecond attempt, by a folemn application to the
Pope, for that purpofe; and the great Michael Angelo, an enthufiaftic
admirer of Dante, very liberally offered to execute a magnificent monument to the Poet. The hopes of the Florentines were again unfuccefsful. The particulars of their fingular petition may be found in the
notes to Condivi's Life of Michael Angelo.

The perfon and manners of Dante are thus reprefented by the defcriptive pen of Boccacio: — " Fu adunque quefto noftro Poeta di Mezzana
ftatura; e poichè alla matura età fu pervenuto, andò alquanto gravetto,
ed era il fuo andar grave, e manfueto, di oneftiffimi panni fempre veftito,

Z   in

in quello abito, che era alla sua matura età convenevole; il suo volto fu
lungo, il naso aquilino, gli occhi anzi grossi, che piccioli, le mascelle
grandi, e dal labbro di sotto, era quel di sopra avanzato; il colore era
bruno, i capelli, e la barba spessi neri e crespi, e sempre nella faccia ma-
linconico e pensoso——Ne costumi publici e domestici mirabilmente
fu composto e ordinato; più che niuno altro cortese e civile; nel cibo
e nel

A GUIDO CAVALCANTI.

Guido, vorrei, che tu, e Lappo, ed io,
    Fossimo presi per incantamento,
    E messi ad un vassel, ch'ad ogni vento
    Per mare andasse a voler vostro e mio;
Sicché fortuna, od altro tempo rio,
    Non ci potesse dare impedimento:
    Anzi vivendo sempre in noi talento
    Di stare insieme crescesse 'l disio.
E monna Vanna, e monna Bice poi,
    Con quella su il numer delle trenta,
    Con noi ponesse il buono incantatore:
E quivi ragionar sempre d'amore:
    E ciascuna di lor fosse contenta,
    Siccome io credo che fariamo noi.

These lively verses were evidently written before the Poet lost the
object of his earliest attachment, as she is mentioned by the name of
Bice. At what time, and in what place, he executed the great and singular work which has rendered him immortal, his numerous Commentators seem unable to determine. Boccacio asserts, that he began it in
his thirty-fifth year, and had finished seven Cantos of his Inferno before
his exile; that in the plunder of his house, on that event, the begin-

e nel poto fu modeſtiſſimo.——Though Dante is deſcribed as much inclined to melancholy, and his genius particularly delighted in the gloomy and ſublime, yet in his early period of life he ſeems to have poſſeſſed all the lighter graces of ſprightly compoſition, as appears from the following airy and ſportive ſonnet:

IMITATION.

Henry! I wiſh that you, and Charles, and I,
    By ſome ſweet ſpell within a bark were plac'd,
    A gallant bark with magic virtue grac'd,
    Swift at our will with every wind to fly:
So that no changes of the ſhifting ſky,
    No ſtormy terrors of the watery waſte,
    Might bar our courſe, but heighten ſtill our taſte
    Of ſprightly joy, and of our ſocial tie:
Then, that my Lucy, Lucy fair and free,
    With thoſe ſoft nymphs on whom your ſouls are bent,
    The kind magician might to us convey,
To talk of love throughout the live-long day;
    And that each fair might be as well content
    As I in truth believe our hearts would be.

---

ning of his poem was fortunately preſerved, but remained for ſome time neglected, till its merit being accidentally diſcovered by an intelligent Poet named Dino, it was ſent to the Marquis Maroello Maleſpina, an Italian nobleman, by whom Dante was then protected. The Marquis reſtored theſe loſt papers to the Poet, and intreated him to proceed in a work which opened in ſo promiſing a manner. To this incident we are probably indebted for the poem of Dante, which he muſt have continued

under

under all the difadvantages of an unfortunate and agitated life. It does not appear at what time he completed it; perhaps before he quitted Verona, as he dedicated the Paradife to his Veronefe patron.——The Critics have varioufly accounted for his having called his poem Comedia. He gave it that title, faid one of his fons, becaufe it opens with diftrefs, and clofes with felicity. The very high eftimation in which this production was held by his country, appears from a fingular inftitution. The republic of Florence, in the year 1373, affigned a public ftipend to a perfon appointed to read lectures on the poem of Dante: Boccacio was the firft perfon engaged in this office; but his death happening in two years after his appointment, his Comment extended only to the feventeen firft Cantos of the Inferno. The critical differtations that have been written on Dante are almoft as numerous as thofe to which Homer has given birth: the Italian, like the Grecian Bard, has been the fubject of the higheft panegyric, and of the groffeft invective. Voltaire has fpoken of him with that precipitate vivacity, which fo frequently led that lively Frenchman to infult the reputation of the nobleft writers. In one of his entertaining letters, he fays to an Italian Abbé, " Je fais grand cas du courage, avec lequel vous avez ofé dire que Dante etoit un fou, et fon ouvrage un monftre — — — Le Dante pourra entrer dans les bibliotheques des curieux, mais il ne fera jamais lu." But more temperate and candid Critics have not been wanting to difplay the merits of this original Poet. Mr. Warton has introduced into his laft volume on Englifh Poetry, a judicious and fpirited fummary of Dante's performance. We have feveral verfions of the celebrated ftory of Ugolino; but I believe no entire Canto of Dante has hitherto appeared in our language, though his whole work has been tranflated into French, Spanifh, and Latin verfe. The three Cantos which follow, were tranflated a few years ago, to oblige a particular friend. The Author has fince been folicited to execute an entire tranflation of Dante; but the extreme inequality of this Poet would render fuch a work a very laborious undertaking, and it appears very doubtful how far fuch a verfion would intereft our country. Perhaps the reception of thefe Cantos may difcover to the Tranflator the fentiments of the public. At all events, he flatters himfelf that the enfuing portion of a celebrated poem may afford fome pleafure from its novelty, as he has endeavoured to give the Englifh reader an idea of

Dante's

Dante's peculiar manner, by adopting his triple rhyme; and he does not recollect that this mode of verſification has ever appeared before in our language; it has obliged him of courſe to make the number of tranſlated lines correſpond exactly with thoſe of the original. The difficulties attending this metre will ſufficiently ſhew themſelves, and obtain ſome degree of indulgence from the intelligent and candid reader.

DELL'

DELL' INFERNO.

CANTO I.

NEL mezzo del cammin di noſtra vita
  Mi ritrovai per una ſelva oſcura,
Che la diritta via era ſmarrita:
E quanto à dir qual era, è coſa dura,
  Queſta ſelva ſelvaggia ed aſpra e forte,
  Che nel penſier rinnuova la paura.
Tanto è amara, che poco è più morte:
  Ma per trattar del ben, ch'i vi trovai,
  Dirò dell' altre coſe, ch'i v'ho ſcorte.
I non ſo ben ridir, com'i v'entrai;
  Tant'era pien di ſonno in ſu quel punto,
  Che la verace via abbandonai.
Ma po' ch'i fui al piè d'un colle giunto,
  Là ove terminava quella valle,
  Che m'avea di paura il cor compunto;
Guarda'in alto, e vidi le ſue ſpalle
  Veſtite già de' raggi del pianeta,
  Che mena dritto altrui per ogni calle.
Allor fu la paura un poco queta,
  Che nel lago del cor m'era durata,
  La notte, ch'i paſſai con tanta pieta.
E come quei, che con lena affannata
  Uſcito fuor del pelago alla riva,
  Si volge all'aqua periglioſa, e guata;
Coſi l'animo mio, ch'ancor fuggiva,
  Si volſ' à retro à rimirar lo paſſo,
  Che non laſciò giammai perſona viva.

Poi

THE INFERNO OF DANTE.

CANTO I.

IN the mid feafon of this mortal ftrife,
  I found myfelf within a gloomy grove,
  Far wandering from the ways of perfect life:
The place I know not, where I chanc'd to rove,
  It was a wood fo wild, it wounds me fore
  But to remember with what ills I ftrove:
Such ftill my dread, that death is little more.
  But I will tell the good which there I found.
  High things 'twas there my fortune to explore:
Yet how I enter'd on that fecret ground
  I know not to explain; fo much in fleep
  My mortal fenfes at that hour were drown'd.
But when I reach'd the bottom of a fteep,
  That rofe to terminate the dreary vale,
  Which made cold terrors thro' my bofom creep,
I look'd on high, where breath'd a purer gale,
  And faw the fummit gliften with that ray
  Which leads the wand'rer fafe o'er hill and dale.
This foon began to chafe thofe fears away,
  Which held my ftruggling fpirit bound fo faft
  During that night of darknefs and difmay:
And, as th' exhaufted wretch, by fortune caft
  Safe from the ftormy deep upon the fhore,
  Turns to furvey the perils he has paft,
So turn'd my foul, ere yet its dread was o'er,
  Back to contemplate that myfterious ftrait
  Where living mortal never paft before.

Arifing

Poi ch'ebbi ripofato il corpo laffo,
 Riprefi via per la piaggia deferta,
 Si che 'l piè fermo fempre era 'l più baffo.
Ed ecco, quafi al cominciar dell' erta,
 Una lonza leggiera e prefta molto,
 Che di pel maculato era coperta.
E non mi fi partia dinanzi al volto;
 Anz' impediva tanto 'l mio cammino,
 Ch'i fu per ritornar piu volte volto.
Temp' era dal principio del mattino,
 E 'l fol montava in fu con quelle ftelle,
 Ch' eran con lui, quando l'amor divino
Moffe da prima quelle cofe belle
 Si ch'a bene fperar m'era cagione
 Di quella fera la gaietta pelle,
L'ora del tempo, e la dolce ftagione:
 Ma non fi, che paura non mi deffe
 La vifta, che m'apparve d'un leone.
Quefti parea, che contra me veneffe
 Con la teft'alta, e con rabbiofa fame,
 Si che parea, che l'aer ne temeffe:
Ed una lupa, che di tutte brame
 Sembiava carca con la fua magrezza,
 E molte genti fe' già viver grame.
Quefta mi porfe tanto di gravezza
 Con la paura, ch'ufcia di fua vifta,
 Ch'i perde' la fperanza dell' altezza.
E quale è quei, che volentieri acquifta,
 E gingne 'l tempo, che perder lo face,
 Che 'n tutt' i fuoi penfier piange, e s'attrifta;
Tal me fece la beftia fenza pace,
 Che venendomi 'ncontro, a poco a poco
 Mi ripingeva là, dove 'l fol tace.
Mentre ch'i rovinava in baffo loco,
 Dinanzi gli occhi mi fi fu offerto
 Chi per lungo filenzio parea fioco.

Quand'i

Arising soon from this repose elate,
 Up the rough steep my journey I begin,
 My lower foot sustaining all my weight.
Here, while my toilsome way I slowly win,
 Behold a nimble Panther springs to sight!
 And beauteous spots adorn his motley skin:
He at my presence shew'd no signs of fright,
 But rather strove to bar my doubtful way;
 I often turn'd, and oft resolv'd on flight.
'Twas now the chearful hour of rising day;
 The sun advanc'd in that propitious sign
 Which first beheld his radiant beams display
Creation's charms, the work of love divine!
 So that I now was rais'd to hope sublime,
 By these bright omens of a fate benign,
The beauteous Beast and the sweet hour of prime.
 But soon I lost that hope; and shook yet more
 To see a Lion in this lonely clime:
With open jaws, athirst for human gore,
 He rush'd towards me in his hungry ire;
 Air seem'd to tremble at his savage roar.
With him, enflam'd with every fierce desire,
 A famish'd She-wolf, like a spectre, came;
 Beneath whose gripe shall many a wretch expire.
Such sad oppression seiz'd my sinking frame,
 Such horror at these strange tremendous sights,
 My hopes to climb the hill no longer aim;
But, as the wretch whom lucre's lust incites,
 In the curst hour which scatters all his wealth,
 Sinks in deep sorrow, dead to all delights,
So was I robb'd of all my spirit's health,
 And to the quarter where the sun grows mute,
 Driven by this Beast, who crept on me by stealth.
While I retreated from her dread pursuit,
 A manly figure my glad eyes survey'd,
 Whose voice was like the whisper of a lute.

A a

Quando i' vidi coftui nel gran diferto ;
   Miferere di me gridai a lui,
   Qual che tu fii, od ombra, od uomo certo.
Rifpofemi : non uomo, uomo già fui,
   E li parenti miei furon Lombardi,
   E Mantovani, per patria amendui.
Nacqui fub Julio, ancorche foffe tardi,
   E viffi a Roma, fotto 'l buono Agufto,
   Al tempo degli Dei falfi e bugiardi.
Poeta fui, e cantai di quel giufto
   Figlioul d'Anchife, che venne da Troja,
   Poichè 'l fuperbo Ilion fu combufto.
Ma tu, perchè ritorni à tanta noja ?
   Perchè non fali il dilettofo monte,
   Ch'è principio e cagion di tutta gioja ?
Or fe' tu quel Virgilio, e quella fonte,
   Che fpande di parlar sì largo fiume ?
   Rifpofi lui, con vergognofa fronte.
Oh degli altri poeti onore e lume,
   Vagliami 'l lungo ftudio, e'l grande amore,
   Che m'han fatto cercar lo tuo volume.
Tu fe' lo mio maeftro, e'l mio autore :
   Tu fe' folo colui, da cu'io tolfi
   Lo bello ftile, che m'ha fatto onore.
Vedi la beftia, per cu'io mi volfi :
   Ajutami da lei, famofo faggio,
   Ch'ella mi fa tremar le vene e i polfi.
A te convien tenere altro viaggio,
   Rifpofe, poichè lagrimar mi vide,
   Se vuoi campar d'efto luogo felvaggio :
Che quefta beftia, per la qual tu gride,
   Non lafcia altrui paffar per la fua via,
   Ma tanto lo 'mpedifce, che l'uccide :
Ed ha natura sì malvagia e ria,
   Che mai non empie la bramofa voglia,
   E, dopo 'l pafto, ha più fame, che pria.

                           Molti.

Soon as I faw him in this dreary glade,
   Take pity on me, to this form I cry'd,
   Be thou fubftantial man, or fleeting fhade !—
A man I was (the gracious form reply'd)
   And both my parents were of Lombard race;
   They in their native Mantua liv'd and dy'd:
I liv'd at Rome, rich in a monarch's grace,
   Beneath the good Auguftus' letter'd reign,
   While fabled Gods were ferv'd with worfhip bafe.
A Bard I was: the fubject of my ftrain
   That juft and pious Chief who fail'd from Troy,
   Sinking in afhes on the fanguine plain.
But thou, whom thefe portentous fights annoy,
   Why'doft thou turn? why not afcend the mount,
   Source of all good, and fummit of all joy !—
Art thou that Virgil? thou! that copious fount
   Of richeft eloquence, fo clear, fo bright?
   I anfwer'd, blufhing at his kind account;
O thou! of Poets the pure guide and light!
   Now let me profit by that fond efteem
   Which kept thy fong for ever in my fight!
Thou art my Mafter! thou my Bard fupreme,
   From whom alone my fond ambition drew
   That purer ftyle which I my glory deem!
O! from this Beaft, fo hideous to the view,
   Save me! O fave me! thou much-honour'd Sage!
   For growing terrors all my power fubdue.—
A different road muft lead thee from her rage,
   (He faid, obfervant of my ftarting tears)
   And from this wild thy fpirit difengage;
For that terrific Beaft, which caus'd thy fears,
   Worries each wretch that in her road fhe fpies,
   Till death at length, his fole relief, appears.
So keen her nature, fleep ne'er feals her eyes;
   Her ravenous hunger no repaft can fate;
   Food only ferves to make its fury rife.

A a 2

She

Molti fon gli animali, a cui s'ammoglia;
 E più faranno ancora, infin che 'l veltro
 Verrà, che la farà morir di doglia.
Quefti non ciberà terra, nè peltro,
 Ma fapienza, e amore, e virtute,
 E fua nazion farà tra Feltro e Feltro:
Di quell' umile Italia fia falute,
 Per cui morío la Vergine Cammilla,
 Eurialo, e Turno, e Nifo di ferute:
Quefti la caccerà per ogni villa,
 Fin chè l'avrà rimeffa nello 'nferno,
 La onde 'nvidia prima dipartilla.
Ond' io, per lo tuo me', penfo e difcerno,
 Che tu mi fegui, ed io farò tua guida,
 E trarrotti di qui, per luogo eterno,
Ov' udirai le difperate ftrida,
 Vedrai gli antiche fpiriti dolenti,
 Che la feconda morte ciafcun grida:
E poi vedrai color, che fon contenti
 Nel fuoco; perchè fperan di venire,
 Quando che fia, alle beate genti:
Alle qua' poi fe tu vorrai falire,
 Anima fia, a ciò di me più degna:
 Con lei ti lafcerò nel mio partire:
Che quello mperador, che lafsù regna,
 Perch' i' fu' ribellante alla fua legge,
 Non vuol che'n fua città per me fi vegna.
In tutte parti impera, e quivi regge:
 Quivi è la fua cittade, e l'alto feggio:
 O felice colui, cu' ivi elegge!
Ed io a lui: Poeta, i' ti rechieggio,
 Per quello Iddio, che tu non conofcefti,
 Acciocch' i' fugga quefto male e peggio,
Che tu mi meni, là dov'or dicefti,
 Sì ch' i' vegga la porta di fan Pietro,
 E color che tu fai cotanto mefti.
Allor fi moffe, ed io li tenni dietro.

CANTO

She calls from different animals her mate;
   And long shall she produce an offspring base,
   Then from a mighty victor meet her fate.
Nor pomp nor riches shall that victor grace,
   But truth, and love, and all excelling worth;
   He from his rescu'd land all ill shall chase,
The saviour of the realm that gives him birth,
   Of Italy, for whom Camilla fell,
   And Turnus, fighting for his native earth,
And Ninus, with the friend he lov'd so well.
   The Beast this victor to that den shall drive
   Whence Envy let her loose, her native hell!
Now for thy good, well-pleas'd, I will contrive,
   That by my aid, while I thy steps controul,
   Thou shalt in safety at those realms arrive
Where thou shalt see the tortur'd spirits roll,
   And hear each mourn his miserable fate,
   Calling for death on his immortal soul.
Then shalt thou visit those, who in a state
   Of purifying fire are still content,
   And for their promis'd heaven submissive wait:
If to that heaven thy happy course is bent,
   A worthier guard will soon my place supply;
   A purer spirit, for thy guidance sent!
For that Immortal Power, who rules on high,
   Because I ne'er his perfect laws have known,
   His sacred presence will to me deny.
There in the realms of light he fix'd his throne;
   There o'er the world Almighty Lord he reigns:
   O blest the servant whom he deigns to own!—
Poet (I answer'd) by thy living strains,
   And by that God, tho' not reveal'd to thee,
   That I may 'scape from these, and heavier pains,
Be thou my leader, where thy way is free!
   So that my eyes St. Peter's gate may find,
   And all the wonders of the deep may see!
He led, and I attentive march'd behind.

CANTO

C A N T O   II.

LO giorno fe n'andava, e l'aer bruno
    Toglieva gli animai, che fono 'n terra,
Dalle fatiche loro: ed io fol' uno
M'apparecchiava a foftener la guerra,
    Sì del cammino, e sì della pietate,
    Che ritrarrà la mente, che non erra.
O Mufe, o alto 'ngegno, or m'ajutate:
    O mente, che fcrivefti ciò ch'i' vidi,
    Qui fi parrà la tua nobilitate.
Io cominciai: Poeta, che mi guidi,
    Guarda la mia virtù, s'ell' è poffente,
    Prima ch' all' alto paffo tu mi fidi.
Tu dici, che di Silvio lo parente,
    Corrutibile ancora, ad immortale
    Secolo andò, e fu fenfibilmente.
Però fe l'avverfario d'ogni male
    Cortefe fu, penfando l'alto effetto,
    Ch' ufcir dovea di lui, e 'l chi, e 'l quale,
Non pare indegno ad uomo d'intelletto;
    Ch' ei fu dell'alma Roma, e di fuo 'mpero,
    Nell' empireo ciel, per padre, eletto:
La quale, e'l quale (a voler dir lo vero)
    Fur ftabiliti, per lo loco fanto,
    U' fiede il fucceffor del maggior Piero.
Per quefta andata, onde li dai tu vanto,
    Intefe cofe, che furon cagione
    Di fua vittoria, e del papale ammanto.
Andovvi poi lo vas d'elezione,
    Per recarne conforto, a quella fede,
    Ch' è principio alla via di falvazione.

2.   Ma

CANTO II.

THE day was finking, and the dufky air
   On all the animals of earth beftow'd
Reft from their labours.   I alone prepare
To meet new toil, both from my dreary road,
   And pious wifh to paint in worthy phrafe
   The Unerring Mind, and his divine abode.
O facred Mufes! now my genius raife!
   O Memory, who writeft what I faw,
   From hence fhall fpring thy ever-during praife!
Kind Poet (I began, with trembling awe)
   Mark if my foul be equal to this aim!
   Nor into fcenes too hard my weaknefs draw!
Thy Song declares, the Chief of pious fame
   Appear'd among the bleft, retaining ftill
   His mortal fenfes and material frame;
Yet, if the great Oppofer of all ill
   Shew'd grace to him, as knowing what and who
   Should from him rife, and mighty things fulfil,
Moft worthy he appear'd, in Reafon's view,
   That Heaven fhould chufe him as the Roman Sire,
   Source of that empire which fo widely grew,
Mark'd in its growth by the angelic choir
   To be the feat where Sanctity fhould reft,
   And Peter's heirs yet raife dominion higher.
From his dark journey, in thy Song expreft,
   He learn'd myfterious things; from whence arofe
   Rome's early grandeur and the Papal veft.
To Paul, while living, heaven's high powers difclofe
   Their fecret blifs, that he may thence receive
   Strength in that faith from which falvation flows.

                                        But

Ma io, perchè venirvi? o chi 'l concede?
Io non Enea, io non Paolo fono:
Me degno à ciò, nè io, nè altri il crede.
Perchè fe del venire i' m'abbandono,
Temo che la venuta non fia folle:
Se' favio, e 'ntendi me', ch'i' non ragiono.
E quale è quei, che difvuol ciò ch'e' volle,
E per nuovi penfier cangia propofta,
Si che del cominciar tutto fi tolle;
Tal mi fec' io' in quella ofcura cofta:
Perchè, penfando, confumai la 'mprefa,
Che fu, nel cominciar, cotanto tofta.
Se io ho ben la tua parola intefa,
Rifpofe del magnanimo quell' ombra,
L'anima tua è da viltate offefa:
La qual molte fiate l'uomo ingombra,
Si che d'onrata imprefa lo rivolve,
Come falfo veder beftia, quand' ombra.
Da quefta tema acciocché tu ti folve,
Dirotti, perch' i' venni, e quel, ch'io'ntefi,
Nel primo punto, che di te mi dolve.
Io era tra color, che fon fofpefi,
E donna mi chiamò beata e bella,
Tal che di comandare i' la richiefi.
Lucevan gli occhi fuoi più, che la ftella:
E cominciommi a dir foave e piana,
Con angelica voce, in fua favella:
O anima cortefe Mantovana,
Di cui la fama ancor nel mondo dura,
E durerà, quanto 'l moto lontana:
L'amico mio, e non della ventura,
Nella deferta piaggia è impedito
Sì nel cammin, che volto è per paura:
E temo, che non fia già sì fmarrito,
Ch'io mi fia tardi al foccorfo levata,
Per quel, ch' io ho di lui, nel Cielo, udito.

3   Or

But how may I this high exploit atchieve?
  I'm not Æneas, nor the holy Paul:
  Of this unworthy I myself believe:
If then I follow at thy friendly call,
  Midway perchance my trembling soul may sink:
  Wife as thou art, thou may'st foresee my fall.
Now as a man who, shudd'ring on the brink
  Of some great venture, sudden shifts his mind,
  And feels his spirit from the peril shrink;
So, in this scene of doubt and darkness join'd,
  Wavering I wasted thought in wild affright,
  And the first ardour of my soul resign'd.
If thy faint words I understand aright,
  (Reply'd the mighty and magnanimous shade)
  Those mists of fear have dimm'd thy mental sight,
Which oft the seat of human sense invade,
  And make blind mortals from high deeds recoil,
  By Terror's airy phantasies betray'd:
But, that such fears thy soul no more may soil,
  I'll tell thee whence I came; at whose request;
  When first I pitied thy uncertain toil.
From the suspended host in which I rest,
  A lovely Spirit call'd me, fair as light;
  Eager I waited on her high behest;
While eyes beyond the solar radiance bright,
  And with the sweetness of an angel's tongue,
  Thus her soft words my willing aid invite:
O ever gentle shade, from Mantua sprung!
  Whose fame unfading on the earth shall last
  As long as earth in ambient air is hung;
My friend, whose love all base desire surpast,
  In yon drear defart finds his passage barr'd,
  And compass'd round with terrors stands aghast;
And much I fear, beset with dangers hard,
  He may be lost beyond all friendly reach,
  And I from heaven descend too late a guard.

B b

But

Or muovi, e con la tua parola ornata,
   E con ciò, che ha meſtieri al ſuo campare,
   L'ajuta sì, ch'i' ne ſia conſolata.
I' ſon Beatrice, che ti faccio andare :
   Vegno di loco, ove tornar diſio :
   Amor mi moſſe, che mi fa parlare.
Quando ſarò dinanzi al ſignor mio,
   Di te mi loderò ſovente a lui :
   Tacette allora, e poi comincia' io :
O donna di virtù, ſola, per cui,
   L'umana ſpezie eccede ogni contento
   Da quel ciel, ch' ha minor li cerchi ſuoi :
Tanto m'aggrada 'l tuo comandamento,
   Che l'ubbidir, ſe già foſſe, m'è tardi :
   Più non t'è uopo aprirmi 'l tuo talento.
Ma dimmi la cagion, che non ti guardi
   Dello ſcender quaggiuſo, in queſto centro,
   Dall' ampio loco, ove tornar tu ardi.
Da che tu vuoi ſaper cotanto addentro,
   Dirotti brevemente, mi riſpoſe,
   Perch'i' non temo di venir qua entro.
Temer ſi dee di ſole quelle coſe,
   Ch' hanno potenza di fare altrui male :
   Dell' altre nò, che non ſon pauroſe.
Io ſon fatta da Dio, ſua mercè, tale,
   Che la voſtra miſeria non mi tange,
   Nè fiamma d'eſto 'ncendio non m'aſſale.
Donna è gentil nel ciel, che ſi compiange
   Di queſto 'mpedimento, ov' i' ti mando,
   Sì che duro giudicio laſſu frange.
Queſta chieſe Lucía in ſuo dimando,
   E diſſe : Ora abbiſogna il tuo ſedele
   Di te, ed io a te lo raccomando.
Lucía nimica di ciaſcun crudele
   Si moſſe, e venne al loco, dov'i' era,
   Che mi ſedea con l'antica Rachele :

                                   Diſſe,

But go! and with thy foft foul-foothing fpeech,
   And all the aid thy wifdom may infpire,
   The ways of fafety to this wanderer teach!
My name is Beatrice: the heavenly quire
   For this I left, tho' ever left with pain;
   But love fuggefted what I now defire.
When I the prefence of my lord regain,
   On thee my praifes with delight fhall dwell.
   So fpake this angel, in her heavenly ftrain.
Bright Fair, (I cry'd) who didft on earth excel
   All that e'er fhone beneath the lunar fphere,
   And every mind to virtuous love impel!
Had I e'en now perform'd the tafk I hear,
   That fwift performance I fhould think too flow:
   Nor needs there more; your gracious will is clear:
Yet how you venture, I would gladly know,
   From thofe pure realms, to which again you fly,
   So near the center of eternal woe.
What you require (fhe faid, in kind reply)
   I briefly will explain: how thus I dare,
   Unconfcious of alarm, thefe depths to try.
From thefe things only fprings our fearful care,
   By which our haplefs friends may fuffer ill;
   But not from other; for no fear is there.
Such am I form'd, by Heaven's moft gracious will,
   That torture cannot touch my purer frame,
   E'en where fierce fires his flaming region fill.
A gentle fpirit (Lucia is her name)
   In heaven laments the hardfhips of my friend,
   For whom I afk your aid: to me fhe came,
And kindly bade me to his woes attend:
   Behold (fhe faid) thy fervant in diftrefs!
   And I his fafety to thy care commend.
Lucia, the friend of all whom ills opprefs,
   Me, where I fate with penfive Rachel, fought,
   In heavenly contemplation's deep recefs:

Diffe, Beatrice, loda di Dio vera,
    Che non foccorri quei, che t'amò tanto;
    Ch' ufcío per te della volgare fchiera?
Non odi tu la pieta del fuo pianto,
    Non vedi tu la morte, che 'l combatte
    Su la fiumana, ove 'l mar non ha vanto?
Al mondo non fur mai perfone ratte
    A far lor pro, ed a fuggir lor danno,
    Com' io, dopo cotai parole fatte,
Venni quaggiù dal mio beato fcanno,
    Fidandomi nel tuo parlare onefto,
    Ch'onora te, e quei, ch'udito l'hanno.
Pofcia che m'ebbe ragionato quefto,
    Gli occhi lucenti, lagrimando, volfe:
    Perchè mi fece del venir più prefto:
E venni à te così, com'ella volfe:
    Dinanzi a quella fiera ti levai,
    Che del bel monte il corto andar ti tolfe.
Dunque che è? perchè, perchè riftai?
    Perchè tanta viltà nel cuore allette?
    Perchè ardire e franchezza non hai?
Pofcia che tai tre donne benedette
    Curan di te, nella corte del Cielo,
    E 'l mio parlar tanto ben t'impromette?
Quale i fioretti, dal notturno gielo,
    Chinati e chiufi, poi che 'l fol gl'imbianca,
    Si drizzan tutti aperti in loro ftelo,
Tal mi fec' io, di mia virtute ftanca:
    E tanto buono ardire al cuor mi corfe,
    Ch'i' cominciai, come perfona franca:
O pietofa colei, che mi foccorfe,
    E tu cortefe, ch'ubbidifti tofto
    Alle vere parole, che ti porfe!
Tu m'hai con defiderio il cuor difpofto
    Sì al venir, con le parole tue,
    Ch'i' fon tornato nel primo propofto.

                             Or

In mercy's name (she cry'd) thus lost in thought,
  Seeft thou not him who held thy charms so dear,
  Whom Love to rise above the vulgar taught?
And dost thou not his lamentation hear,
  Nor see the horror, which his strength impairs,
  On yon wide torrent, with no haven near?
Never was mind, intent on worldly cares,
  So eager wealth to gain, or loss to shun,
  As, when acquainted with these deadly snares,
I flew from the blest confines of the sun,
  Trusting that eloquence, which to thy name
  And to thy followers such praise has won.
She having thus explain'd her gracious aim,
  Turn'd her bright eyes, which tears of pity fill:
  And hence more swift to thy relief I came;
And, pleas'd to execute her heavenly will,
  I sav'd thee from the fury of that Beast,
  Which barr'd thy journey up the brighter hill.
Why then, O why has all thy ardour ceas'd?
  And whence this faintness in thy feeble mind?
  Why has its noble energy decreas'd,
When these pure Spirits, for thy good combin'd,
  Watch o'er thy safety in their heavenly seat,
  And I reveal the favour thou shalt find?—
As tender flowers, reviv'd by solar heat,
  That thro' the chilling night have sunk deprest,
  Rise and unfold, the welcome ray to meet;
So rose my spirit, of new life possest;
  And, my warm heart on high atchievements bent,
  I thus my animating guide addrest:
Gracious that Spirit who thy succour sent!
  And friendly thou, who freely hast display'd
  Thy zeal to execute her kind intent!
Thy soothing words have to my soul convey'd
  Such keen desire to those bright realms to soar,
  I scorn the terror that my step delay'd.

                                       Now

Or va, ch'un fol volere è d'amendue :
Tu duca, tu fignore, e tu maeftro :
Così li diffi : e poichè moffo fue,
Entrai per lo cammino alto e filveftro.

CANTO III.

" PER me fi va nella città dolente :
Per me fi va nell' eterno dolore :
Per me fi va tra la perduta gente.
Giuftizia moffe 'l mio alto fattore :
Fecemi la divina poteftate,
La fomma fapienzia, e 'l primo amore.
Dinanzi a me non fur cofe create,
Se non eterne, ed io eterno duro :
Lafciate ogni fperanza, voi che 'ntrate."
Quefte parole di colore ofcuro
Vid' io fcritte al fommo d'una porta :
Perch'io, Maeftro, il fenfo lor m'è duro.
Ed egli a me, come perfona accorta,
Qui fi convien lafciare ogni fofpetto :
Ogni viltà convien, che qui fia morta.
Noi fem venuti al luogo, ov' i' t'ho detto,
Che tu vedrai le genti dolorofe,
Ch'hanno perduto 'l ben dello 'ntelletto.
E poichè la fua mano alla mia pofe,
Con lieto volto, ond'i' mi confortai,
Mi mife dentro alle fegrete cofe.
Quivi fofpiri, pianti, e alti guai
Rifonavan, per l'aer fenza ftelle,
Perch'io al cominciar, ne lagrimai.
Diverfe lingue, orribili favelle,
Parole di dolore, accenti d'ira,
Voci alte e fioche, e fuon di man con elle

1   Facevano

Now lead !—thy pleafure I difpute no more.
　My lord, my mafter thou ! and thou my guard !—
　I ended here ; and, while he march'd before,
The gloomy road I enter'd, deep and hard.

C A N T O   III.

" THRO' me you pafs to Mourning's dark domain ;
　　Thro' me to fcenes where Grief muft ever pine ;
　Thro' me, to Mifery's devoted train:
Juftice and power in my Great Founder join,
　And love and wifdom all his fabrics rear ;
　Wifdom above controul, and love divine !
Before me, Nature faw no works appear,
　Save works eternal : fuch was I ordain'd.
　Quit every hope, all ye who enter here !"
Thefe charaƈters, where mifty darknefs reign'd,
　High o'er a lofty gate I faw engrav'd.
　Ah Sire ! (faid I) hard things are here contain'd.
He, fapient Guide ! my farther queftion fav'd,
　With fpirit anfwering, " Here all doubt refign,
　All weak diftruft, and every thought deprav'd ;
At length we've reach'd that gloomy drear confine,
　Where, as I faid, thou'lt fee the mournful race.
　For ever robb'd of Reafon's light benign."
Then, ftretching forth his hand with gentle grace,
　From whence new comfort through my bofom flows,
　He led me in to that myfterious place.
There fighs, and wailings, and fevereft woes,
　Deeply refounded through the ftarlefs air ;
　And as I firft advanc'd, my fears arofe.
Each different cry, the murmuring notes of care,
　Accents of mifery, and words of ire,
　　With all the founds of difcord and defpair,

　　　　　　　　　　　　　　　　　　To

Facevano un tumulto, il qual s'aggira
   Sempre 'n quell' aria, senza tempo, tinta,
   Come la rena quando 'l turbo spira.
Ed io, ch' avea d'error la testa cinta,
   Dissi, Maestro, che è quel, ch' i' odo?
   E che gent' è, che par nel duol sì vinta?
Ed egli a me: Questo misero modo
   Tengon l' anime triste di coloro,
   Che visser sanza infamia, e sanza lodo.
Mischiate sono a quel cattivo coro
   Degli angeli, che non furon ribelli,
   Nè fur fedeli a Dio, ma per se foro.
Cacciarli i ciel, per non esser men belli:
   Nè lo profondo inferno gli riceve,
   Ch'alcuna gloria i rei avrebber d'elli.
Ed io: Maestro, che è tanto greve
   A lor, che lamentar gli fa sì forte?
   Rispose: Dicerolti molto breve.
Questi non hanno speranza di morte:
   E la lor cieca vita è tanto bassa,
   Che 'nvidiosi son d'ognì altra sorte.
Fama di loro il mondo esser non lassa:
   Misericordia e giustizia gli sdegna.
   Non ragioniam di lor, ma guarda, e passa.
Ed io, che riguardai, vidi una insegna,
   Che, girando, correva tanto ratta,
   Che d'ogni posa mi pareva indegna •
E dietro le venía sì lunga tratta
   Di gente, ch'i' non avrei mai creduto,
   Che morte tanta n' avesse disfatta.
Poscia ch' io v'ebbi alcun riconosciuto,
   Guardai, e vidi l'ombra di colui,
   Che fece, per viltate, il gran rifiuto.
Incontanente intese, e certo fui,
   Che quest' era la setta de' cattivi
   A Dio spiacenti, ed a' nemici sui.

6

Questi

To form such tumult in this scene conspire,
   As flies for ever round the gloomy waste,
   Like sand when quicken'd by the whirlwind's fire.
I then (my mind with error still disgrac'd)
   Exclaim'd—O Sire! what may this trouble mean?
   What forms are these, by sorrow so debas'd?—
He soon reply'd—Behold, these bounds between,
   All who without or infamy or fame
   Clos'd the blank business of their mortal scene!
They join those angels, of ignoble name,
   Who not rebell'd, yet were not faithful found;
   Without attachment! self alone their aim!
Heaven shuts them out from its unsullied bound;
   And Hell refuses to admit this train,
   Lest e'en the damn'd o'er these their triumph sound.—
O Sire! (said I) whence then this grievous pain,
   That on our ears their lamentations grate?—
   This (he reply'd) I will in brief explain:
These have no hope that death may mend their fate;
   And their blind days form so confus'd a mass,
   They pine with envy of each other's state:
From earth their name has perish'd, like the grass;
   E'en Mercy views them with a scornful eye.
   We'll speak of them no more: Behold! and pass!—
I look'd, and saw a banner rais'd on high,
   That whirl'd, unconscious of a moment's stand,
   With rapid circles in the troubled sky:
Behind it, driven by Fate's supreme command,
   Came such a host! I ne'er could have believ'd
   Death had collected so complete a band.
When now I had the forms of all perceiv'd,
   I saw the shade of that ignoble priest,
   Of sovereign power by indolence bereav'd.
Instant I knew, from every doubt releas'd,
   These were the base, the miscreated crew
   To whom the hate of God had never ceas'd.

C c

Vile

Queſti ſciaurati, che mai non fur vivi,
 Erano ignudi, e ſtimolati molto
 Da moſconi, e da veſpe, ch'erano ivi.
Elle rigavan lor di ſangue il volto,
 Che miſchiato di lagrime, a' lor piedi,
 Da faſtidioſi vermi era ricolto.
E poi, ch'a riguardare oltre mi diedi,
 Vidi gente alla riva d'un gran fiume ;
 Perch' i' diſſi : Maeſtro, or mi concedi,
Ch'io ſappia, quali ſono, e qual coſtume
 Le fa parer di trapaſſar ſì pronte,
 Com'io diſcerno per lo fioco lume.
Ed egli a me : Le coſe ti fien conte,
 Quando noi fermerem li noſtri paſſi
 Su la triſta riviera d'Acheronte.
Allor con gli occhi vergognoſi e baſſi
 Temendo, no 'l mio dir gli fuſſe grave,
 Infino al fiume di parlar mi traſſi.
Ed ecco verſo noi venir, per nave,
 Un vecchio bianco, per antico pelo,
 Gridando, Guai à voi anime prave :
Non iſperate mai veder lo cielo :
 I' vegno, per menarvi all' altra riva
 Nelle tenebre eterne, in caldo e'n gielo :
E tu, che ſe' coſtì, anima viva,
 Partiti da coteſti, che ſon morti :
 Ma poi ch' e' vide, ch i' non mi partiva,
Diſſe : Per altre vie, per altri porti
 Verrai a piaggia, non qui, per paſſare :
 Più lieve legno convien, che ti porti.
E 'l duca a lui : Caron, non ti crucciare :
 Vuolſi coſì colà, dove ſi puote
 Ciò che ſi vuole, e più non dimandare.
Quinci fur quete le lanoſe gote
 Al nocchier della livida palude,
 Che 'ntorno agli occhi ave' di fiamme ruote.

Ma

Vile forms ! ne'er honor'd with exiftence true !
    Naked they march'd, and forely were they ftung
    By wafps and hornets, that around them flew ;
Thefe the black blood from their gall'd faces wrung ;
    Blood mixt with tears, that, trickling to their feet,
    Fed the faftidious worms which round them clung.
When now I farther pierc'd the dark retreat,
    Numbers I faw befide a mighty ftream :
    Sudden I cry'd—Now, Sire, let me entreat
To know what forms in diftant profpect feem
    To pafs fo fwiftly o'er a flood fo wide,
    As I difcern by this imperfect gleam ?—
That fhalt thou know (return'd my gracious Guide)
    When the near refpite from our toil we reach.
    On fullen Acheron's infernal tide.—
With downcaft eyes, that pardon now befeech,
    And hoping filence may that pardon win,
    E'en to the river I abftain'd from fpeech.
And lo ! towards us, with a fhrivell'd fkin,
    A hoary boatman fteers his crazy bark,
    Exclaiming, " Woe to all ye fons of fin '
Hope not for heaven, nor light's celeftial fpark !
    I come to waft you to a different lot ;
    To Torture's realm, with endlefs horror aark :
And thou, who living view'ft this facred fpot,
    Hafte to depart from thefe, for thefe are dead !"
    But when he faw that I departed not,
In wrath he cry'd, " Thro' other paffes led,
    Not here, fhalt thou attempt the farther fhore ;
    But in a bark to bear thy firmer tread."—
O Charon, faid my Guide, thy ftrife give o'er ;
    For thus 'tis will'd in that fuperior fcene
    Where will is power.   Seek thou to know no more !—
Now grew the bearded vifage more ferene
    Of the ftern boatman on the livid lake,
    Whofe eyes fo lately glar'd with anger keen :

Ma quell' anime, ch'eran laffe e nude,
   Cangiar colore, e dibattero i denti,
   Ratto che 'ntefer le parole crude.
Beftemmiavano Iddio, e i lor parenti,
   L'umana fpezie, il luogo, il tempo, e'l feme,
   Di lor femenza, e di lor nafcimenti.
Poi fi ritraffer tutte quante infieme
   Forte piangendo, alla riva malvagia,
   Ch'attende ciafcun'uom, che Dio non teme.
Caron dimonio, con occhi di bragia,
   Loro accennando, tutte le raccoglie:
   Batte col remo, qualunque s'adagia.
Come d' Autunno fi levan le foglie,
   L' una appreffo dell' altra, infin che 'l ramo
   Rende alla terra tutte le fue fpoglie;
Similemente il mal feme d' Adamo:
   Gittanfi di quel lito ad una ad una,
   Per cenni, com' augel, per fuo richiamo.
Così fen vanno fu per l'onda bruna,
   E avanti che fien di là difcefe,
   Anche di qua nova fchiera s'aduna.
Figliuol mio, diffe il maeftro cortefe,
   Quelli, che muojon nell' ira di Dio,
   Tutti convegnon qui d' ogni paefe:
E pronti fono al trapaffar del rio,
   Che la divina giuftizia gli fprona,
   Sì che la tema fi volge in difio.
Quinci non paffa mai anima buona:
   E però fe Caron di te fi lagna,
   Ben puoi faper omai, che'l fuo dir fuona.
Finito quefto la buja campagna
   Tremò sì forte, che dello fpavento
   La mente di fudore ancor mi bagna.
La terra lagrimofa diede vento,
   Che balenò una luce vermiglia,
   La qual mi vinfe ciafcun fentimento:
E caddi, come l' uom, cui fonno piglia.

But all the naked fhades began to quake;
  Their fhuddering figures grew more pale than earth,
  Soon as they heard the cruel words he fpake:
God they blafphem'd, their parents' injur'd worth,
  And all mankind; the place, the hour, that faw
  Their firft formation, and their future birth.
Then were they driven, by Fate's refiftlefs law,
  Weeping, to that fad fcene prepar'd for all
  Who fear not God with pure devotion's awe.
Charon, with eyes of fire and words of gall,
  Collects his crew, and high his oar he wields,
  To ftrike the tardy wretch who flights his call.
As leaves in autumn thro' the woody fields
  Fly in fucceffion, when each trembling tree
  Its ling'ring honors to the whirlwind yields;
So this bad race, condemn'd by Heaven's decree,
  Succeffive haften from that river's fide:
  As birds, which at a call to bondage flee,
So are they wafted o'er the gloomy tide;
  And ere from thence their journey is begun,
  A fecond crew awaits their hoary guide.—
My gracious Mafter kindly faid—My fon!
  All thofe who in the wrath of God expire,
  From every clime hafte hither, one by one;
Nor would their terrors from this ftream retire,
  Since heavenly juftice fo impels their mind,
  That fear is quicken'd into keen defire.
Here may no fpirit pafs, to good inclin'd;
  And hence, if Charon feem'd to thwart thy will,
  Hence wilt thou deem his purpofe not unkind.—
He paus'd; and horrors of approaching ill
  Now made the mournful troop fo ftand aghaft,
  Their fears yet ftrike me with a deadly chill!
The groaning earth fent forth a hollow blaft,
  And flafh'd a fiery glare of gloomy red!
  The horrid fcene my fainting power furpaft:
I fell, and, as in fleep, my fenfes fled.

                                          NOTE

NOTE V. Verse 127.

The gay Boccacio, tempts th' Italian Mufe.] Boccacio was almoft utterly unknown to our country as a Poet, when two of our moft accomplifhed Critics reftored his poetical reputation.

Mr. Tyrwhitt, to whom Chaucer is as deeply indebted as a Poet can be to the judgment and erudition of his commentator, has given a fketch of Boccacio's Thefeida, in his introductory difcourfe to the Canterbury Tales; and Mr. Warton has enriched the firft volume of his Hiftory of Englifh Poetry with a confiderable fpeci men of this very rare Italian Epic poem, of which our country is faid to poffefs but a fingle copy.—The father of Boccacio was an Italian merchant, a native of Certaldo, near Florence, who in his travels attached himfelf to a young woman of Paris; and our Poet is fuppofed to have been the illegitimate offspring of that connection. He was born in 1313, and educated as a ftudent of the canon law; but a fight of Virgil's tomb, according to Filippo Villani, his moft ancient Biographer, made him refolve to relinquifh his more irkfome purfuits, and devote himfelf entirely to the Mufes. His life feems to have been divided between literature and love, as he was equally remarkable for an amorous difpofition, and a paffionate attachment to ftudy. His moft celebrated miftrefs was Mary of Arragon, the natural daughter of Robert, King of Naples, the generous and enthufiaftic patron of Petrarch. To this lady, diftinguifhed by the name of The Fiammetta, Boccacio addreffed his capital poem, the Thefeida; telling her, in an introductory letter, that it contained many allufions to the particular circumftances of their own fecret attachment. In his latter days he retired to Certaldo, and died there in the year 1475, of a diforder fuppofed to have arifen from exceffive application. Few authors have rendered more effential fervice to the republic of letters than Boccacio, as he not only contributed very much to the improvement of his native language, but was particularly inftrumental in promoting the revival of ancient learning : a merit which he fhared with Petrarch. The tender and generous friendfhip which fubfifted between thefe two engaging authors, reflects the higheft honour on both; and their letters to each other may be ranked among the moft interefting productions of that period. Boccacio compofed, according

to

to Quadrio, no lefs than thirty-four volumes. His Novels are univerfally known: his Poetical Works are as follow: 1. La Thefeida in
Ottava Rima. 2. L'Amorofa Vifione in Terza Rima. 3. Il Filoftrato
in Ottava Rima. 4. Il Ninfale Fiefolano in Ottava Rima.—He piqued
himfelf on being the firft Poet who fung of martial fubjects in Italian
verfe; and he has been generally fuppofed the inventor of the Ottava
Rima, the common Heroic meafure of the Italian Mufe; but Quadrio
has fhewn that it was ufed by preceding writers; and Pafquier, in his
Recherches, has quoted two ftanzas of Thibaud king of Navarre, written in the fame meafure, on Blanch queen of France, who died in
1252. The neglect into which the Poems of Boccacio had fallen appears the more ftriking, as he peculiarly prided himfelf on his poetical
character; informing the world, by an infcription on his tomb, that
Poetry was his favourite purfuit—Studium fuit alma Poefis, are the laft
words of the epitaph which he compofed for himfelf.

NOTE VI. VERSE 142.

She fpoke exulting, and Triffino fung.] Giovanni Giorgio **Triffino**
was born of a noble family in Vicenza, 1478: he was particularly diftinguifhed by a paffion for Poetry and Architecture; and one of the very
few Poets who have been rich enough to build a palace. This he is faid
to have done from a defign of his own, under the direction of the celebrated Palladio. He had the merit of writing the firft regular tragedy
in the Italian language, entitled Sophonifba; but in his Epic poem he is
generally allowed to have failed, though fome learned Critics (and
Gravina amongft them) have endeavoured to fupport the credit of that
performance. His fubject was the expulfion of the Goths from Italy
by Belifarius; and his poem confifts of twenty-feven books, in blank
verfe. He addreffed it to the Emperor Charles the Vth; and profeffes
in his Dedication to have taken Ariftotle for his preceptor, and Homer
for his guide.

The reader will excufe a trifling anachronifm, in my naming **Triffino**
before Ariofto, for poetical reafons. The Italia Liberata of the former
was firft publifhed in 1548; the Orlando Furiofo, in 1515. **Triffino**
died at Rome, 1550; Ariofto at Ferrara, 1533.

NOTE

NOTE VII. VERSE 194.

Of a poetic Sire the more poetic Son.] The reputation of Torquato
Taſſo has almoſt eclipſed that of his father Bernardo, who was himſelf a
conſiderable Poet, and left two productions of the Epic kind, L'Amadigi,
and Il Floridante : the latter remained unfiniſhed at his death, but was
afterwards publiſhed in its imperfect ſtate by his ſon ; who has ſpoken
of his father's poetry with filial regard, in his different critical works.
The Amadigi was written at the requeſt of ſeveral Spaniſh Grandees, in
the court of Charles the Vth, and firſt printed in Venice by Giolito,
1560. The curious reader may find an entertaining account of the
Author's ideas in compoſing this work, among his Letters, volume the
firſt, page 198. I cannot help remarking, that the letter referred to
contains a ſimile which Torquato has introduced in the opening of his
Jeruſalem Delivered.

The Italians have formed a very pleaſing and valuable work, by collecting the letters of their eminent Painters ; which contain much information on points relating to their art. The letters of their Poets, if
properly ſelected, might alſo form a few intereſting volumes : as a proof
of this, I ſhall inſert a ſhort letter of the younger Taſſo, becauſe it ſeems
to have eſcaped the notice of his Biographers, and relates the remarkable
circumſtance of his having deliberated on five different ſubjects before
he decided in favour of Goffredo :

Al M. Illuſtre Sig. Conte Ferrante Eſtenſe Taſſone.

Io ho ſcritto queſta mattina a V. S. che io deſidero di far due Poemi a
mio guſto ; e ſebben per elezione non cambierci il ſoggetto che una volta
preſi ; nondimeno per ſoddisfar il ſignor principe gli do l' elezione di
tutti queſti ſoggetti, i quali mi paijono ſovra gli altri atti a ricever
la forma eroica.

Eſpedizion di Goffredo, e degli altri principi contra gl' Infedeli,
e ritorno. Dove avrò occaſione di lodar le famiglie d' Europa, che io
vorrò.

Eſpedizion di Beliſario contra i Goti.

Di Narſete contra i Goti, e diſcorro d' un principe. E in queſti

6   avrei

vrei grandiſſima occaſione di lodar le coſe di Spagna e d' Italia e di Grecia e l' origine di caſa d' Auſtria.

Eſpedizion di Carlo il magno contra Lanſoni.

Eſpedizion di Carlo contra i Longobardi.   In queſti troverei l' origine di tutte le famiglie grandi di Germania, di Francia, e d' Italia, e 'l ritorno d' un principe.

E ſebben alcuni di queſti ſoggetti ſono ſtati preſi, non importa; perche io cercherei di trattarglimeglio, e a giudicio d' Ariſtotele.

Opere di Torquato Taſſo, tom. ix. p. 240.

This letter is the more worthy of notice, as the ſubject on which Taſſo fixed has been called by Voltaire, and perhaps very juſtly, Le plus grand qu'on ait jamais choiſi.   Le Taſſe l'a traité dignement, adds the lively Critic, with unuſual candour; yet in his ſubſequent remarks he is peculiarly ſevere on the magic of the Italian Poet.   The merits of Taſſo are very ably defended againſt the injuſtice of French criticiſm, and particularly that of Boileau and Voltaire, in the well-known Letters on Chivalry and Romance.   Indeed the genius of this injured Poet ſeems at length to triumph in the country where he was moſt inſulted, as the French have lately attempted a poetical verſion of his Jeruſalem.

I enter not into the hiſtory of Taſſo, or that of his rival Arioſto, becauſe the public has lately received from Mr. Hoole a judicious account of their lives, prefixed to his elegant verſions of their reſpective Poems.

NOTE VIII. VERSE 197.

Shall gay Taſſoni want his feſtive crown.]   Aleſſandro Taſſoni, the ſuppoſed inventor of the modern Heroi-comic Poetry, was born at Modena, 1565.   His family was noble; but his parents dying during his infancy, left him expoſed to vexatious law-ſuits, which abſorbed a great part of his patrimony, and rendered him dependant.   In 1599 he was engaged as Secretary to Cardinal Aſcanio Colonna, whom he attended on an embaſſy into Spain.   He was occaſionally diſpatched into Italy on the ſervice of that Prelate, and in the courſe of one of theſe expeditions wrote his Obſervations on Petrarch.   In 1605 he is ſuppoſed

D d

to have quitted the fervice of the Cardinal, and to have lived in a state of freedom at Rome, where, in 1607, he became the chief of a literary fociety, entitled Academia degli Umorifti. He was afterwards employed in the fervice of Charles Emanuel, Duke of Savoy; which, after fuffering many vexations in it, he quitted with a defign of devoting himfelf to ftudy and retirement. But this defign he was induced to relinquifh, and to ferve the Cardinal Lodovifio, nephew of Pope Gregory XV. from whom he received a confiderable ftipend. On the death of this patron, in 1632, he was recalled to his native city by Francis the Firft, Duke of Modena, and obtained an honourable eftablifhment in the court of that Prince. Age had now rendered him unable to enjoy his good fortune: his health declined in the year of his return, and he expired in April 1635. His genius was particularly difpofed to lively fatire; and the incidents of his life had a tendency to increafe that difpofition. After having paffed many vexatious and unprofitable years in the fervice of the Great, he had his portrait painted, with a fig in his hand; and Muratori fuppofes him to have written thefe two lines on the occafion:

> Dextera cur ficum, quæris, mea geftet inanem:
> Longi operis merces hæe fuit; aula dedit.

His celebrated Poem, La Secchia rapita, was written, as he has himfelf declared, in 1611; begun in April, and finifhed in October. It was circulated in MS. received with the utmoft avidity, and firft printed at Paris 1622. In a catalogue of the numerous editions of the Secchia, which Muratori has prefixed to his Life of Taffoni, he includes an Englifh tranflation of it, printed 1715.

NOTE IX. VERSE 209.

And rafhly judges that her Vega's lyre.] The famous Lope de Vega, frequently called the Shakefpear of Spain, is perhaps the moft fertile Poet in the annals of Parnaffus; and it would be difficult to name any author, ancient or modern, fo univerfally idolized while living by all ranks of people, and fo magnificently rewarded by the liberality of the Great. He was the fon of Felix de Vega and Francifca Fernandez,

6

who

who were both descended from honourable families, and lived in the neighbourhood of Madrid. Our Poet was born in that city, on the 25th of November 1562. He was, according to his own expression, a Poet from his cradle; and, beginning to make verses before he had learned to write, he used to bribe his elder school-fellows with a part of his breakfast, to commit to paper the lines he had composed. Having lost his father while he was still a child, he engaged in a frolic, very natural to a lively boy, and wandered with another lad to various parts of Spain, till, having spent their money, and being conducted before a magistrate at Segovia, for offering to sell a few trinkets, they were sent home again to Madrid. Soon after this adventure, our young Poet was taken under the protection of Geronimo Manrique, Bishop of Avila, and began to distinguish himself by his dramatic compositions, which were received with great applause by the public, though their author had not yet completed his education ; for, after this period, he became a member of the university of Alcala, where he devoted himself for four years to the study of philosophy. He was then engaged as Secretary to the Duke of Alva, and wrote his Arcadia in compliment to that patron; who is frequently mentioned in his Occasional Poems. He quitted that employment on his marriage with Isabel de Urbina, a lady (says his friend and biographer Perez de Montalvan) beautiful without artifice, and virtuous without affectation. His domestic happiness was soon interrupted by a painful incident :—Having written some lively verses in ridicule of a person who had taken some injurious freedom with his character, he received a challenge in consequence of his wit ; and happening, in the duel which ensued, to give his adversary a dangerous wound, he was obliged to fly from his family, and shelter himself in Valencia. He resided there a considerable time ; but connubial affection recalled him to Madrid. His wife died in the year of his return. His affliction on this event led him to relinquish his favourite studies, and embark on board the Armada which was then preparing for the invasion of England. He had a brother who served in that fleet as a lieutenant ; and being shot in an engagement with some Dutch vessels, his virtues were celebrated by our afflicted Poet, whose heart was peculiarly alive to every generous affection. After the ill success of the Armada, the disconsolate Lope de Vega returned to Madrid, and became Secretary to the Marquis

D d 2   of

of Malpica, to whom he has addreſſed a grateful Sonnet. From the ſervice of this Patron he paſſed into the houſehold of the Count of Lemos, whom he celebrates as an inimitable Poet. He was once more induced to quit his attendance on the Great, for the more inviting comforts of a married life. His ſecond choice was Juana de Guardio, of noble birth and ſingular beauty. By this lady he had two children; a ſon, who died in his infancy, and a daughter, named Feliciana, who ſurvived her father. The death of his little boy is ſaid to have haſtened that of his wife, whom he had the misfortune to loſe in about ſeven years after his marriage. Having now experienced the precariouſneſs of all human enjoyments, he devoted himſelf to a religious life, and fulfilled all the duties of it with the moſt exemplary piety; ſtill continuing to produce an aſtoniſhing variety of poetical compoſitions. His talents and his virtues procured him many unſolicited honours. Pope Urban the VIIIth ſent him the Croſs of Malta, with the title of Doctor in Divinity, and appointed him to a place of profit in the Apoſtolic Chamber; favours for which he expreſſed his gratitude by dedicating his Corona Tragica (a long poem on the fate of Mary Queen of Scots) to that liberal Pontiff. In his ſeventy-third year he felt the approaches of death, and prepared himſelf for it with the utmoſt compoſure and devotion. His laſt hours were attended by many of his intimate friends, and particularly his chief patron the Duke of Seſſa, whom he made his executor; leaving him the care of his daughter Feliciana, and of his various manuſcripts. The manner in which he took leave of thoſe he loved was moſt tender and affecting. He ſaid to his Diſciple and Biographer, Montalvan, That true fame conſiſted in being good; and that he would willingly exchange all the applauſes he had received, to add a ſingle deed of virtue to the actions of his life. Having given his dying benediction to his daughter, and performed the laſt ceremonies of his religion, he expired on the 25th of Auguſt 1635.

The ſplendor of his funeral was equal to the reſpect paid to him while living.—His magnificent patron, the Duke of Seſſa, invited the chief nobility of the kingdom to attend it. The ceremony was prolonged through the courſe of ſeveral days; and three ſermons in honour of the deceaſed were delivered by three of the moſt celebrated preachers. Theſe

3

are

are printed with the works of the Poet, and may be confidered as curious fpecimens of the falfe eloquence which prevailed at that time. A volume of encomiaftic verfes, chiefly Spanifh, and written by more than a hundred and fifty of the moft diftinguifhed characters in Spain, was publifhed foon after the death of this lamented Bard. To this collection his friend and difciple Perez de Montalvan prefixed a circumftantial account of his life and death, which I have chiefly followed in the preceding narrative. An ingenious Traveller, who has lately publifhed a pleafing volume of Letters on the Poetry of Spain, has imputed the duel in which Lope de Vega was engaged to the gallantries of his firft wife; but Montalvan's relation of that adventure clears the honor of the lady, whofe innocence is ftill farther fupported by a poem written in her praife by Pedro de Medina Medinilla: it is printed in the works of our Poet, who is introduced in it, under the name of Belardo, celebrating the excellencies and lamenting the lofs of his departed Ifabel.

Of the perfon and manners of Lope de Vega, his friend Montalvan has only given this general account:—that his frame of body was particularly ftrong, and preferved by temperance in continued health;—that in converfation he was mild and unafluming; courteous to all, and to women peculiarly gallant;—very eager when engaged in the bufinefs of his friends, and fomewhat carelefs in the management of his own. Of his wealth and charity I fhall have occafion to fpeak in a fubfequent note. The chief expences in which he indulged himfelf were books and pictures; of the latter, he diftributed a few as legacies to his intimate friends: to the Duke of Seffa, a fine portrait of himfelf; and to me, fays Montalvan, another, painted when he was young, furrounded by dogs, monkies, and other monfters, and writing in the midft of them, without attending to their noife.——Of the honours paid to this extraordinary Poet, his Biographer afferts that no perfon of eminence vifited Spain without feeking his perfonal acquaintance; that men yielded him precedence when they met him in the ftreets, and women faluted him with benedictions when he paffed under their windows. If fuch homage can be deferved by the moft unwearied application to poetry, Lope de Vega was certainly entitled to it. He declared that he conftantly wrote five fheets a day; and his biographers, who have formed a calculation from this account, conclude the number of his verfes to be

no

no lefs than 21,316,000. His country has very lately publifhed an elegant edition of his poems in 19 quarto volumes; his dramatic works are to be added to this collection, and will probably be ftill more voluminous. I fhall fpeak only of the former.—Among his poems there are feveral of the Epic kind; the three following appear to me the moft remarkable. 1. La Dragontea. 2. La Hermofura de Angelica. 3. La Jerufalem Conquiftada. The Dragontea confifts of ten cantos, on the laft expedition and death of our great naval hero Sir Francis Drake, whom the Poet, from his exceffive partiality to his country, confiders as an avaricious pirate, or rather, as he chufes to call him, a marine Dragon: and it may be fufficient to obferve that he has treated him accordingly. The poem on Angelica feems to have been written in emulation of Ariofto, and it is founded on a hint in that Poet: it was compofed in the early part of our Author's life, and contains many compliments to his fovereign Philip the IId: it confifts of 20 cantos, and clofes with Angelica's being reftored to her beloved Medoro. In his Jerufalem Conquiftada he enters the lifts with Taffo, whom he mentions in his preface as having fung the firft part of the hiftory which he had chofen for his fubject. From the great name of Lope de Vega, I had fome thoughts of prefenting to the reader a fketch of this his moft remarkable poem; but as an Epic Poet he appears to me fo much inferior to Taffo, and to his countryman and cotemporary Ercilla, that I am unwilling to fwell thefe extenfive notes by an enlarged defcription of fo unfuccefsful a work: the Author has prophefied in the clofe of it, that, although neglected by his own age, it would be efteemed by futurity:—a fingular proof that even the moft favoured writers are frequently difpofed to declaim againft the period in which they live. If Lope de Vega could think himfelf neglected, what Poet may ever expect to be fatisfied with popular applaufe?—But to return to his Jerufalem Conquiftada. Richard the Second of England, and Alphonfo the Eighth of Caftile, are the chief heroes of the poem; which contains twenty cantos; and clofes with the unfortunate return of thefe confederate Kings, and the death of Saladin. It was firft printed 1609, more than twenty years after the firft appearance of Taffo's Jerufalem.——One of the moft amiable peculiarities in the character of Lope de Vega, is the extreme liberality with which he commends the merit of his rivals. In his Laurel de Apollo, he celebrates

brates all the eminent Spanish and Portugueze Poets; he speaks both of Camoens and Ercilla with the warmest applause. Among the most pleasing passages in this poem is a compliment which he pays to his father, who was, like the father of Tasso, a Poet of considerable talents.

Among the smaller pieces of Lope de Vega, there are two particularly curious; a descriptive poem on the garden of his patron the Duke of Alva, and a sonnet in honour of the Invincible Armada: the latter may be considered as a complete model of Spanish bombast: " Go forth and burn the world," says the Poet, addressing himself to that mighty fleet; " my sighs will furnish your sails with a never-failing wind; and my breast will supply your cannon with inexhaustible fire."——Perhaps this may be equalled by a Spanish character of our Poet, with which I shall close my imperfect account of him. It is his friend and biographer Montalvan, who, in the opening of his life, bestows on him the following titles: El Doctor Frey Lope Felix de Vega Carpio, Portento del Orbe, Gloria de la Nacion, Lustre de la Patria, Oracula de la Lengua, Centro de la Fama, Assumpio de la Invidia, Cuydado de la Fortuna, Fenix de los Siglos, Principe de los Versos, Orfeo de las Ciencias, Apolo de las Musas, Horacio de los Poetas, Virgilio de los Epicos, Homero de los Heroycos, Pindaro de los Lyricos, Sofocles de los Tragicos, y Terencio de los Comicos, Unico entre los Mayores, Mayor entre los Grandes, y Grande a todas Luzes, y en todas Materias.

NOTE X. Verse 239.

The brave Ercilla sounds, with potent breath,

His Epic trumpet in the fields of death.] Don Alonzo de Ercilla y Zuniga was equally distinguished as a Hero and a Poet; but this exalted character, notwithstanding his double claim to our regard, is almost totally unknown in our country, and I shall therefore endeavour to give the English reader the best idea that I can, both of his gallant life, and of his singular poem.—He was born in Madrid, on the 7th of August 1533, the third son of Fortun Garcia de Ercilla, who, though descended from a noble family, pursued the profession of the law, and was so remarkable for his talents, that he acquired the appellation of "The subtle Spaniard." The mother of our Poet was also noble, and from her he inherited his
second

second title, Zuniga : Ercilla was the name of an ancient caſtle in Biſcay, which had been long in the poſſeſſion of his paternal anceſtors. He loſt his father while he was yet an infant, a circumſtance which had great influence on his future life ; for his mother was received, after the deceaſe of her huſband, into the houſehold of the Empreſs Iſabella, the wife of Charles the Vth, and had thus an early opportunity of introducing our young Alonzo into the palace. He ſoon obtained an appointment there, in the character of page to the Infant Don Philip, to whoſe ſervice he devoted himſelf with the moſt heroic enthuſiaſm, though Philip was a maſter who little deſerved ſo generous an attachment. At the age of fourteen, he attended that Prince in the ſplendid progreſs which he made, at the deſire of his Imperial father, through the principal cities of the Netherlands, and through parts of Italy and Germany. This ſingular expedition is very circumſtantially recorded in a folio volume, by a Spaniſh hiſtorian named Juan Chriſtoval Calvete de Eſtrella, whoſe work affords a very curious and ſtriking picture of the manners and ceremonies of that martial and romantic age. All the cities which were viſited by the Prince contended with each other in magnificent feſtivity : the brilliant ſeries of literary and warlike pageants which they exhibited, though they anſwered not their deſign of conciliating the affection of the ſullen Philip, might probably awaken the genius of our youthful Poet, and excite his ambition to acquire both poetical and military fame. In 1551, he returned with the Prince into Spain, and continued there for three years ; at the end of which he attended his royal maſter to England on his marriage with Queen Mary, which was celebrated at Wincheſter in the ſummer of 1554. At this period Ercilla firſt aſſumed the military character ; for his ſovereign received advice, during his reſidence at London, that the martial natives of Arauco, a diſtrict on the coaſt of Chile, had revolted from the Spaniſh government, and diſpatched an experienced officer, named Alderete, who attended him in England, to ſubdue the inſurrection, inveſting him with the command of the rebellious province. Ercilla embarked with Alderete ; but that officer dying in his paſſage, our Poet proceeded to Lima. Don Hurtado de Mendoza, who commanded there as Viceroy of Peru, appointed his ſon Don Garcia to ſupply the place of Alderete, and ſent him with a conſiderable force to oppoſe the Araucanians. Ercilla was engaged in this enterprize, and

greatly

greatly diftinguifhed himfelf in the obftinate conteft which enfued.
The noble character of the Barbarians who maintained this unequal
ftruggle, and the many fplendid feats of valour which this fcene afforded,
led our author to the fingular defign of making the war, in which he
was himfelf engaged, the fubject of an Heroic poem; which he entitled
" La Araucana," from the name of the country. As many of his own particular adventures may be found in the following fummary of his work,
I fhall not here enlarge on his military exploits ; but proceed to one of
the moft mortifying events of his life, which he briefly mentions in the
conclufion of his poem. After pafling with great honour through many
and various perils, he was on the point of fuffering a difgraceful death,
from the rafh orders of his young and inconfiderate Commander.
On his return from an expedition of adventure and difcovery, to the
Spanifh city of Imperial, he was prefent at a fcene of public feftivity
difplayed there, to celebrate the acceffion of Philip the IId to the crown
of Spain ; at a kind of tournament, there arofe an idle difpute between
Ercilla and Don Juan de Pineda, in the heat of which the two difputants
drew their fwords; many of the fpectators joined in the broil; and, a
report arifing that the quarrel was a mere pretence, to conceal fome mu-
tinous defign, the hafty Don Garcia, their General, committed the two
antagonifts to prifon, and fentenced them both to be publicly beheaded.
Ercilla himfelf declares, he was conducted to the fcaffold before his precipitate judge difcovered the iniquity of the fentence ; but his innocence
appeared juft time enough to fave him ; and he feems to have been
fully reinftated in the good opinion of Don Garcia, as, among the com-
plimentary fonnets addreffed to Ercilla, there is one which bears the name
of his General, in which he ftyles him the Divine Alonzo, and celebrates both his military and poetical genius. But Ercilla feems to
have been deeply wounded by this affront; for, quitting Chile, he went
to Callao, the port of Lima, and there embarked on an expedition
againft a Spanifh rebel, named Lope de Aguirre, who, having murdered
his captain, and ufurped the chief power, was perpetrating the moft
cruel enormities in the fettlement of Venezuela. But Ercilla learned,
on his arrival at Panama, that this barbarous ufurper was deftroyed ;
he therefore refolved, as his health was much impaired by the hardfhips he had paffed, to return to Spain. He arrived there in the twenty-

E e   ninth

ninth year of his age; but foon left it, and travelled, as he himfelf informs us, through France, Italy, Germany, Silefia, Moravia, and Pannonia; but the particulars of this expedition are unknown. In the year 1570 he appeared again at Madrid, and was married to Maria Bazan, a lady whom he contrives to celebrate in the courfe of his military poem. He is faid to have been afterwards gentleman of the bed-chamber to the Emperor Rodolph the IId, a prince who had been educated at Madrid; but the connection of our Poet with this Monarch is very indiftinctly recorded; and indeed all the latter part of his life is little known. In the year 1580 he refided at Madrid, in a ftate of retirement and poverty. The time and circumftances of his death are uncertain: it is proved that he was living in the year 1596, by the evidence of a Spanifh writer named Mofquera, who, in a treatife of military difcipline, fpeaks of Ercilla as engaged at that time in celebrating the victories of Don Alvaro Bazan, Marques de Santa Cruz, in a poem which has never appeared, and is fuppofed to have been left imperfect at his death. Some anecdotes related of our Poet afford us ground to hope that his various merits were not entirely unrewarded. It is faid, that in fpeaking to his fovereign Philip, he was fo overwhelmed by diffidence that language failed him: " Don Alonzo! (replied the King) fpeak to me in writing."—He did fo, and obtained his requeft. The Spanifh Hiftorian Ovalle, who has written an account of Chile, in which he frequently fupports his narration by the authority of Ercilla, affirms that our Poet prefented his work to Philip with his own hand, and received a recompence from the King. But in this circumftance I fear the Hiftorian was miftaken, as he fuppofes it to have happened on the return of Ercilla from Chile; and our Poet, in a diftinct portion of his work, which was not publifhed till many years after that period, exprefsly declares, in addreffing himfelf to Philip, that all his attempts to ferve him had been utterly unrequited. Ercilla left no legitimate family; but had fome natural children, the moft eminent of which was a daughter, who was advantageoufly married to a nobleman of Portugal.

In that elegant collection of Spanifh Poets, "*Parnafo Efpañol*," there is a pleafing little amorous poem, written by Ercilla in his youth, which is peculiarly commended by Lope de Vega; who has beftowed a very generous encomium on our Poet, in his "*Laurel de Apolo.*" But the great
and

and fingular work which has juftly rendered Ercilla immortal, is his
Poem entitled Araucana, which was publifhed in three feparate parts : the
firft appeared in 1577; he added the fecond in the fucceeding year; and
in 1590 he printed a complete edition of the whole. It was applauded
by the moft eminent writers of Spain; and Cervantes, in fpeaking of
Don Quixote's Library, has ranked it among the choiceft treafures of
the Caftilian Mufe. Voltaire, who fpeaks of Ercilla with his ufual
fpirit and inaccuracy, has the merit of having made our Poet more generally known, though his own acquaintance with him appears to have
been extremely flight; for he affirms that Ercilla was in the battle of
Saint Quintin : a miftake into which he never could have fallen, had he
read the Araucana. Indeed the undiftinguifhing cenfure which he paffes
on the poem in general, after commending one particular paffage, fufficiently proves him a perfect ftranger to many fubfequent parts of the
work; yet his remark on the inequality of the Poet is juft. Ercilla is
certainly unequal; but, with all his defects, he appears to me one of the
moft extraordinary and engaging characters in the poetical world. Perhaps I am a little partial to him, from the accidental circumftance of
having firft read his poem with a departed friend, whofe opinions are
very dear to me, and who was particularly fond of this military Bard.
However this may be, my idea of Ercilla's merit has led me to hazard
the following extenfive fketch of his Work : — it has fwelled to a much
larger fize than I at firft intended; for I was continually tempted to extend it, by the defire of not injuring the peculiar excellencies of this
wonderful Poet. If I have not utterly failed in that defire, the Englifh
reader will be enabled to judge, and to enjoy an author, who, confidering
his fubject and its execution, may be faid to ftand fingle and unparal-
leled in the hoft of Poets. His beauties and his defects are of fo obvious a nature, that I fhall not enlarge upon them; but let it be remembered, that his poem was compofed amidft the toils and perils of
the moft fatiguing and hazardous fervice, and that his verfes were fometimes written on fcraps of leather, from the want of better materials.
His ftyle is remarkably pure and perfpicuous, and, notwithftanding the
reftraint of rhyme, it has frequently all the eafe, the fpirit, and the volu-
bility of Homer. I wifh not, however, to conceal his defects; and I
have therefore given a very fair account of the ftrange epifode he intro-

duces

duces concerning the hiſtory of Dido, which has juſtly fallen under the ridicule of Voltaire. I muſt however obſerve, as an apology for Ercilla, that many Bards of his country have conſidered it as a point of honour to defend the reputation of this injured lady, and to attack Virgil with a kind of poetical Quixotiſm for having ſlandered the chaſtity of ſo ſpotleſs a heroine. If my memory does not deceive me, both Lope de Vega and Quevedo have employed their pens as the champions of Dido. We may indeed very readily join the laugh of the lively Frenchman

against

S O N E T O

DE LA SEÑORA DOÑA LEONOR DE ICIZ,

SEÑORA DE LA BARONIA DE RAFALES

A DON ALONSO DE ERCILLA.

Mil bronces para eſtatuas ya forxados,
Mil lauros de tus obras premio honroſo
Te ofrece Eſpaña, Ercilla generoſo,
Por tu pluma y tu lanza tan ganados.
Houreſe tu valor entre ſoldados,
Invidie tu nobleza el valeroſo,
Y buſque en tí el poeta mas famoſo
Lima para ſus verſos mas limados.
Derrame por el mundo tus loores
La fama, y eternice tu memoria,
Porque jamás el tiempo la conſuma.
Gocen ya, ſin temor de que hay mayores
Tus hechos, y tus libros de igual gloria,
Pues la han ganado igual la eſpada y pluma.

against our Poet on this occasion ; but let us recollect that Ercilla has infinitely more Homeric spirit, and that his poem contains more genuine Epic beauties, than can be found in Voltaire.

Ercilla has been honoured with many poetical encomiums by the writers of his own country ; and, as I believe the most elegant compliment which has been paid to his genius is the production of a Spanish lady, I shall close this account of him with a translation of the Sonnet, in which she celebrates both the Hero and the Poet.

SONNET

FROM THE LADY LEONORA DE ICIZ,
BARONESS OF RAFALES,
TO DON ALONZO DE ERCILLA.

Marble, that forms the Hero's mimic frame,
And laurels, that reward the Poet's strain,
Accept, Ercilla, from thy grateful Spain!
Thy sword and pen alike this tribute claim.
Our Warriors honor thy heroic name ;
Thy birth is envy'd by Ambition's train ;
Thy verses teach the Bard of happiest vein
A finer polish, and a nobler aim.
May glory round the world thy merit spread!
In Memory's volume may thy praises stand
In characters that time shall ne'er destroy!
Thy songs, and thy exploits, without the dread
To be surpass'd by a superior hand,
With equal right their equal fame enjoy!

A SKETCH

A SKETCH OF THE ARAUCANA.

THE Poem of Ercilla opens with the following expofition of his fubject :

I Sing not love of ladies, nor of fights
   Devis'd for gentle dames by courteous knights,
Nor feafts, nor tourneys, nor that tender care
Which prompts the Gallant to regale the Fair ;
But the bold deeds of Valor's fav'rite train,
Thofe undegenerate fons of warlike Spain,
Who made Arauco their ftern laws embrace,
And bent beneath their yoke her untam'd race.
Of tribes diftinguifh'd in the field I fing ;
Of nations who difdain the name of King ;
Courage, that danger only taught to grow,
And challenge honour from a generous foe ;
And perfevering toils of pureft fame,
And feats that aggrandize the Spanifh name :
For the brave actions of the vanquifh'd fpread
The brighteft glory round the victor's head.

He then addreffes his work to his fovereign, Philip the Second, and devotes his firft Canto to the defcription of that part of the new world which forms the fcene of his action, and is called Arauco ; a diftrict in the province of Chile. He paints the fingular character and various cuftoms of its warlike inhabitants with great clearnefs and fpirit. In many points they bear a ftriking refemblance to the ancient Germans, as they are drawn with a kind of poetical energy by the ftrong pencil of Tacitus. The firft Canto clofes with a brief account how this martial province was fubdued by a Spanifh officer named Valdivia ; with an

intimation

intimation that his negligence in his new dominion gave birth to thofe important exploits which the Poet propofes to celebrate.

C A N T O   II.

ERCILLA begins his Cantos much in the manner of Ariofto, with a moral reflection; fometimes rather too much dilated, but generally ex-preffed in eafy, elegant, and fpirited verfe.—The following lines faintly imitate the two firft ftanzas of his fecond Canto :

> Many there are who, in this mortal ftrife,
> Have reach'd the flippery heights of fplendid life :
> For Fortune's ready hand its fuccour lent;
> Smiling fhe rais'd them up the fteep afcent,
> To hurl them headlong from that lofty feat
> To which fhe led their unfufpecting feet;
> E'en at the moment when all fears difperfe,
> And their proud fancy fees no fad reverfe.
> Little they think, beguil'd by fair fuccefs,
> That Joy is but the herald of Diftrefs :
> The hafty wing of time efcapes their fight,
> And thofe dark evils that attend his flight :
> Vainly they dream, with gay prefumption warm,
> Fortune for them will take a fteadier form;
> She, unconcern'd at what her victims feel,
> Turns with her wonted hafte her fatal wheel.

After blaming his countrymen for abufing their good fortune, the Poet celebrates, in the following fpirited manner, the eagernefs and in-dignation with which the Indians prepared to wreak their vengeance on their Spanifh oppreffors :

> The Indians firft, by novelty difmay'd,
> As Gods rever'd us, and as Gods obey'd;
> But when they found we were of woman born,
> Their homage turn'd to enmity and fcorn :

Their

Their childifh error, when our weaknefs fhow'd,
They blufh'd at what their ignorance beftow'd ;
Fiercely they burnt, with anger and with fhame,
To fee their mafters but of mortal frame.
Difdaining cold and cowardly delay,
They feek atonement, on no diftant day :
Prompt and refolv'd, in quick debate they join,
To form of deep revenge their dire defign.
Impatient that their bold decree fhould fpread,
And fhake the world around with fudden dread,
Th' affembling Chieftains led fo large a train,
Their ready hoft o'erfpread th' extenfive plain.
No fummons now the foldier's heart requires ;
The thirft of battle every breaft infpires ;
No pay, no promife of reward, they afk,
Keen to accomplifh their fpontaneous tafk ;
And, by the force of one avenging blow,
Crufh and annihilate their foreign foe.
Of fome brave Chiefs, who to this council came,
Well may'ft thou, Memory, preferve the name ;
Tho' rude and favage, yet of noble foul,
Juftly they claim their place on Glory's roll,
Who robbing Spain of many a gallant fon,
In fo confin'd a fpace fuch victories won ;
Whofe fame fome living Spaniards yet may fpread,
Too well attefted by our warlike dead.

The Poet proceeds to mention, in the manner of Homer, but in a much fhorter catalogue, the principal chieftains, and the number of their refpective vaffals.

Uncouthly as their names muft found to an Englifh ear, it feems neceffary to run through the lift, as thefe free and noble-minded favages act fo diftinguifhed a part in the courfe of the poem.—Tucapel ftands firft ; renowned for the moft inveterate enmity to the Chriftians, and leader of three thoufand vaffals : Angol, a valiant youth, attended by four thoufand : Cayocupil, with three ; and Millarapue, an elder chief,

with five thoufand: Paycabi, with three thoufand; and Lemolemo, with
fix: Maregnano, Gualèmo, and Lebopia, with three thoufand each:
Elicura, diftinguifhed by ftrength of body and deteftation of fervitude,
with fix thoufand; and the ancient Colocolo with a fuperior number:
Ongolmo, with four thoufand; and Puren, with fix; the fierce and
gigantic Lincoya with a ftill larger train. Peteguelen, lord of the valley
of Arauco, prevented from perfonal attendance by the Chriftians, difpatches fix thoufand of his retainers to the affembly: the moft diftinguifhed of his party are Thomè and Andalican. The Lord of the mari-
time province of Pilmayquen, the bold Caupolican, is alfo unable to
appear at the opening of the council. Many other Chieftains attended,
whofe names the Poet fuppreffes, left his prolixity fhould offend. As
they begin their bufinefs in the ftyle of the ancient Germans, with
a plentiful banquet, they foon grow exafperated with liquor, and a violent quarrel enfues concerning the command of the forces for the projected war: an honour which almoft every chieftain was arrogant
enough to challenge for himfelf. In the midft of this turbulent debate,
the ancient Colocolo delivers the following harangue, which Voltaire
prefers (and I think with great juftice) to the fpeech of Neftor, on a
fimilar occafion, in the firft Iliad.

> Affembled Chiefs! ye guardians of the land!
> Think not I mourn from thirft of loft command,
> To find your rival fpirits thus purfue
> A poft of honour which I deem my due.
> Thefe marks of age, you fee, fuch thoughts difown
> In me, departing for the world unknown;
> But my warm love, which ye have long poffeft,
> Now prompts that counfel which you'll find the beft.
> Why fhould we now for marks of glory jar?
> Why wifh to fpread our martial name afar?
> Crufh'd as we are by Fortune's cruel ftroke,
> And bent beneath an ignominious yoke,
> Ill can our minds fuch noble pride maintain,
> While the fierce Spaniard holds our galling chain.
> Your generous fury here ye vainly fhew;
> Ah! rather pour it on th' embattled foe!

F f What

What frenzy has your fouls of fenfe bereav'd ?
Ye rufh to felf-perdition, unperceiv'd.
'Gainft your own vitals would ye lift thofe hands,
Whofe vigor ought to burft oppreffion's bands ?

  If a defire of death this rage create,
O die not yet in this difgraceful ftate !
Turn your keen arms, and this indignant flame, ⎫
Againft the breaft of thofe who fink your fame, ⎬
Who made the world a witnefs of your fhame. ⎭
Hafte ye to caft thefe hated bonds away,
In this the vigor of your fouls difplay ;
Nor blindly lavifh, from your country's veins,
Blood that may yet redeem her from her chains.

  E'en while I thus lament, I ftill admire
The fervor of your fouls ; they give me fire :
But, juftly trembling at their fatal bent,
I dread fome dire calamitous event ;
Left in your rage Diffention's frantic hand
Should cut the finews of our native land.
If fuch its doom, my thread of being burft,
And let your old compeer expire the firft !
Shall this fhrunk frame, thus bow'd by age's weight,
Live the weak witnefs of a nation's fate ?
No : let fome friendly fword, with kind relief,
Forbid its finking in that fcene of grief.
Happy whofe eyes in timely darknefs clofe,
Sav'd from that worft of fights, his country's woes !
Yet, while I can, I make your weal my care,
And for the public good my thoughts declare.

  Equal ye are in courage and in worth ;
Heaven has affign'd to all an equal birth :
In wealth, in power, and majefty of foul,
Each Chief feems worthy of the world's controul.
Thefe gracious gifts, not gratefully beheld,
To this dire ftrife your daring minds impell'd.

  But on your generous valor I depend,
That all our country's woes will fwiftly end.

A Leader

A Leader ftill our prefent ftate demands,
To guide to vengeance our impatient bands ;
Fit for this hardy tafk that Chief I deem,
Who longeft may fuftain a maffive beam :
Your rank is equal, let your force be try'd,
And for the ftrongeft let his ftrength decide.

The Chieftains acquiefce in this propofal ; which, as Voltaire juftly
obferves, is very natural in a nation of favages.   The beam is produced,
and of a fize fo enormous, that the Poet declares himfelf afraid to fpecify
its weight.   The firft Chieftains who engage in the trial fupport it on
their fhoulders five and fix hours each ; Tucapel fourteen ; and Lincoza
more than double that number ; when the affembly, confidering his
ftrength as almoft fupernatural, is eager to beftow on him the title of
General ; but in the moment he is exulting in this new honour,
Caupolican arrives without attendants.   His perfon and character are
thus defcribed by the Poet :

Tho' from his birth one darken'd eye he drew
(The viewlefs orb was of the granate's hue)
Nature, who partly robb'd him of his fight,
Repaid this failure by redoubled might.
This noble youth was of the higheft ftate ;
His actions honour'd, and his words of weight :
Prompt and refolv'd in every generous caufe,
A friend to Juftice and her fterneft laws :
Fafhion'd for fudden feats, or toils of length,
His limbs poffefs'd both fupplenefs and ftrength :
Dauntlefs his mind, determin'd and adroit
In every quick and hazardous exploit.

This accomplifhed Chieftain is received with great joy by the affembly ; and, having furpaffed Lincoza by many degrees in the trial, is in-
vefted with the fupreme command.   He difpatches a fmall party to attack a neighbouring Spanifh fort : they execute his orders, and make
a vigorous

a vigorous affault.   After a fharp conflict they are repulfed; but in the
moment of their retreat Caupolican arrives with his army to their fupport.   The Spaniards in defpair evacuate the fort, and make their efcape
in the night : the news is brought to Valdivia, the Spanifh Commander
in the city of Conception ;—and with his refolution to punifh the Barbarians the canto concludes.

C A N T O   III.

O CURELESS malady ! Oh fatal peft !
    Embrac'd with ardor and with pride careft ;
Thou common vice, thou moft contagious ill,
Bane of the mind, and frenzy of the will !
Thou foe to private and to public health ;
Thou dropfy of the foul, that thirfts for wealth,
Infatiate Avarice !—'tis from thee we trace
The various mifery of our mortal race.

With this fpirited and generous invective againft that prevailing vice
of his countrymen, which fullied the luftre of their moft brilliant exploits, Ercilla opens his 3d canto.   He does not fcruple to affert, that the
enmity of the Indians arofe from the avaricious feverity of their Spanifh
oppreffors ; and he accufes Valdivia on this head, though he gives him
the praife of a brave and gallant officer. —— This Spaniard, on the firft
intelligence of the Indian infurrection, difpatched his fcouts from the
city where he commanded.   They do not return.   Preffed by the impatient gallantry of his troops, Valdivia marches out :—they foon difcover
the mangled heads of his meffengers fixed up as a fpectacle of terror on
the road.   Valdivia deliberates what meafures to purfue.   His army entreat him to continue his march.   He confents, being piqued by their
infinuations of his difgracing the Spanifh arms.   An Indian ally brings him
an account that twenty thoufand of the confederated Indians are waiting
to deftroy him in the valley of Tucapel.   He ftill preffes forward ; arrives

rives in fight of the fort which the Indians had deftroyed, and engages them in a moft obftinate battle; in the defcription of which, the Poet introduces an original and ftriking fimile, in the following manner:

The fteady pikemen of the favage band,
Waiting our hafty charge, in order ftand;
But when th' advancing Spaniard aim'd his ftroke,
Their ranks, to form a hollow fquare, they broke;
An eafy paffage to our troop they leave,
And deep within their lines their foes receive;
Their files refuming then the ground they gave,
Bury the Chriftians in that clofing grave.
    As the keen Crocodile, who loves to lay
His filent ambufh for his finny prey,
Hearing the fcaly tribe with fportive found
Advance, and caft a muddy darknefs round,
Opens his mighty mouth, with caution, wide,
And, when th' unwary fifh within it glide,
Clofing with eager hafte his hollow jaw,
Thus fatiates with their lives his rav'nous maw:
So, in their toils, without one warning thought,
The murd'rous foe our little fquadron caught
With quick deftruction, in a fatal ftrife,
From whence no Chriftian foldier 'fcap'd with life.

Such was the fate of the advanced guard of the Spaniards. The Poet then defcribes the conflict of the main army with great fpirit:—ten Spaniards diftinguifh themfelves by fignal acts of courage, but are all cut in pieces. The battle proceeds thus:

The hoftile fword, now deeply dy'd in blood,
Drench'd the wide field with many a fanguine flood;
Courage ftill grows to form the fierce attack,
But wafted vigor makes the combat flack:
No paufe they feek, to gain exhaufted breath,
No reft, except the final reft of death:

The

The warieſt combatants now only try
To ſnatch the ſweets of vengeance ere they die.

The fierce diſdain of death, and ſcorn of flight,
Give to our ſcanty troop ſuch wond'rous might,
The Araucanian hoſt begin to yield;
They quit with loſs and ſhame the long-fought field:
They fly; and their purſuers ſhake the plain
With joyous ſhouts of Victory and Spain.
But dire miſchance, and Fate's reſiſtleſs ſway,
Gave a ſtrange iſſue to the dreadful day.

An Indian Youth, a noble Chieftain's ſon,
Who as our friend his martial feats begun,
Our Leader's Page, by him to battle train'd,
Who now beſide him the hard fight ſuſtain'd,
As he beheld his kindred Chiefs retire,
Felt an indignant flaſh of patriot fire;
And thus incited to a glorious ſtand
The flying champions of his native land:

Miſguided Country, by vain fear poſſeſt,
Ah whither doſt thou turn thy timid breaſt?
Ye brave compatriots, ſhall your ancient fame
Be vilely buried in this field of ſhame?
Thoſe laws, thoſe rights, ye gloried to defend,
All periſh, all by this ignoble end?
From Chiefs of dreaded power, and honor'd worth,
Ye ſink to abject ſlaves, the ſcorn of earth!
To the pure founders of your boaſted race
Ye give the cureleſs wound of deep diſgrace!
Behold the waſted vigor of your foe!
See, bath'd in ſweat and blood, their courſers blow!
Loſe not your mental force, your martial fires,
Our beſt inheritance from generous ſires;
Sink not the noble Araucanian name,
From glory's ſummit to the depths of ſhame;
Fly, fly the ſervitude your ſouls deteſt!
To the keen ſword oppoſe the dauntleſs breaſt.

Why

Why ſhew ye frames endued with manly power,
Yet ſhrink from danger in the trying hour?
Fix in your minds the friendly truth I ſpeak;
Vain are your fears, your terror blind and weak:
Now make your names immortal; now reſtore
Freedom's loſt bleſſings to your native ſhore:
Now turn, while Fame and Victory invite,
While proſp'rous Fortune calls you to the fight;
Or yet a moment ceaſe, O ceaſe to fly,
And for our country learn of me to die!

As thus he ſpeaks, his eager ſteps advance,
And 'gainſt the Spaniſh Chief he points his lance;
To lead his kindred fugitives from flight,
Singly he dares to tempt th' unequal fight:
Againſt our circling arms, that round him ſhine,
Eager he darts amidſt the thickeſt line,
Keen as, when chaf'd by ſummer's fiery beam,
The young Stag plunges in the cooling ſtream.

The Poet proceeds to relate the great agility and valor diſplayed by Lautaro, for ſuch is the name of this gallant and patriotic Youth: and, as Ercilla has a ſoul ſuſficiently heroic to do full juſtice to the virtues of an enemy, he gives him the higheſt praiſe. Having mentioned on the occaſion many heroes of ancient hiſtory, he exclaims:

Say, of theſe famous Chiefs can one exceed
Or match this young Barbarian's noble deed?
Vict'ry for them, her purpoſe unexplor'd,
Tempted by equal chance their happy ſword:
What riſk, what peril did they boldly meet,
Save where Ambition urg'd the ſplendid feat;
Or mightier Int'reſt fir'd the daring mind,
Which makes a Hero of the fearful Hind?
Many there are who with a brave diſdain
Face all the perils of the deathful plain,

2

Who,

Who, fir'd by hopes of glory, nobly dare,
Yet fail the ftroke of adverfe chance to bear;
With animated fire their fpirit fhines,
Till the fhort fplendor of their day declines;
But all their valor, all their ftrength expires,
When fickle Fortune from their fide retires.
This youthful Hero, when the die was caft,
War's dire decree againft his country paft,
Made the ftern Power the finifh'd caufe refume,
And finally reverfe the cruel doom :
He, by his efforts in the dread debate,
Forc'd the determin'd will of adverfe Fate,
From fhouting Triumph rufh'd the palm to tear,
And fix'd it on the brow of faint Defpair.

Caupolican, leading his army back to the charge, in confequence of Lantaro's efforts in their favour, obtains a complete victory. The Spaniards are all flain in the field, except their Commander Valdivia, who flies, attended only by a prieft; but he is foon taken prifoner, and conducted before the Indian Chief, who is inclined to fpare his life; when an elder favage, called Leocato, in a fudden burft of indignation, kills him with his club.

All the people of Arauco affemble in a great plain to celebrate their victory : old and young, women and children, unite in the feftival; and the trees that furround the fcene of their affembly are decorated with the heads and fpoils of their flaughtered enemies.

They meditate the total extermination of the Spaniards from their country, and even a defcent on Spain. The General makes a prudent fpeech to reftrain their impetuofity; and afterwards, beftowing juft applaufe on the brave exploit of the young Lantaro, appoints him his lieutenant. In the midft of the feftivity, Caupolican receives advice that a party of fourteen Spanifh horfemen had attacked fome of his forces with great havoc. He difpatches Lantaro to oppofe them.

CANTO

CANTO IV.

A PARTY of fourteen gallant Spaniards, who had set forth from the city of Imperial to join Valdivia, not being apprized of his unhappy fate, are surprized by the enemy where they expected to meet their Commander;—they defend themselves with great valor. They are informed by a friendly Indian of the fate of Valdivia. They attempt to retreat; but are surrounded by numbers of the Araucanians:—when the Poet introduces the following instance of Spanish heroism, which I insert as a curious stroke of their military character:

> Here, cried a Spaniard, far unlike his race,
> Nor shall his abject name my verse debase,
> Marking his few associates march along,
> O that our band were but a hundred strong!
> The brave Gonsalo with disdain replied:
> Rather let two be sever'd from our side,
> Kind Heaven! that Memory may our feats proclaim
> And call our little troop The Twelve of Fame!

They continue to fight with great bravery against superior numbers, when Lantaro arrives with a fresh army against them. Still undaunted, they only resolve to sell their lives as dear as possible. Seven of them are cut to pieces.—In the midst of the slaughter a furious thunder and hail storm arises, by which incident the surviving seven escape. The tempest is described with the following original simile:

> Now in the turbid air a stormy cloud
> Spreads its terrific shadow o'er the crowd;
> The gathering darkness hides the solar ray,
> And to th' affrighted earth denies the day;
> The rushing winds, to which the forests yield,
> Rive the tall tree, and desolate the field:

G g

In drops diftinct and rare now falls the rain;
And now with thickening fury beats the plain.
As the bold mafter of the martial drum,
Ere to the fhock th' advancing armies come,
In awful notes, that fhake the heaven's high arch,
Intrepid ftrikes the flow and folemn march;
But, when the charging heroes yield their breath,
Doubles the horrid harmony of death:
So the dark tempeft, with encreafing found,
Pours the loud deluge on the echoing ground.

The few Spaniards that efcape take refuge in a neighbouring fort; which they abandon the following day on hearing the fate of Valdivia. Lantaro returns, and receives new honors and new forces from his General, to march againft a Spanifh army, which departs from the city of Penco under the command of Villagran, an experienced officer, to revenge the death of Valdivia. The departure of the troops from Penco is defcribed, and the diftrefs of the women.—Villagran marches with expedition towards the frontiers of Arauco. He arrives at a dangerous pafs, and finds Lantaro, with his army of 10,100 Indians, advantageoufly pofted on the heights, and waiting with great fteadinefs and difcipline to give him battle.

CANTO V.

LANTARO with great difficulty reftrains the eager Indians in their poft on the rock. He fuffers a few to defcend and fkirmifh on the lower ground, where feveral diftinguifh themfelves in fingle combat. The Spaniards attempt in vain to diflodge the army of Lantaro by an attack of their cavalry:—they afterwards fire on them from fix pieces of cannon.

The vext air feels the thunder of the fight,
And fmoke and flame involve the mountain's height;

                                                    Earth

Earth seems to open as the flames aspire,
And new volcano's spout destructive fire.

Lantaro saw no hopes of life allow'd,
Save by dispersing this terrific cloud,
That pours its lightning with so dire a shock,
Smiting his lessen'd host, who strew the rock;
And to the troop of Leucoton the brave
His quick command the skilful Leader gave:
He bids them fiercely to the charge descend,
And thus exhorts aloud each ardent friend:

My faithful partners in bright victory's meed,
Whom fortune summons to this noble deed,
Behold the hour when your prevailing might
Shall prove that Justice guards us in the fight!
Now firmly fix your lances in the rest,
And rush to honor o'er each hostile breast;
Through every bar your bloody passage force,
Nor let a brother's fall impede your course;
Be yon dread instruments of death your aim;
Possest of these you gain eternal fame:
The camp shall follow your triumphant trace,
And own you leaders in the glorious chace.

While these bold words their ardent zeal exalt,
They rush impetuous to the rash assault.

The Indians, undismayed by a dreadful slaughter, gain possession of the cannon.—Villagran makes a short but spirited harangue to his flying soldiers. He is unable to rally them: and, chusing rather to die than to survive so ignominious a defeat, rushes into the thickest of the enemy :— when the Poet, leaving his fate uncertain, concludes the canto.

CANTO

C A N T O   VI.

THE valiant mind is privileg'd to feel
    Superior to each turn of Fortune's wheel;
Chance has no power its value to debase,
Or brand it with the mark of deep difgrace:
So thought the noble Villagran, our Chief,
Who chofe that death fhould end his prefent grief,
And fmooth the horrid path, with thorns o'erfpread,
Which Deftiny condemn'd his feet to tread.

With the preceding encomium on the fpirit of this unfortunate officer
the Poet opens his 6th Canto.   Thirteen of the moft faithful foldiers
of Villagran, perceiving their Leader fallen motionlefs under the fury of
his enemies, make a defperate effort to preferve him.—Being placed
again on his horfe by thefe generous deliverers, he recovers from the
blow which had ftunned him; and by fingular exertion, with the affift-
ance of his fpirited little troop, effects his efcape, and rejoins his main
army; whom he endeavours in vain to lead back againft the triumphant
Araucanians.   The purfuit becomes general, and the Poet defcribes the
horrid maffacre committed by the Indians on all the unhappy fugitives
that fell into their hands.—The Spaniards in their flight are ftopt by a
narrow pafs fortified and guarded by a party of Indians.   Villagran
forces the rude entrenchment in perfon, and conducts part of his army
fafe through the pafs; but many attempting other roads over the moun-
tainous country, are either loft among the precipices of the rocks, or
purfued and killed by the Indians.

C A N T O   VII.

THE remains of the Spanifh army, after infinite lofs and fatigue,
    at laft reach the city of Concepcion.

    Their entrance in thefe walls let fancy paint,
    O'erwhelm'd with anguifh, and with labor faint:

                              Thefe

These gash'd with ghastly wounds, those writh'd with pain,
And some their human semblance scarce retain;
They seem unhappy spirits 'scap'd from hell,
Yet wanting voice their misery to tell.
Their pangs to all their rolling eyes express,
And silence most declares their deep distress.
　　When weariness and shame at length allow'd
Their tongues to satisfy th' enquiring crowd,
From the pale citizens, amaz'd to hear
A tale surpassing e'en their wildest fear,
One general sound of lamentation rose,
That deeply solemniz'd a nation's woes;
The neighbouring mansions to their grief reply,
And every wall return'd the mournful cry.

　　The inhabitants of Concepcion, expecting every instant the triumphant Lantaro at their gates, resolve to abandon their city. A gallant veteran upbraids their cowardly design. They disregard his reproaches, and evacuate the place:—when the Poet introduces the following instance of female heroism:

'Tis just that Fame a noble deed display,
Which claims remembrance, even to the day
When Memory's hand no more the pen shall use,
But sink in darkness and her being lose:
The lovely Mencia, an accomplish'd Dame,
A valiant spirit in a tender frame,
Here firmly shew'd, as this dread scene began,
Courage now found not in the heart of man.
The bed of sickness 'twas her chance to press;
But when she heard the city's loud distress,
Snatching such weapons as the time allow'd,
She rush'd indignant midst the flying crowd.
　　Now up the neighbouring hill they slowly wind,
And, bending oft their mournful eyes behind,

Cast

Caſt a ſad look, of every hope bereft,
On thoſe rich plains, the precious home they left.

    More poignant grief ſee generous Mencia feel,
More noble proof ſhe gives of patriot zeal:
Waving a ſword in her heroic hand,
In their tame march ſhe ſtopt the timid band;
Croſs'd the aſcending road before their van,
And, turning to the city, thus began:

    Thou valiant nation, whoſe unequall'd toils
Have dearly purchas'd fame and golden ſpoils,
Where is the courage ye ſo oft diſplay'd
Againſt this foe, from whom ye ſhrink diſmay'd?
Where thoſe high hopes, and that aſpiring flame,
Which made immortal praiſe your conſtant aim?
Where your firm ſouls, that every chance defied,
And native ſtrength, that form'd your noble pride?
Ah whither would you fly, in ſelfiſh fear,
In frantic haſte, with no purſuer near?

    How oft has cenſure to your hearts aſſign'd
Ardor too keenly brave and raſhly blind;
Eager to dart amid the doubtful fray,
Scorning the uſeful aid of wiſe delay?
Have we not ſeen you with contempt oppoſe,
And bend beneath your yoke unnumber'd foes;
Attempt and execute deſigns ſo bold,
Ye grew immortal as ye heard them told?

    Turn! to your people turn a pitying eye,
To whom your fears theſe happy ſeats deny!
Turn! and ſurvey this fair, this fertile land,
Whoſe ready tribute waits your lordly hand;
Survey its pregnant mines, its ſands of gold;
Survey the flock now wandering from its fold,
Mark how it vainly ſeeks, in wild deſpair,
The faithleſs ſhepherd, who forſakes his care.

    E'en the dumb creatures, of domeſtic kind,
Though not endow'd with man's diſcerning mind,

Now

Now fhew the femblance of a reafoning foul,
And in their mafters mifery condole:
The ftronger animals, of fterner heart,
Take in this public woe a feeling part;
Their plaintive roar, that fpeaks their fenfe aright,
Juftly upbraids your ignominious flight.

　Ye fly from quiet, opulence, and fame,
Purchas'd by valor, your acknowledg'd claim;
From thefe ye fly, to feek a foreign feat,
Where daftard fugitives no welcome meet.
How deep the fhame, an abject life to fpend
In poor dependance on a pitying friend!
Turn! let the brave their only choice await,
Or honourable life, or inftant fate.

　Return! return! O quit this path of fhame!
Stain not by fear your yet unfullied name;
Myfelf I offer, if our foes advance,
To rufh the foremoft on the hoftile lance;
My actions then fhall with my words agree,
And what a woman dares your eyes fhall fee.
Return! return! fhe cried; but cried in vain;
Her fire feem'd frenzy to the coward train.

The daftardly inhabitants of the city, unmoved by this remon-
ftrance of the noble Donna Mencia de Nidos, continue their precipitate flight, and, after twelve days of confufion and fatigue, reach the
city of Santiago, in the valley of Mapocho. Lantaro arrives in the
mean time before the walls they had deferted:—and the Poet concludes
his canto with a fpirited defcription of the barbaric fury with which the
Indians entered the abandoned city, and deftroyed by fire the rich and
magnificent manfions of their Spanifh oppreffors.

CANTO

C A N T O   VIII.

LANTARO is recalled from his victorious exploits, to assist at a general assembly of the Indians, in the valley of Arauco. The different Chieftains deliver their various sentiments concerning the war, after their Leader Caupolican has declared his design to pursue the Spaniards with unceasing vengeance. The veteran Colocolo proposes a plan for their military operations. An ancient Augur, named Puchecalco, denounces ruin on all the projects of his countrymen, in the name of the Indian Dæmon Eponamon. He recites the omens of their destruction. The fierce Tucapel, provoked to frenzy by this gloomy prophet, strikes him dead in the midst of his harangue, by a sudden blow of his mace. Caupolican orders the murderous Chieftain to be led to instant death. He defends himself with success against numbers who attempt to seize him. Lantaro, pleased by this exertion of his wonderful force and valour, intreats the General to forgive what had passed; and, at his intercession, Tucapel is received into favour. Lantaro then closes the business of the assembly, by recommending the plan proposed by Colocolo, and intreating that he may himself be entrusted with a detached party of five hundred Indians, with which he engages to reduce the city of Santiago. His proposal is accepted. The Chieftains, having finished their debate, declare their resolutions to their people; and, after their usual festivity, Caupolican, with the main army, proceeds to attack the city of Imperial.

C A N T O   IX.

THE Poet opens this Canto with an apology for a miracle, which he thinks it necessary to relate, as it was attested by the whole Indian army; and, though it does not afford him any very uncommon or sub-

lime

lime imagery, he embellishes the wonder he describes, by his easy and spirited versification, of which the following lines are an imperfect copy :

When to the city's weak defenceless wall
Its foes were rushing, at their trumpet's call,
The air grew troubled with portentous sound,
And mournful omens multiplied around ;
With furious shock the elements engage,
And all the winds contend in all their rage.
　　From clashing clouds their mingled torrents gush,
And rain and hail with rival fury rush.
Bolts of loud thunder, floods of lightning rend
The opening skies, and into earth descend.
　　O'er the vast army equal terrors spread ;
No mind escapes the universal dread ;
No breast, tho' arm'd with adamantine power,
Holds its firm vigor in this horrid hour ;
For now the fierce Eponamon appears,
And in a Dragon's form augments their fears ;
Involving flames around the Dæmon swell,
Who speaks his mandate in a hideous yell :
He bids his votaries with haste invest
The trembling city, by despair deprest.
Where'er th' invading squadrons force their way,
He promises their arms an easy prey.
Spare not (he cry'd) in the relentless strife,
One Spanish battlement, one Christian life !
He spoke, and, while the host his will adore,
Melts into vapour, and is seen no more.
　　Quick as he vanish'd Nature's struggles cease ;
The troubled elements are sooth'd to peace :
The winds no longer rage with boundless ire,
But, hush'd in silence, to their caves retire :
The clouds disperse, restoring as they fly
The unobstructed sun and azure sky :

H h

Fear

Fear only held its place, and ftill poffeft
Ufurp'd dominion o'er the boldeft breaft.

    The tempeft ceas'd, and heaven, ferenely bright,
Array'd the moiften'd earth in joyous light :
When, pois'd upon a cloud that fwiftly flew,
A Female form defcended to their view,
Clad in the radiance of fo rich a veil,
As made the fun's meridian luftre pale ;
For it outfhone his golden orb as far
As his full blaze outfhines the twinkling ftar.
Her facred features banifh all their dread,
And o'er the hoft reviving comfort fhed.
An hoary Elder by her fide appear'd,
For age and fanctity of life rever'd ;
And thus fhe fpoke, with foft perfuafive grace :
Ah ! whither rufh ye, blind devoted race ?
Turn, while you can, towards your native plain,
Nor 'gainft yon city point your arms in vain ;
For God will guard his faithful Chriftian band,
And give them empire o'er your bleeding land,
Since, thanklefs, falfe, and obftinate in ill,
You fcorn fubmiffion to his facred will.
Yet fhun thofe walls ; th' Almighty, there ador'd,
There arms his people with Deftruction's fword.

    So fpoke the Vifion, with an angel's tongue,
And thro' the fpacious air to heaven fhe fprung.

The Indians, confounded by this miraculous interpofition, difperfe
in diforder to their feveral homes ; and the Poet proceeds very gravely
to affirm, that, having obtained the beft information, from many individuals, concerning this miracle, that he might be very exact in his account of it, he finds it happened on the twenty-third of April, four
years before he wrote the verfes that defcribe it, and in the year of our
Lord 1554. The Vifion was followed by peftilence and famine among
the Indians. They remain inactive during the winter, but affemble
again the enfuing fpring in the plains of Arauco, to renew the war.
                                       They

They receive intelligence that the Spaniards are attempting to rebuild the city of Concepcion, and are requested by the neighbouring tribes to march to their affistance, and prevent that defign. Lantaro leads a chofen band on that expedition, hoping to furprize the fort the Spaniards had erected on the ruins of their city; but the Spanifh commander, Alvarado, being apprized of their motion, fallies forth to meet the Indian party: a fkirmifh enfues; the Spaniards retire to their fort; Lantaro attempts to ftorm it; a moft bloody encounter enfues; Tucapel fignalizes himfelf in the attack; the Indians perfevere with the moft obftinate valour, and, after a long conflict (defcribed with a confiderable portion of Homeric fpirit) gain poffeffion of the fort; Alvarado and a few of his followers efcape; they are purfued, and much galled in their flight: a fingle Indian, named Rengo, harraffes Alvarado and two of his attendants; the Spanifh officer, provoked by the infult, turns with his two companions to punifh their purfuer; but the wily Indian fecures himfelf on fome rocky heights, and annoys them with his fling, till, defpairing of revenge, they continue their flight.

CANTO X.

THE Indians celebrate their victory with public games; and prizes are appointed for fuch as excel in their various martial exercifes. Leucoton is declared victor in the conteft of throwing the lance, and receives a fcimitar as his reward. Rengo fubdues his two rivals, Cayeguan and Talco, in the exercife of wreftling, and proceeds to contend with Leucoton. After a long and fevere ftruggle, Rengo has the misfortune to fall by an accidental failure of the ground, but, fpringing lightly up, engages his adverfary with increafing fury; and the canto ends without deciding the conteft.

CANTO XI.

LANTARO separates the two enraged antagonists, to prevent the ill effects of their wrath. The youth Orompello, whom Leucoton had before surpassed in the contest of the lance, challenges his successful rival to wrestle : they engage, and fall together : the victory is disputed. Tucapel demands the prize for his young friend Orompello, and insults the General Caupolican. The latter is restrained from avenging the insult, by the sage advice of the veteran Colocolo, at whose request he distributes prizes of equal value to each of the claimants. To prevent farther animosities, they relinquish the rest of the appointed games, and enter into debate on the war. Lantaro is again appointed to the command of a chosen troop, and marches towards the city of St. Jago. The Spaniards, alarmed at the report of his approach, send out some forces to reconnoitre his party : a skirmish ensues : they are driven back to the city, and relate that Lantaro is fortifying a strong post at some distance, intending soon to attack the city. Villagran, the Spaniard who commanded there, being confined by illness, appoints an officer of his own name to sally forth, with all the forces he can raise, in quest of the enemy. The Spaniards fix their camp, on the approach of night, near the fort of Lantaro : they are suddenly alarmed, and summoned to arms ; but the alarm is occasioned only by a single horse without a rider, which Lantaro, aware of their approach, had turned loose towards their camp, as an insulting mode of proclaiming his late victory, in which he had taken ten of the Spanish horses.

The Spaniards pass the night under arms, resolving to attack the Indians at break of day. Lantaro had issued orders that no Indian should sally from the fort under pain of death, to prevent the advantage which the Spanish cavalry must have over his small forces in the open plain. He also commanded his soldiers to retreat with an appearance of dismay, at the first attack on the fort, and suffer a considerable number of the enemy to enter the place. This stratagem succeeds : the Spaniards rush forward with great fury : the Indians give ground, but,

I   soon

soon turning with redoubled violence on those who had passed their lines, destroy many, and oblige the rest to save themselves by a precipitate flight. The Indians, forgetting the orders of their Leader, in the ardour of vengeance sally forth in pursuit of their flying enemy. Lantaro recalls them by the sound of a military horn, which he blows with the utmost violence. They return, but dare not appear in the presence of their offended Commander. He issues new restrictions; and then, summoning his soldiers together, addresses them, in a spirited, yet calm and affectionate harangue, on the necessity of martial obedience. While he is yet speaking, the Spaniards return to the attack, but are again repulsed with great loss. They retreat, and encamp at the foot of a mountain, unmolested by any pursuers.

C A N T O   XII.

THE Spaniards remain in their camp, while two of their adventurous soldiers engage to return once more to the fort, and examine the state of it. On their approach, one of them, called Marcos Vaez, is saluted by his name, and promised security, by a voice from within the walls. Lantaro had formerly lived with him on terms of friendship, and now invites him into the fort. The Indian Chief harangues on the resolution and the power of his countrymen to exterminate the Spaniards, unless they submit. He proposes, however, terms of accommodation to his old friend Marcos, and specifies the tribute he should expect. The Spaniard answers with disdain, that the only tribute the Indians would receive from his countrymen would be torture and death. Lantaro replies, with great temper, that arms, and the valour of the respective nations, must determine this point; and proceeds to entertain his guest with a display of six Indians, whom he had mounted and trained to exercise on Spanish horses. The Spaniard challenges the whole party : Lantaro will not allow him to engage in any conflict, but dismisses him in peace. He recalls him, before he had proceeded far from the fort, and, telling him that his soldiers were much distressed by the want of provision, entreats him to send a supply, affirming it to be true

heroism

heroifm to relieve an enemy from the neceffities of famine. The Spaniard fubfcribes to the fentiment, and engages, if poffible, to comply
with the requeft. Returning to his camp, he acquaints his Commander
Villagran with all that had paffed ; who, fufpecting fome dangerous
defign from Lantaro, decamps haftily in the night to regain the city.
The Indian Chief is feverely mortified by their departure, as he had
formed a project for cutting off their retreat, by letting large currents of
water into the marfhy ground on which the Spaniards were encamped.
Defpairing of being able to fucceed againft their city, now prepared to
refift him, he returns towards Arauco, moft forely galled by his difap-
pointment, and thus venting his anguifh :

What can redeem Lantaro's wounded name ?
What plea preferve his failing arms from fhame ?
Did not my ardent foul this tafk demand,
Which now upbraids my unperforming hand ?
On me, on me alone can cenfure fall ;
Myfelf th' advifer and the guide of all.
Am I the Chief who, in Fame's bright career,
Afk'd to fubdue the globe a fingle year ?
    While, at the head of this my glittering train,
I weakly threaten Spanifh walls in vain,
Thrice has pale Cynthia, with replenifh'd ray,
Seen my ill-order'd troop in loofe array ;
And the rich chariot of the blazing fun
Has from the Scorpion to Aquarius run.
At laft, as fugitives thefe paths we tread,
And mourn twice fifty brave companions dead.
Could Fate's kind hand this hateful ftain efface,
Could death redeem me from this worfe difgrace,
My ufelefs fpear fhould pierce this abject heart,
Which has fo ill fuftain'd a foldier's part.
Unworthy thought ! the mean ignoble blow
Would only tempt my proud and vaunting foe
To boaft that I preferr'd, in fear's alarm,
My own weak weapon to his ftronger arm.

By

By Hell I fwear, who rules the fanguine ftrife,
If Chance allow me yet a year of life,
I'll chafe thefe foreign lords from Chile's ftrand,
And Spanifh blood fhall faturate our land.
No changing feafon, neither cold nor heat,
Shall make the firmer ftep of War retreat;
Nor fhall the earth, nor hell's expanding cave,
From this avenging arm one Spaniard fave.

Now the brave Chief, with folemn ardor, fwore
To his dear native home to turn no more;
From no fierce fun, no ftormy winds to fly,
But patiently abide the varying fky,
And fpurn all thoughts of pleafure and of eafe,
Till refcu'd fame his tortur'd foul appeafe;
Till earth confefs the brave Lantaro's hand
Has clos'd the glorious work his fpirit plann'd.
In thefe refolves the Hero found relief,
And thus relax'd the o'erftrain'd cord of grief;
Whofe preffure gall'd him with fuch mental pain,
That frenzy almoft feiz'd his burning brain.

Lantaro continues his march into an Indian diftrict, from which he collects a fmall increafe of force; and, after addreffing his foldiers concerning the expediency of ftrict military difcipline, and the caufe of their late ill fuccefs, he turns again towards the city of St. Jago; but, receiving intelligence on his road of its preparations for defence, he again fufpends his defign, and fortifies a poft, which he chufes with the hope of collecting ftill greater numbers to affift him in his projected enterprize. The Spaniards at St. Jago are eager to fally in queft of Lantaro, but their Commander Villagran was abfent on an expedition to the city of Imperial. In returning from thence he paffes near the poft of Lantaro. An Indian ally acquaints him with its fituation, and, at the earneft requeft of the Spanifh officer, agrees to conduct him, by a fhort though difficult road, over a mountain, to attack the fort by furprize. The Poet fufpends his narration of this interefting event, to relate the arrival of new forces from Spain in America; and he now be-

gins

gins to appear himself on the field of action. "Hitherto," says he, "I have described the scenes in which I was not present; yet I have collected my information from no partial witnesses, and I have recorded only those events in which both parties agree. Since it is known that I have shed so much blood in support of what I affirm, my future narration will be more authentic; for I now speak as an ocular witness of every action, unblinded by partiality, which I disdain, and resolved to rob no one of the praise which he deserves."

After pleading his youth as an apology for the defects of his style, and after declaring that his only motive for writing was the ardent desire to preserve so many valiant actions from perishing in oblivion, the Poet proceeds to relate the arrival of the Marquis de Canete as Viceroy in Peru, and the spirited manner in which he corrected the abuses of that country. The canto concludes with reflections on the advantages of loyalty, and the miseries of rebellion.

CANTO XIII.

SPANISH deputies from the province of Chile implore assistance from the new Viceroy of Peru: he sends them a considerable succour, under the conduct of Don Garcia, his son. The Poet is himself of this band, and relates the splendid preparations for the enterprize, and the embarkation of the troops in ten vessels, which sail from Lima towards the coast of Chile. Having described part of this voyage, he returns to the bold exploit of Villagran, and the adventures of Lantaro, the most interesting of all the Araucanian Heroes, whom he left securing himself in his sequestered fort.

> A path where watchful centinels were spread,
> A single path, to this lone station led:
> No other signs of human step were trac'd;
> For the vex'd land was desolate and waste.
> It chanc'd that night the noble Chieftain prest
> His anxious mistress to his gallant breast,

The

The fair Guacolda, for whose charms he burn'd,
And whose warm heart his faithful love return'd.
That night beheld the warlike savage rest,
Free from th' incumbrance of his martial vest;
That night alone allow'd his eyes to close
In the deceitful calm of short repose:
Sleep prest upon him like the weight of death;
But soon he starts, alarm'd, and gasps for breath.
The fair Guacolda, with a trembling tongue,
Anxious enquires from whence his anguish sprung.

My lovely Fair! the brave Lantaro cries,
An hideous vision struck my scornful eyes:
Methought that instant a fierce Chief of Spain
Mock'd my vain spear with insolent disdain;
His forceful arm my failing powers o'ercame,
And strength and motion seem'd to quit my frame.
But still the vigor of my soul I keep,
And its keen anger burst the bonds of sleep.

With quick despair, the troubled Fair one said,
Alas! thy dreams confirm the ills I dread.
'Tis come—the object of my boding fears!
Thy end, the source of my unceasing tears.
Yet not so wretched is this mournful hour,
Nor o'er me, Fortune, canst thou boast such power,
But that kind death may shorten all my woes,
And give the agonizing scene to close.
Let my stern fate its cruel rage employ,
And hurl me from the throne of love and joy;
Whatever pangs its malice may devise,
It cannot rend affection's stronger ties.
Tho' horrible the blow my fears foresee,
A second blow will set my spirit free;
For cold on earth thy frame shall ne'er be found,
While mine with useless being loads the ground.

The Chief, transported with her tender charms,
Closely around her neck entwin'd his arms;

I i   And,

And, while fond tears her ſnowy breaſt bedew'd,
Thus with redoubled love his ſpeech purſu'd :
   My generous Fair, thy gloomy thoughts diſmiſs ;
Nor let dark omens interrupt our bliſs,
And cloud theſe moments that with tranſport ſhine,
While my exulting heart thus feels thee mine.
Thy troubled fancy prompts my mutual ſigh ;
Not that I think the hour of danger nigh :
But Love ſo melts me with his ſoft controul,
Impoſſibilities alarm my ſoul.
If thy kind wiſhes bid Lantaro live,
Who to this frame the wound of death can give ?
Tho' 'gainſt me all the powers of earth combine,
My life is ſubject to no hand but thine.
Who has reſtor'd the Araucanian name,
And rais'd it, ſinking in the depths of ſhame,
When alien lords our nation's ſpirit broke,
And bent its neck beneath a ſervile yoke ?
I am the Chief who burſt our galling chain,
And freed my country from oppreſſive Spain ;
My name alone, without my ſword's diſplay,
Humbles our foes, and fills them with diſmay.
Theſe happy arms while thy dear beauties fill,
I feel no terror, I foreſee no ill.
Be not by falſe and empty dreams depreſt,
Since truth has nothing to afflict thy breaſt.
Oft have I 'ſcap'd, inur'd to every ſtate,
From many a darker precipice of fate ;
Oft in far mightier perils riſk'd my life,
And iſſued glorious from the doubtful ſtrife.
   With leſſ'ning confidence, and deeper grief,
Trembling ſhe hung upon the ſoothing Chief,
His lip with ſupplicating ſoftneſs preſt,
And urg'd with many a tear this fond requeſt :
   If the pure love, which, prodigal and free,
When freedom moſt was mine, I gave to thee ;

If truth, which Heaven will witnefs and defend,
Weigh with my fovereign lord and gentle friend ;
By thefe let me adjure thee ; by the pain
Which at our parting pierc'd my every vein,
And all the vows, if undifpers'd in air,
Which then with many a tear I heard thee fwear;
To this my only wifh at leaft agree,
If all thy wifhes have been laws to me :
Hafte, I entreat thee, arm thyfelf with care,
And bid thy foldiers for defence prepare.

The brave Barbarian quick reply'd—'Tis clear
How low my powers are rated by thy fear.
Canft thou fo poorly of Lantaro deem ?
And is this arm fo funk in thy efteem ?
This arm, which, refcuing thy native earth,
So prodigally prov'd its valiant worth !
In my try'd courage how complete thy truft,
Whofe terror weeps thy living lord as duft !

In thee, fhe cries, with confidence moft pure,
My foul is fatisfy'd, yet not fecure.
What will thy arm avail in danger's courfe,
If my malignant fate has mightier force ?
But let the mis'ry I forebode arife ;
On this firm thought my conftant love relies :
The fword whofe ftroke our union may disjoin,
Will teach my faithful foul to follow thine.
Since my hard deftiny, with rage fevere,
Thus threatens me with all that love can fear ;
Since I am doom'd the worft of ills to fee,
And lofe all earthly good in lofing thee ;
O ! fuffer me to pafs, ere death appears,
The little remnant of my life in tears !
The heart that finks not in diftrefs like this,
Could never feel, could never merit blifs.

Here from her eyes fuch floods of forrow flow,
Compaffion weeps in gazing on her woe !

The

The fond Lantaro, tho' of firmest power,
Sheds, as she speaks, a sympathetic shower.
But, to the tender scenes of love unus'd,
My artless pen, embarrass'd and confus'd,
From its sad task with diffidence withdraws,
And in its labour asks a little pause.

CANTO XIV.

WHAT erring wretch, to Truth and Beauty blind,
Shall dare to satirize the Female kind,
Since pure affection prompts their anxious care,
Their lovely weakness, and their fond despair?
This fair Barbarian, free from Christian ties,
A noble proof of perfect love supplies,
By kindest words, and floods of tears that roll
From the clear source of her impassion'd soul.

The chearing ardor of the dauntless Chief
Fails to afford her troubled mind relief;
Nor can the ample trench and guarded wall
Preserve her doubtful heart from fear's enthrall:
Her terrors, rushing with love's mighty force,
Level whatever would impede their course.
She finds no shelter from her cruel doom,
Save the dear refuge of Lantaro's tomb.

Thus their two hearts, where equal passion reign'd,
A fond debate with tender strife maintain'd;
Their differing words alike their love display,
Feed the sweet poison, and augment its sway.

The sleepy soldiers now their stories close,
And stretch'd around their sinking fires repose.
The path in front with centinels was lin'd,
And the high mountain was their guard behind;

But

But o'er that mountain, with advent'rous tread,
Bold Villagran his silent forces led.
His hasty march with painful toil he made;
Toil is the price that must for fame be paid.
Now near the fort, and halting in its sight,
He waits the coming aid of clearer light.
The stars yet shining, but their fires decay,
And now the reddening east proclaims the day.
Th' advancing troop no Indian eye alarms,
For friendly darkness hover'd o'er their arms;
And on the quarter where the mountain rose,
The careless guard despis'd the thought of foes.
No panting horse their still approach betray'd;
Propitious Fortune lent the Spaniards aid;
Fortune, who oft bids drowsy Sloth beware,
And lulls to sleep the watchful eye of Care.

When Night's obscure dominion first declines,
And glimmering light the dusky air refines,
The weary guards, who round the wall were plac'd,
Hail the new day, and from their station haste;
Secure of ill, no longer watch they keep,
Quick to forget their nightly toils in sleep:
Thro' all the fort there reign'd a calm profound;
In wine and slumber all its force was drown'd.

The Spanish Chief, who saw the fav'ring hour,
Led on by slow degrees his silent power.
No Indian eyes perceiv'd his near advance;
Fate seem'd to bind them in a cruel trance;
Each in sound slumber draws his easy breath,
Nor feels his slumber will be clos'd by Death.
So blind are mortals to that tyrant's sway,
They deem him distant, while they sink his prey.

Our eager soldiers now no longer halt,
While kind occasion prompts the keen assault;
A shout they raise, terrific, loud, and long,
Swell'd by the voice of all the ardent throng;

Whose

Whofe ranks, obedient to their Leader's call,
Rufh with light ardor o'er th' unguarded wall,
And gain the fort, where Sleep's oppreffive weight
Expos'd his wretched victims, blind to fate.

As villains, confcious of their life impure,
Find in their guilty courfe no fpot fecure ;
For vice is ever doom'd new fears to feel,
And tremble at each turn of Fortune's wheel ;
At every noife, at each alarm that ftirs,
Death's penal horror to their mind occurs ;
Quick to their arms they fly with wild difmay,
And rufh where hafty terror points the way :
So quick the Indians to the tumult came,
With fleep and valour ftruggling in their frame.
Unaw'd by danger's unexpected fight,
They roufe their fellows, and they rufh to fight.
Tho' their brave bofoms are of armour bare,
Their manly hearts their martial rage declare.
No furious odds their gallant fouls appall,
But refolute they fly to guard the wall.

It was the feafon when, with tender care,
Lantaro reafon'd with his anxious Fair ;
Careft, confol'd, and, in his anger kind,
Mildly reprov'd her weak miftrufting mind.
Spite of his chearing voice fhe trembles ftill ;
Severer terrors now her bofom fill :
For fterner founds their foft debate o'ercome,
Drown'd in the rattle of th' alarming drum.
But not fo quick, on Apprehenfion's wings,
The wretched mifer from his pillow fprings,
Whofe hoarded gold forbids his mind to reft,
If doubtful noife the nightly thief fuggeft :
Nor yet fo hafty, tho' with terror wild,
Flies the fond mother to her wounded child,
Whofe painful cry her fhuddering foul alarms,
As flew Lantaro at the found of arms.

His

His mantle rapidly around him roll'd,
And, grasping a light sword with hasty hold,
Too eager for his heavier arms to wait,
The fierce Barbarian hurried to the gate.
O faithless Fortune! thou deceitful friend!
Of thy false favours how severe the end!
How quick thou cancell'st, when thy frown appears,
Th' accumulated gifts of long triumphant years!
    To aid the Spaniards in their bold emprize,
Four hundred Indians march'd, their firm allies,
Who on the left their line of battle close,
And haste to combat with their painted bows;
Launching adroitly, in their rapid course,
Unnumber'd arrows with unerring force.
As brave Lantaro issued from his tent,
A shaft to meet the sallying Chief was sent;
Thro' his left side (ye valiant, mourn his lot!)
Flew the keen arrow, with such fury shot
It pierc'd his heart, the bravest and the best
That e'er was lodg'd within a human breast.
Proud of the stroke that laid such valor low,
Death seem'd to glory in th' important blow;
And, that no Mortal might his triumph claim,
In darkness hid the doubtful Archer's name.
Such force the keen resistless weapon found,
It stretch'd the mighty Chieftain on the ground,
And gave large outlet to his ardent blood,
That gush'd apace in a tumultuous flood.
From his sunk cheek its native colour fled;
His sightless eyes roll'd in his ghastly head;
His soul, that felt its glorious hopes o'erthrown,
Retir'd, indignant, to the world unknown.

The noble savages, not dismayed by the death of their Leader, continue
to defend the fort with great fury.

CANTO

C A N T O   XV.

THE Poet opens this canto with a lively panegyric on **Love**: he
affirms that the greateſt Poets have derived their glory from their
vivid deſcriptions of this enchanting paſſion; and he laments that he is
precluded by his ſubject from indulging his imagination in ſuch ſcenes
as are more likely to captivate a reader.

He ſeems to intend this as an apology (but I muſt own it is an un-
ſatisfactory one) for deſerting the fair Guacolda, whom he mentions
no more. He proceeds to deſcribe the ſharp conteſt which the undaunted
Indians ſtill maintained in their fort :—they refuſe quarter, which is offered them by the Spaniſh Leader, and all reſolutely periſh with the
brave and beloved Lantaro. The Poet then reſumes his account of the
naval expedition from Peru to Chile; and concludes the canto with a
ſpirited deſcription of a ſtorm, which attacked the veſſels as they arrived
in ſight of the province to which they were ſteering.

C A N T O   XVI.

THE ſtorm abates. The Spaniards land, and fortify themſelves on
an iſland near the country of the Araucanians. The latter hold a
council of war in the valley of Ongolmo. Caupolican, their General,
propoſes to attack the Spaniards in their new poſt. The elder Chieftains
diſſuade him from the deſign. A quarrel enſues between Tucapel and
the aged Peteguelen :—they are appeaſed by a ſpeech of the venerable
Colocolo; by whoſe advice a ſpirited and adroit young Indian, named
Millalanco, is diſpatched, as a peaceful ambaſſador, to learn the ſitua-
tion and deſigns of the Spaniards. He embarks in a large galley with
oars, and ſoon arrives at the iſland. He ſurveys the Spaniſh implements
of war with aſtoniſhment, and is conducted to the tent of the General,
Don Garcia.

CANTO

CANTO XVII.

THE Indian addresses the Spanish officers with a proposal of peace and amity. He is dismissed with presents. The Chieftains, on his return, pretend to relinquish hostilities; but prepare secretly for war. The Spaniards remain unmolested on the island during the stormy season. They send a select party of a hundred and thirty, including our Poet, to raise a fort on the continent: these execute their commission with infinite dispatch, and all the Spanish troops remove to this new post. The Araucanians are alarmed. An intrepid Youth, named Gracolano, proposes to the Indian General, Caupolican, to storm the fort. The Indians advance near it, under shelter of the night. The Poet describes himself, at this juncture, as oppressed by the excessive labours of the day, and unable to pursue his poetical studies according to his nightly custom: the pen falls from his hand: he is seized with violent pains and tremblings: his strength and senses forsake him: but soon recovering from this infirmity, he enjoys a refreshing sleep. Bellona appears to him in a vision, and encourages him both as a soldier and a poet. She conducts him, through a delicious country, to the summit of a most lofty mountain; when, pointing to a spot below, she informs him it is St. Quintin, and that his countrymen, under the command of their sovereign Philip, are just marching to attack it: she adds, that her presence is necessary in the midst of that important scene; and leaves the Poet on the eminence to survey and record the battle.

CANTO XVIII.

AFTER the Poet has described the success of his royal master at St. Quintin, a female figure of a most venerable appearance, but without a name, relates to him prophetically many future events of great importance to his country. She touches on the disturbances in the

K k   Netherlands,

Netherlands, the enterprizes of the Turks, and the exploits of Don John of Auſtria, at that time unknown to fame. Theſe ſhe hints very imperfectly, telling the Poet, that if he wiſhes for farther information, he muſt follow the ſteps of a tame deer, which he will find in a particular ſpot; this animal will lead him to the cell of an ancient hermit, formerly a ſoldier, who will conduct him to the ſecret cave of the unſocial Fiton, a mighty magician, who will diſplay to him the moſt miraculous viſions. His female Inſtructor then adviſes him to mix ſofter ſubjects with the horrors of war, and to turn his eyes and his thoughts to the charms of the many Beauties who then flouriſhed in Spain. He beholds all theſe lovely fair ones aſſembled in a delicious paradiſe; and he is particularly attracted by a young lady, whoſe name he diſcovers to be Donna Maria Bazan (his future wife): in the moment that he begins to queſtion his Guide concerning this engaging Beauty, he is rouſed from his viſion by the ſound of an alarm. He ſnatches up his arms, and hurries to his poſt:—while the morning dawns, and the Indians begin to attack the fort.

CANTO XIX.

THE Indians advance in three ſquadrons. The Youth Gracolano o'erleaps the trench, ſupported on a lofty pike, by which he alſo paſſes the wall. He defends himſelf in the midſt of the Spaniards with great ſpirit; but, finding himſelf unſupported, he wrenches a lance from a Spaniſh ſoldier, and tries to leap once more over the trench; but he is ſtruck by a ſtone while vaulting through the air, and falls, covered, as the Poet expreſsly declares, with two-and-thirty wounds. Some of his friends are ſhot near him; but the Indians get poſſeſſion of the Spaniſh lance with which he had ſprung over the wall, and brandiſh it in triumph. The Spaniard, named Elvira, who had loſt his weapon, piqued by the adventure, ſallies from the fort, and returns, amid the ſhouts of his countrymen, with an Indian ſpear which he won in ſingle combat from a Barbarian, whom he had perceived detached from his

5.   party.

party. The Indians attempt to ftorm the fort on every fide : many are deftroyed by the Spanifh fire-arms. The head of the ancient Peteguelen is fhot off ; but Tucapel paffes the wall, and rufhes with great flaughter into the midft of the enemy. The Spaniards who were in the fhips that anchored near the coaft haften on fhore, and march to affift their countrymen in the fort, but are attacked by a party of Indians in their march. The conflict continues furious on the walls; but the Indians at length retreat, leaving Tucapel ftill fighting within the fort.

CANTO XX.

TUCAPEL, though feverely wounded, efcapes with life, and rejoins the Indian army, which continues to retreat. The Spaniards fally from the fort, but foon return to it, from the apprehenfion of an ambufcade. They clear their trench, and ftrengthen the weaker parts of their fortification. Night comes on. The Poet defcribes himfelf ftationed on a little eminence in the plain below the fort, which was feated on high and rocky ground:—fatigued with the toils of the day, and oppreffed by the weight of his armour, which he continues to wear, he is troubled with a lethargic heavinefs; which he counteracts by exercife, declaring that his difpofition to flumber in his poft arofe not from any intemperance either in diet or in wine, as mouldy bifcuit and rainwater had been for fome time his chief fuftenance; and that he was accuftomed to make the moift earth his bed, and to divide his time between his poetical and his military labours. He then relates the following nocturnal adventure, which may perhaps be confidered as the moft ftriking and pathetic incident in this fingular poem :

> While thus I ftrove my nightly watch to keep,
> And ftruggled with th' oppreffive weight of fleep,
> As my quick feet, with many a filent ftride,
> Travers'd th' allotted ground from fide to fide,
> My eye perceiv'd one quarter of the plain
> White with the mingled bodies of the flain ;

K k 2

For

For our inceffant fire, that bloody day,
Had flaughter'd numbers in the ftubborn fray.

As oft I paus'd each diftant noife to hear,
Gazing around me with attentive ear,
I heard from time to time a feeble found
Towards the breathlefs Indians on the ground,
Still clofing with a figh of mournful length;
At every interval it gather'd ftrength;
And now it ceas'd, and now again begun,
And ftill from corfe to corfe it feem'd to run.
As night's encreafing fhade my hope deftroys,
To view the fource of this uncertain noife,
Eager my mind's unquiet doubts to ftill,
And more the duties of my poft fulfil,
With crouching fteps I hafte, and earneft eyes,
To the low fpot from whence the murmurs rife;
And fee a dufky Form, that feems to tread
Slow, on four feet, among the gory dead.

With terror, that my heart will not deny,
When this ftrange vifion ftruck my doubtful eye,
Towards it, with a prayer to Heav'n, I preft,
Arms in my hand, my corfelet on my breaft;
But now the dufky Form, on which I fprung,
Upright arofe, and fpoke with plaintive tongue:

Mercy! to mercy hear my juft pretence;
I am a woman, guiltlefs of offence!
If my diftrefs, and unexampled plight,
No generous pity in thy breaft excite;
If thy blood-thirfty rage, by tears uncheck'd,
Would pafs thofe limits which the brave refpect;
Will fuch a deed encreafe thy martial fame,
When Heaven's juft voice fhall to the world proclaim,
That by thy ruthlefs fword a woman died,
A widow, funk in forrow's deepeft tide?
Yet I implore thee, if 'twas haply thine,
Or for thy curfe, as now I feel it mine;

If

If e'er thy lot, in any state, to prove
How firm the faithful ties of tender love,
O let me bury one brave warrior slain,
Whose corse lies blended with this breathless train!
Remember, he who thwarts the duteous will
Becomes th' approver and the cause of ill.

Thou wilt not hinder these my pious vows;
War, fiercest war, this just demand allows:
The basest tyranny alone is driven
To use the utmost power that chance has given.
Let but my soul its dear companion find,
Then sate thy fury, if to blood inclin'd;
For in such grief I draw my lingering breath,
Life is my dread, beyond the pangs of death.
There is no ill that now can wound my breast,
No good, but what I in my Love possest:
Fly then, ye hours! that keep me from the dead;
For he, the spirit of my life, is fled.
If adverse Heaven my latest wish deny,
On his dear corse to fix my closing eye,
My tortur'd soul, in cruel Fate's despight,
Will soar, the faithful partner of his flight.

And now her agony of heart implor'd
An end of all her sorrows from my sword.
Doubt and distrust my troubled mind assail,
That fears deceit in her affecting tale;
Nor was I fully of her faith secure,
Till oft her words the mournful truth insure;
Suspicion whisper'd, that an artful spy
By this illusion might our state descry.

Howe'er inclin'd to doubt, yet soon I knew,
Though night conceal'd her features from my view,
That truth was stamp'd on every word she said;
So full of grief, so free from guilty dread:
And that bold love, to every danger blind,
Had sent her forth her slaughter'd Lord to find,

Who,

Who, in the onset of our bloody strife,
For brave distinction sacrific'd his life.

    Fill'd with compassion, when I saw her bent
To execute her chaste and fond intent,
I led her weeping to the higher spot,
To guard whose precincts was that night my lot;
Securely there I begg'd her to relate
The perfect story of her various fate:
From first to last her touching woes impart,
And by the tale relieve her loaded heart.

    Ah! she replied, relief I ne'er can know,
Till Death's kind aid shall terminate my woe!
Earth for my ills no remedy supplies,
Beyond all suff'rance my afflictions rise:
Yet, though the task will agonize my soul,
Of my sad story I will tell the whole;
Grief, thus inforc'd, my life's weak thread may rend,
And in the killing tale my pangs may end.

    The fair Indian then relates to Ercilla the particulars of her life, in a speech of considerable length:—she informs him, that her name is Tegualda;—that she is the daughter of the Chieftain Brancól;—that her father had often pressed her to marry, which she had for some time declined, though solicited by many of the noblest Youths in her country; till, being appointed, in compliment to her beauty, to distribute the prizes, in a scene of public festivity, to those who excelled in the manly exercises, she was struck by the accomplishments of a gallant Youth, named Crepino, as she bestowed on him the reward of his victories;—that she declared her choice to her father, after perceiving the Youth inspired with a mutual affection for her;—that the old Chieftain was delighted by her chusing so noble a character, and their marriage had been publicly solemnized but a month from that day. On this conclusion of her story, she bursts into new agonies of grief, and intreats Ercilla to let her pay her last duties to her husband; or rather, to unite them again in a common grave. Ercilla endeavours to console her, by repeated promises of all the assistance in his power. In the most passionate excess of sorrow,

she

she still entreats him to end her miserable life.—In this distressing scene, our Author is relieved by the arrival of a brother officer, who had been also stationed on the plain, and now informs Ercilla that the time of their appointed watch is expired. They join in comforting the unhappy Mourner, and conduct her into the fort; where they consign her, for the remainder of the night, to *the decent care of married women,* to use the chaste expression of the generous and compassionate Ercilla.

C A N T O   XXI.

IN pure affection who has soar'd above
  The tender pious proof of faithful love,
Which thus awak'd our sympathetic care
For this unhappy, fond, barbarian Fair?
O that just Fame my humble voice would raise
To swell in loudest notes her lasting praise!
To spread her merits, in immortal rhyme,
Through every language, and through every clime!

  With pitying females she the night remain'd,
Where no rude step their privacy profan'd;
Though wretched, thankful for their soothing aid,
With hopes her duty would at length be paid.

  Soon as the welcome light of morning came,
Though soundest sleep had seiz'd my jaded frame,
Though my tir'd limbs were still to rest inclin'd,
Solicitude awak'd my anxious mind.
Quick to my Indian Mourner I repair,
And still in tears I find the restless Fair;
The varying hours afford her no relief,
No transient momentary pause of grief.
With truest pity I her pangs assuage;
To find her slaughter'd Lord my word engage;
Restore his corse, and, with a martial band,
Escort her safely to her native land.

With

With blended doubt and forrow, weeping ftill,
My promis'd word fhe pray'd me to fulfil.

　　Affembling now a menial Indian train,
I led her to explore the bloody plain:
Where heaps of mingled dead deform'd the ground,
Near to the fort the breathlefs Chief we found;
Clay-cold and ftiff, the gory earth he preft,
A fatal ball had pafs'd his manly breaft.

　　Wretched Tegualda, who before her view'd
The pale disfigur'd form, in blood imbru'd,
Sprung forward, and with inftantaneous force
Frantic fhe darted on the precious corfe,
And prefs'd his lips, where livid death appears,
And bath'd his wounded bofom in her tears,
And kifs'd the wound, and the wild hope purfues
That her fond breath may yet new life infufe.

　　Wretch that I am! at length fhe madly cried,
Why does my foul thefe agonies abide?
Why do I linger in this mortal ftrife,
Nor pay to Love his juft demand, my life?
Why, poor of fpirit! at a fingle blow
Do I not clofe this bitter fcene of woe?
Whence this delay? will Heaven to me deny
The wretch's choice and privilege, to die?

　　While, bent on death, in this defpair fhe gafp'd,
Her furious hands her fnowy neck inclafp'd;
Failing her frantic wifh, they do not fpare
Her mournful vifage nor her flowing hair.
Much as I ftrove to ftop her mad intent,
Her fatal purpofe I could fcarce prevent:
So loath'd fhe life, and with fuch fierce controul
The raging thirft of death inflam'd her foul.

　　When by my prayers, and foft perfuafion's balm,
Her pangs of forrow grew a little calm,
And her mild fpeech confirm'd my hope, at laft,
That her delirious agony was paft,

　　　　　　　　　　　　　　　　　　　　　　My

My ready Indian train, with duteous hafte,
On a firm bier the clay-cold body plac'd,
And bore the Warrior, in whofe fate we griev'd,
To where her vaffals the dear charge receiv'd.
But, left from ruthlefs War's outrageous fway
The mourning Fair might fuffer on her way,
O'er the near mountains, to a fafer land,
I march'd to guard her with my warlike band;
And there fecure, for the remaining road
Was clear and open to her own abode,
She gratefully declin'd my farther care,
And thank'd and blefs'd me in a parting prayer.

As I have been tempted to dwell much longer than I intended on fome of the moft pathetic incidents of this extraordinary poem, I fhall give a more concife fummary of the remaining cantos.——On Ercilla's return, the Spaniards continue to ftrengthen their fort. They receive intelligence from an Indian ally, that the Barbarian army intend a frefh affault in the night. They are relieved from this alarm by the arrival of a large reinforcement from the Spanifh cities in Chile:—on which event Colocolo prevails on the Indians to fufpend the attack. Caupolican, the Indian General, reviews all his forces; and the various Chieftains are well defcribed. The Spanifh Commander, Don Garcia, being now determined to march into the hoftile diftrict of Arauco, addreffes his foldiers in a fpirited harangue, requefting them to remember the pious caufe for which they fight, and to fpare the life of every Indian who is difpofed to fubmiffion. They remove from their poft, and pafs in boats over the broad river Biobio.

CANTO XXII.

THE Spaniards are attacked in their new quarters — a furious battle enfues. The Spaniards are forced to give ground, but at laft prevail. The Indian Chief, Rengo, fignalizes himfelf in the action; defends himfelf in a marfh, and retreats in good order with his forces.

L l   The

The Spaniards, after the conflict, seize an unhappy straggling Youth, named Galvarino, whom they punish as a rebel in the most barbarous manner, by cutting off both his hands. The valiant Youth defies their cruelty in the midst of this horrid scene; and, brandishing his bloody stumps, departs from his oppressors with the most insulting menaces of revenge.

C A N T O   XXIII.

GALVARINO appears in the Assembly of the Indian Chieftains, and excites them, in a very animated speech, to revenge the barbarity with which he has been treated. He faints from loss of blood, in the close of his harangue, but is recovered by the care of his friends, and restored to health. The Indians, exasperated by the sight of his wounds, unanimously determine to prosecute the war. The Spaniards, advancing in Arauco, send forth scouts to discover the disposition of the neighbouring tribes. Ercilla, engaging in this service, perceives an old Indian in a sequestered spot, apparently sinking under the infirmities of age; but, on his approach, the ancient figure flies from him with astonishing rapidity. He endeavours in vain, though on horseback, to overtake this aged fugitive, who soon escapes from his sight. He now discovers the tame Deer foretold in his vision; and, pursuing it, is conducted through intricate paths to a retired cottage, where a courteous old man receives him in a friendly manner. Ercilla enquires after the Magician Fiton: the old man undertakes to guide him to the secret mansion of that wonderful Necromancer, to whom he declares himself related. He adds, that he himself was once a distinguished warrior; but, having the misfortune to sully his past glory, without losing his life, in a conflict with another Chieftain, he had withdrawn himself from society, and lived twenty years as a hermit. He now leads Ercilla through a gloomy grove to the cell of the Magician, whose residence and magical apparatus are described with great force of imagination. Fiton appears from a secret portal, and proves to be the aged figure who had escaped so swiftly from the sight of Ercilla. At the request of

his

his relation, the old Warrior, he condefcends to fhew Ercilla the wonders of his art. He leads him to a large lucid globe, felf-fufpended in
the middle of an immenfe apartment. He tells him it is the work of
forty years ftudy, and contains an exact reprefentation of the world,
with this fingular power, that it exhibits, at his command, any fcene of
futurity which he wifhes to behold :—that, knowing the heroic compofition of Ercilla, he will give him an opportunity to vary and embellifh
his poem by the defcription of a moft important fea-fight, which he will
difplay to him moft diftinctly on that fphere. He then invokes all the
powers of the infernal world. Ercilla fixes his eye on the globe, and
perceives the naval forces of Spain, with thofe of the Pope and the
Venetians, prepared to engage the great armament of the Turks.

CANTO XXIV.

DESCRIBES circumftantially the naval battle of Lepanto, and celebrates the Spanifh admiral, Don John of Auftria. Ercilla gazes
with great delight on this glorious action, and beholds the complete
triumph of his countrymen ; when the Magician ftrikes the globe with
his wand, and turns the fcene into darknefs. Ercilla, after being entertained with other marvellous fights, which he omits from his dread of
prolixity, takes leave of his two aged friends, and regains his quarters.
The Spaniards continue to advance : on their pitching their camp in a
new fpot, towards evening, an Araucanian, fantaftically dreft in armour,
enquires for the tent of Don Garcia, and is conducted to his prefence.

CANTO XXV.

THE Araucanian delivers a defiance to Don Garcia, in the name of
Caupolican, who challenges the Spanifh General to end the war
by a fingle combat. The meffenger adds, that the whole Indian army
will defcend into the plain, on the next morning, to be fpectators of the

duel.

duel. Don Garcia difmiffes him with an acceptance of the challenge.
At the dawn of day the Indian forces appear in three divifions. A party
of Spanifh horfe precipitately attack their left wing, before which
Caupolican was advancing. They are repulfed. A general and obftinate
engagement enfues. The mangled Galvarino appears at the head of one
Indian fquadron, and excites his countrymen to revenge his wrongs.
Many Spaniards are named who diftinguifh themfelves in the battle.
Among the Indian Chiefs Tucapel and Rengo difplay the moft fplendid
acts of valour; and, though perfonal enemies, they mutually defend
each other. Caupolican alfo, at the head of the left fquadron, obliges
the Spaniards to retreat; and the Araucanians are on the point of gain-
ing a decifive victory, when the fortune of the day begins to turn.

C A N T O   XXVI.

THE referved guard of the Spaniards, in which Ercilla was ftationed,
advancing to the charge, recover the field, and oblige the main body
of the Indians to fly. Caupolican, though victorious in his quarter,
founds a retreat when he perceives this event. The Indians fly in great
diforder. Rengo for fome time fuftains an unequal conflict, and at laft
retreats fullenly into a wood, where he collects feveral of the fcattered
fugitives. As Ercilla happened to advance towards this fpot, a
Spaniard, called Remon, exhorts him by name to attempt the dangerous
but important exploit of forcing this Indian party from the wood. His
honour being thus piqued, he rufhes forward with a few followers,
and, after an obftinate engagement, in which many of the Indians are
cut to pieces, the Spaniards obtain the victory, and return to their camp
with feveral prifoners. After this great defeat of the Indian army, the
Spaniards, to deter their enemies from all future refiftance, barbaroufly
refolve to execute twelve Chieftains of diftinction, whom they find
among their captives, and to leave their bodies expofed on the trees that
furrounded the field of battle. The generous Ercilla, lamenting this
inhuman fentence, intercedes particularly for the life of one, alledging

                                                                    that

that he had feen him united with the Spaniards. This perfon proves to be Galvarino; who, on hearing the interceffion for his life, produces his mangled arms, which he had concealed in his bofom, and, giving vent to his deteftation of the Spaniards, infifts on dying with his country-men. Ercilla perfifts in vain in his endeavour to fave him. As no executioner could be found among the Spanifh foldiers, a new mode of deftruction, fays our Poet, was invented; and every Indian was ordered to terminate his own life by a cord which was given him. Thefe brave men haftened to accomplifh their fate with as much alacrity, continues Ercilla, as the moft fpirited warrior marches to an attack. One alone of the twelve begins to hefitate, and pray for mercy; declaring himfelf the lineal defcendant of the moft ancient race and fovereign of the country. He is interrupted by the reproaches of the impetuous Galva-rino, and, repenting his timidity, atones for it by inftant death.

The Spaniards advance ftill farther in the country, and raife a fort where Valdivia had perifhed. Ercilla finds his old friend the Magician once more, who tells him that Heaven thought proper to punifh the pride of the Araucanians by their late defeat; but that the Spaniards would foon pay dearly for their prefent triumph. The Wizard retires after this prophecy, and, with much intreaty, allows Ercilla to follow him. Coming to a gloomy rock, he ftrikes it with his wand; a fecret door opens, and they enter into a delicious garden, which the Poet commends for its fymmetry, expreffly declaring that every hedge *has its brother*. The Magician leads him into a vault of alabafter; and, perceiving his wifh, though he does not exprefs it, of feeing the miraculous globe again, the courteous Fiton conducts him to it.

CANTO XXVII.

THE Magician difplays to our Poet the various countries of the globe; particularly pointing out to him the ancient caftle of Ercilla, the feat of his anceftors in Bifcay, and the fpot where his fove-reign Philip the Second was foon to build his magnificent palace, the Efcurial. Having fhewn him the various nations of the earth on his marvellous fphere, Fiton conducts his gueft to the road leading to the
Spanifh

Spanish camp, where the soldiers of Ercilla were seeking their officer. The Spaniards in vain attempt to sooth and to terrify the Araucanians into peace ; and, finding the importance of their present post, they determine to strengthen it. Ercilla proceeds with a party to the city of Imperial, to provide necessaries for this purpose. On his return, as he is marching through the country of some pacific Indians, he discovers, at the close of day, a distrest female, who attempts to fly, but is overtaken by Ercilla.

C A N T O   XXVIII.

THE fair fugitive, whom our Poet describes as singularly beautiful, relates her story. She tells him her name is Glaura, the daughter of an opulent Chieftain, with whom she lived most happily, till a brother of her father's, who frequently resided with him, persecuted her with an unwarrantable passion ;—that she in vain represented to him the impious nature of his love ;—he persisted in his frantic attachment, and, on the appearance of a hostile party of Spaniards, rushed forth to die in her defence, intreating her to receive his departing spirit. He fell in the action ; her father shared the same fate : she herself escaped at a postern gate into the woods. Two negroes, laden with spoil, discovered, and seized her. Her cries brought a young Indian, named Cariolano, to her rescue: he shot an arrow into the heart of the first ruffian, and stabbed the second. Glaura expressed her gratitude by receiving her young deliverer as her husband. Before they could regain a place of safety, they were alarmed by the approach of Spaniards. The generous Youth intreated Glaura to conceal herself in a tree, while he ventured to meet the enemy. In her terror she submitted to this expedient, which, on recovery from her panic, she bitterly repented; for when she issued from her retreat, she sought in vain for Cariolano, and supposed, from the clamour she had heard, that he must have perished. She continued to wander in this wretched state of mind, still unable to hear any tidings of her protector. While the fair Indian thus closes her narrative, Ercilla is alarmed by the approach of a large party of Barbarians. One of his faithful Indian attendants, whom he had lately attached to him,

intreats

intreats him to escape with the utmost haste; adding, that he can save him from pursuit by his knowledge of the country; and that he will risque his own life most willingly, to preserve that of Ercilla. Glaura bursts into an agony of joy, in discovering her lost Cariolano in this faithful attendant. Ercilla exclaims, " Adieu, my friends; I give you " both your liberty, which is all I have at present to bestow," and rejoins his little troop. Before he enters on the account of what followed, he relates the circumstance by which he attached Cariolano to his service; whom he had found alone, as he himself was marching with a small party, and a few prisoners that he had taken. The Youth at first defended himself, and shot two Spaniards with his arrows, and continued to resist the numbers that pressed upon him, with his mantle and his dagger evading their blows by his extreme agility, and wounding several. Ercilla generously rushed in to his rescue, and declared he deserved a reward for his uncommon bravery, instead of being destroyed so unfairly. The Youth, in consequence of this treatment, flung down his dagger, and became the affectionate attendant of Ercilla. Our Poet, after relating this incident, returns to the scene where his party was surprized in a hollow road, and severely galled by the enemy, who attacked them with showers of stones from the higher ground. Ercilla forces his way up the precipice, and, after dispersing part of the Indian force, effects his escape with a few followers; but all are wounded, and obliged to leave their baggage in the possession of their numerous enemies.

CANTO XXIX.

OPENS with an encomium on the love of our country, and the signal proofs of this virtue which the Araucanians displayed; who, notwithstanding their loss of four great battles in the space of three months, still continue firm in their resolution of defending their liberty. Caupolican proposes, in a public assembly, to set fire to their own habitations, and leave themselves no alternative, but that of killing or being killed. The Chieftains all agree in this desperate determination. Tucapel,

capel, before they proceed to action againſt the Spaniards, inſiſts on ter-
minating his difference with Rengo, a rival Chieftain, by a ſingle combat. A plain is appointed for this purpoſe : all the people of Arauco
aſſemble as ſpectators : the Chiefs appear in complete armour, and engage in a moſt obſtinate and bloody conflict.

C A N T O   XXX.

AFTER many dreadful wounds on each ſide, the two Chieftains,
cloſing with each other, fall together, and, after a fruitleſs ſtruggle
for victory, remain ſpeechleſs on the ground. Caupolican, who preſided
as judge of the combat, deſcends from his ſeat, and, finding ſome ſigns
of life in each, orders them to be carried to their reſpective tents. They
recover, and are reconciled. The Spaniards, leaving a garriſon in their
new fort, under a captain named Reynoſo, had proceeded to the city of
Imperial. Caupolican endeavours to take advantage of this event. He
employs an artful Indian, named Pran, to examine the ſtate of the fort.
Pran inſinuates himſelf among the Indian ſervants belonging to the
Spaniards. He views the fort, and endeavours to perſuade a ſervile
Indian, named Andreſillo, to admit Caupolican and his forces while
the Spaniards are ſleeping. Andreſillo promiſes to meet Caupolican in
ſecret, and converſe with him on this project.

C A N T O   XXXI.

OPENS with a ſpirited invective againſt treachery in war, and particularly thoſe traitors who betray their country. Andreſillo reveals
all that had paſſed to his Spaniſh captain ; who promiſes him a great
reward if he will aſſiſt in making the ſtratagem of the Indians an inſtru-
ment of deſtruction to thoſe who contrived it. They concert a plan for
this purpoſe. Andreſillo meets Caupolican in ſecret, and promiſes to
                                                        introduce

introduce the Indian forces into the fort when the Spaniards are sleeping, in the heat of the day. Pran is sent forward, to learn from Andresillo if all things are quiet, just before the hour appointed for the assault. He examines the state of the fort, and, finding the Spaniards apparently unprepared for defence, hastens back to the Indian General, who advances by a quick and silent march. The Spaniards in the interim point all their guns, and prepare for the most bloody resistance.

CANTO XXXII.

AFTER a panegyric on clemency, and a noble censure of those enormous cruelties, by which his countrymen sullied their military fame, the Poet relates the dreadful carnage which ensued as the Indians approached the fort. The Spaniards, after destroying numbers by their artillery, send forth a party of horse, who cut the fugitives to pieces. They inhumanly murder thirteen of their most distinguished prisoners, by blowing them from the mouths of cannon: but none of the confederate Chieftains, whom the Poet has particularly celebrated, were included in this number; for those high-spirited Barbarians had refused to attend Caupolican in this assault, as they considered it as disgraceful to attack their enemies by surprize. The unfortunate Indian Leader, seeing his forces thus unexpectedly massacred, escapes with ten faithful followers, and wanders through the country in the most calamitous condition. The Spaniards endeavour, by all the means they can devise, to discover his retreat: the faithful inhabitants of Arauco refuse to betray him.

Ercilla, in searching the country with a small party, finds a young wounded female. She informs him, that marching with her husband, she had the misfortune of seeing him perish in the late slaughter;—that a friendly soldier, in pity to her extreme distress, had tried to end her miserable life in the midst of the confusion, but had failed in his generous design, by giving her an ineffectual wound;—that she had been removed from the field of battle to that sequestered spot, where she lan-

M m   guished

guished in the hourly hope of death, which she now implores from the
hand of Ercilla. Our Poet confoles her; dreffes her wound, and leaves
one of his attendants to protect her. On his return to the fort, he dif-
courfes to his foldiers in praife of the fidelity and fpirit difplayed by the
Indian females, comparing them to the chafte and conftant Dido. A
young foldier of his train expreffes his furprize on hearing Ercilla commend the Carthaginian Queen for a virtue to which, he conceived, she
had no pretence. From hence our Poet takes occafion to vindicate
the injured Eliza from the flanderous mifreprefentation of Virgil; and
flatters himfelf that the love of juftice, fo natural to man, will induce
every reader to liften with pleafure to his defence of the calumniated
Queen. He then enters on her *real hiftory*, and relates circumftantially
her lamentation over the murdered Sichæus, and the artifice by which
she efcaped with her treafures from her inhuman brother Pygmalion:—she
engages many of his attendants to fhare the chances of her voyage ; and,
having collected a fupply of females from the ifland of **Cyprus**, she directs her courfe to the coaft of **Africa**.

C A N T O   XXXIII.

DIDO, as our Poet continues her *more authentic ftory*, purchafes her
dominion and raifes her flourifhing city. The ambaffadors of Iarbas arrive at Carthage, to offer this celebrated Queen the alternative of
marriage or war. The Senate, who are firft informed of the propofal,
being fearful that the chafte refolutions of their fair Sovereign may
ruin their country, attempt to engage her, by a fingular device, to
accept the hand of Iarbas. They tell her, that this haughty Monarch
has fent to demand twenty of her privy counfellors to regulate his kingdom ; and that, in confideration of their age and infirmities, they muft
decline fo unpleafant a fervice. The Queen reprefents to them the danger of their refufal, and the duty which they owe to their country ;
declaring, that she would moft readily facrifice her own life for the fafety
or advantage of her fubjects. The Senators then reveal to her the real
demand

demand of Iarbas, and urge the neceſſity of her marriage for the preſer-
vation of the ſtate. The faithful Dido knows not what to reſolve, and
demands three months to conſider of this delicate and important point:
—at the cloſe of that period, ſhe aſſembles her ſubjects; and, taking
leave of them in a very affectionate harangue, declares her reſolution to
die, as the only means by which ſhe can at once ſatisfy both Heaven
and earth, by diſcharging her duty to her people, and at the ſame
time preſerving her faith inviolate to her departed Sichæus. Invoking his name, ſhe plunges a poniard in her breaſt; and throws
herſelf on a flaming pile, which had been kindled for a different ſacrifice.
Her grateful ſubjects lament her death, and pay divine honours to her
memory. " This * (ſays our Poet) is the true and genuine ſtory of
the famous defamed Dido, whoſe moſt honoured chaſtity has been belied
by the inconſiderate Virgil, to embelliſh his poetical fictions."

Our Poet returns from this digreſſion on Dido, to the fate of the Indian
Leader Caupolican.—One of the priſoners, whom the Spaniards had
taken in their ſearch after this unfortunate Chief, is at laſt tempted by
bribes to betray his General. He conducts the Spaniards to a ſpot near
the ſequeſtered retreat of Caupolican, and directs them how to diſcover
it; but refuſes to advance with them, overcome by his dread of the
Hero whom he is tempted to betray. The Spaniards ſurround the houſe
in which the Chieftain had taken refuge with his ten faithful aſſociates.
Alarmed by a centinel, he prepares for defence; but being ſoon wounded
in the arm, ſurrenders, endeavouring to conceal his high character, and
to make the Spaniards believe him an ordinary ſoldier.

> With their accuſtom'd ſhouts, and greedy toil,
> Our furious troops now riot in their ſpoil;

---

* Eſte es el cierto y verdadero cuento,
De la famoſa Dido disfamada
Que Virgilio Maron ſin miramiento
Falſeó ſu hiſtoria y caſtidad preciada
Por dar a ſus ficciones ornamento
Pues vemos que eſta Reyna importunada
Pudiéndoſe caſar y no quemarſe
Antes quemarſe quiſo, que caſarſe.

M m 2

Through

Through the lone village their quick rapine fpread,
Nor leave unpillag'd e'en a fingle fhed:
When, from a tent, that, plac'd on fafer ground,
The neighbouring hill's uncultur'd fummit crown'd,
A woman rufh'd, who, in her hafty flight,
Ran through the rougheft paths along the rocky height.
A Negro of our train, who mark'd her way,
Soon made the haplefs fugitive his prey;
For thwarting crags her doubtful fteps impede,
And the fair form was ill prepar'd for fpeed;
For at her breaft fhe bore her huddled fon;
To fifteen months the infant's life had run:
From our brave captive fprung the blooming boy,
Of both his parents the chief pride and joy.
The Negro carelefsly his victim brought,
Nor knew th' important prize his hafte had caught.

Our foldiers now, to catch the cooling tide,
Had fallied to the murmuring river's fide:
When the unhappy Wife beheld her Lord,
His ftrong arms bound with a difgraceful cord,
Stript of each enfign of his paft command,
And led the pris'ner of our fhouting band;
Her anguifh burft not into vain complaint,
No female terrors her firm foul attaint;
But, breathing fierce difdain, and anger wild,
Thus fhe exclaim'd, advancing with her child:

The ftronger arm that in this fhameful band
Has tied thy weak effeminated hand,
Had nobler pity to thy ftate expreft
If it had bravely pierc'd that coward breaft.
Wert thou the warrior whofe heroic worth
So fwiftly flew around the fpacious earth,
Whofe name alone, unaided by thy arm,
Shook the remoteft clime with fear's alarm?
Wert thou the victor whofe triumphant ftrain
Promis'd with rapid fword to vanquifh Spain;

To

To make new realms Arauco's power revere,
And spread her empire o'er the Arctic sphere?
Wretch that I am! how was my heart deceiv'd,
In all the noble pride with which it heav'd,
When through the world my boasted title ran,
Tresia, the wife of great Caupolican!
Now, plung'd in misery from the heights of fame,
My glories end in this detested shame,
To see thee captive in a lonely spot,
When death and honour might have been thy lot!

What now avail thy scenes of happier strife,
So dearly bought by many a nobler life;
The wondrous feats, that valour scarce believ'd,
By thee with hazard and with toil atchiev'd?
Where are the vaunted fruits of thy command,
The laurels gather'd by this fetter'd hand?
All sunk! all turn'd to this abhorr'd disgrace,
To live the slave of this ignoble race!
Say, had thy soul no strength, thy hand no lance,
To triumph o'er the fickle pow'r of chance?
Dost thou not know, that, to the Warrior's name,
A gallant exit gives immortal fame?

Behold the burthen which my breast contains,
Since of thy love no other pledge remains!
Hadst thou in glory's arms resign'd thy breath,
We both had follow'd thee in joyous death:
Take, take thy son! he was a tie most dear,
Which spotless love once made my heart revere;
Take him!—by generous pain, and wounded pride,
The currents of this fruitful breast are dried:
Rear him thyself, for thy gigantic frame,
To woman turn'd, a woman's charge may claim:
A mother's title I no more desire,
Or shameful children from a shameful sire!

As thus she spoke, with growing madness stung,
The tender nursling from her arms she flung

With

With ſavage fury, haſt'ning from our ſight,
While anguiſh ſeem'd to aid her rapid flight.
Vain were our efforts; our indignant cries,
Nor gentle prayers, nor angry threats, ſuffice
To make her breaſt, where cruel frenzy burn'd,
Receive the little innocent ſhe ſpurn'd.

The Spaniards, after providing a nurſe for this unfortunate child, return with their priſoner Caupolican to their fort, which they enter in triumph.

The Indian General, perceiving that all attempts to conceal his quality are ineffectual, deſires a conference with the Spaniſh Captain Reynoſo.

C A N T O   XXXIV.

CAUPOLICAN entreats Reynoſo to grant his life, but without any ſigns of terror. He affirms it will be the only method of appeaſing the ſanguinary hatred by which the contending nations are inflamed; and he offers, from his great influence over his country, to introduce the Chriſtian worſhip, and to bring the Araucanians to conſider themſelves as the ſubjects of the Spaniſh Monarch. His propoſals are rejected, and he is ſentenced to be impaled, and ſhot to death with arrows. He is unappall'd by this decree; but firſt deſires to be publicly baptized: after which ceremony, he is inhumanly led in chains to a ſcaffold. He diſplays a calm contempt of death; but, on ſeeing a wretched Negro appointed his executioner, his indignation burſts forth, and he hurls the Negro from the ſcaffold, entreating to die by a more honourable hand. His horrid ſentence is however executed. He ſupports the agonies of the ſtake with patient intrepidity, till a choſen band of archers put a period to his life.

Our brave Ercilla expreſſes his abhorrence of this atrocious ſcene; and adds, that if he had been preſent, this cruel execution ſhould not have taken place.

The conſequence of it was ſuch as Caupolican foretold:—the Araucanians determine to revenge his death, and aſſemble to elect a new General. The Poet makes an abrupt tranfition from their debate, to relate the adventures of Don Garcia, with whom he was himfelf marching to explore new regions. The inhabitants of the diftricts they invade, alarmed at the approach of the Spaniards, confult on the occafion. An Indian, named Tunconabala, who had ferved under the Araucanians, addreffes the affembly, and recommends to them a mode of eluding the fuppofed avaricious defigns of the Spaniards, by fending meffengers to them, who fhould affume an appearance of extreme poverty, and reprefent their country as barren, and thus induce the invaders to turn their arms towards a different quarter. He offers to engage in this fervice himfelf. The Indians adopt the project he recommends, and remove their valuable effects to the interior parts of their country.

C A N T O   XXXV.

DON GARCIA being arrived at the boundaries of Chile, which no Spaniard had paffed, encourages his foldiers, in a fpirited harangue, to the acquifition of the new provinces which lay before them. They enter a rude and rocky country, in which they are expofed to many hazards by their deceitful guides. Tunconabala meets them, as he had projected, with the appearance of extreme poverty; and, after many affurances of the fterility of that region, advifes them to return, or to advance by a different path, which he reprefents to them as dangerous, but the only practicable road. On finding them refolved to prefs forward, he fupplies them with a guide. They advance, with great toil and danger. Their guide efcapes from them. They continue their march, through various hardfhips, in a defolate region. They at length difcover a fertile plain, and a large lake with many little inhabited iflands. As they approach the lake, a large gondola, with twelve oars, advances to meet them: the party it contained leap afhore, and falute the Spaniards with expreffions of amity.

CANTO XXXVI.

THE young Chieftain of the gondola fupplies the Spaniards with provifions, refufing to accept any reward : and our Poet celebrates all the inhabitants of this region, for their amiable fimplicity of manners. He vifits one of the principal iflands, where he is kindly entertained. He difcovers that the lake had a communication with the fea, by a very rough and dangerous channel : this circumftance obliges the Spaniards, though reluctant, to return. They lament the neceffity of paffing again through the hardfhips of their former road. A young Indian undertakes to conduct them by an eafier way. But our adventurous Ercilla, before the little army fet forth on their return, engages ten chofen affociates to embark with him in a fmall veffel, and pafs the dangerous channel. He lands on a wild and fandy fpot, and, advancing half a mile up the country, engraves a ftanza, to record this adventure, on the bark of a tree. He repaffes the channel, and rejoins the Spanifh troops; who, after much difficulty, reach the city of Imperial. Our Poet then touches on fome particulars of his perfonal hiftory, which I mention in the flight fketch of his life. He afterwards promifes his reader to relate the iffue of the debate among the Araucanian Chieftains, on the election of their new General ; but, recollecting in the inftant that Spain herfelf is in arms, he entreats the favour of his Sovereign to infpire him with new fpirit, that he may devote himfelf to that higher and more interefting fubject.

CANTO XXXVII.

OUR Poet, in this his laft canto, feems to begin a new work. He enters into a difcuffion of Philip's right to the dominion of Portugal, and his acquifition of that kingdom ; when, finking under the weight of this new fubject, he declares his refolution of leaving it to fome happier Poet. He recapitulates the various perils and hardfhips of his own life, and, remarking that he has ever been unfortunate, and that all his labours are unrewarded, he confoles himfelf with the reflection, that

honour

honour confifts not in the poffeffion of rewards, but in the confcioufnefs of having deferved them. He concludes with a pious refolution to withdraw himfelf from the vain purfuits of the world, and to devote himfelf to God.

NOTE XI. VERSE 280.

At once the Bard of Glory and of Love.] The Epic powers of Camoens have received their due honour in our language, by the elegant and fpirited tranflation of Mr. Mickle; but our country is ftill a ftranger to the lighter graces and pathetic fweetnefs of his fhorter compofitions. Thefe, as they are illuftrated by the Spanifh notes of his indefatigable Commentator, *Manuel de Faria*, amount to two volumes in folio. I fhall prefent the reader with a fpecimen of his Sonnets, for which he is celebrated as the rival of Petrarch. Of the three tranflations which follow, I am indebted for the two firft to an ingenious friend, from whom the public may wifh me to have received more extenfive obligations of a fimilar nature. It may be proper to add, that the firft Sonnet of Camoens, like that of Petrarch, is a kind of preface to the amorous poetry of its author.

S O N E T O   I.

E M quanto quis Fortuna que tiveſſe
    Eſperanca de algum contentamento,
   O goſto de hum ſuave penſamento
   Me fez que ſeus effeytos eſcreveſſe.
Porèm temendo Amor que aviſo deſſe
    Minha eſcritura a algum juizo iſento,
   Eſcureccome o engenho co' o tormento,
   Para que ſeus enganos naõ diſſeſſe
O vós, que amor obriga a ſer ſogeytos
    A diverſas vontades ! quando lerdes
   Num breve livro caſos taõ diverſos ;
Verdades puras faõ, & naõ defeytos.
   Entendey que ſegundo o amor tiverdes,
   Tircis o entendimento de meus verſos.

S O N E T O   XIX.

A LMA minha gentil, que te partiſte
    Taõ cedo deſta vida deſcontente,
   Repouſa lâ no ceo eternamente,
   E viva eu câ na terra ſempre triſte.
Se là no aſſento etereo, onde ſubiſte,
    Memoria deſta vida ſe conſente,
   Naõ te eſqueças de aquelle amor ardente
   Que já nos olhos meus taõ puro viſte.
Eſe vires que póde merecerte
    Algũa couſa a dor queme ficou
   Da magoa, ſem remedio, de perderte,
Roga a Deos que teus annos encurtou,
   Que taõ cedo de câ me leve a verte,
   Quaõ cedo de meus olhos te levou.

SONNET

SONNET I.

WHILE on my head kind Fortune deign'd to pour
    Her lavish boons, and through my willing soul
Made tides of extasy and pleasure roll,
I sung the raptures of each passing hour.
But Love, who heard me praise the golden shower,
Resolv'd my fond presumption to controul;
And painful darkness o'er my spirit stole,
Lest I should dare to tell his treacherous power.
O ye, whom his hard yoke compels to bend
To others' will, if in my various lay
Sad plaints ye find, and fears, and cruel wrong,
To suffering nature and to truth attend;
For in the measure ye have felt his sway,
Your sympathizing hearts will feel my song.

SONNET XIX.

ON THE DEATH OF THE POET'S MISTRESS, DONNA CATALINA DE ATAIDE, WHO DIED AT THE AGE OF TWENTY.

GO, gentle spirit! now supremely blest,
    From scenes of pain and struggling virtue go:
From thy immortal seat of heavenly rest
Behold us lingering in a world of woe!
And if beyond the grave, to saints above,
Fond memory still the transient past pourtrays,
Blame not the ardor of my constant love,
Which in these longing eyes was wont to blaze.
But if from virtue's source my sorrows rise,
For the sad loss I never can repair,
Be thine to justify my endless sighs,
And to theThrone of Grace prefer thy prayer,
That Heaven, who made thy span of life so brief,
May shorten mine, and give my soul relief.

N n 2   SONETO

SONETO LXXII.

QUANDO de minhas magoas ẽ comprida
 Maginaçaõ os olhos me adormece,
 Em sonhos aquella alma me aparece
 Que para mi foy sonho nesta vida.
Lá numa soidade, onde estendida
 A vista por o campo desfallece,
 Corro apos ella ; & ella entaõ parece
 Que maes de mi se alonga, compelida,
Brado : Naõ me fujays, sombra benina.
 Ella (os olhos em mi c'hum brado pejo,
 Como quem diz, que ja naõ pode ser)
Torna a fugirme : torno a bradar ; dina :
 E antes q acabe em mene, acordo, & vejo
 Que nem hum breve engano posso ter.

The Spanish Commentator of Camoens considers this vision as the most exquisite Sonnet of his author, and affirms that it is superior to the much longer poem of Petrarch's, on a similar idea. It may amuse a curious reader to compare both Camoens and Petrarch, on this occasion, with Milton, who has also written a Sonnet on the same subject. The Commentator Faria has a very pleasant remark on this species of composition. He vindicates the dignity of the amorous Sonnet, by producing an alphabetical list of two hundred great Poets, who have thus complimented the object of their affection ; and he very gravely introduces Achilles as the leader of this choir, for having celebrated Briseis. If the Sonnets of the Portugueze Poet are worthy of attention, his Elegies are perhaps still more so, as they illustrate many particulars of his interesting life, which ended in 1579, under the most cruel circumstances of neglect and poverty.

Portugal has produced no less than fourteen Epic poems ; twelve in

SONNET LXXII.

WHILE preft with woes from which it cannot flee,
  My fancy finks, and flumber feals my eyes,
Her fpirit haftens in my dreams to rife,
Who was in life but as a dream to me.
O'er a drear wafte, fo wide no eye can fee
How far its fenfe-evading limit lies,
I follow her quick ftep; but ah! fhe flies!
Our diftance widening by ftern Fate's decree.
Fly not from me, kind fhadow! I exclaim:
She, with fix'd eyes, that her foft thoughts reveal,
And feem to fay, "Forbear thy fond defign!"
Still flies:—I call her; but her half-form'd name
Dies on my falt'ring tongue.—I wake, and feel
Not e'en one fhort delufion may be mine.

---

her own language, and two in that of Spain. At the head of thefe
ftands the Lufiad of Camoens. The Malaca Conquiftada of Francifco
de Sa' de Menefis—and the Ulyffea, or Lifboa Edificada, of Gabriel
Pereira de Caftro, are two of the moft eminent among its fucceffors.—
For a lift of the Portugueze Epic Poets, and for an elegant copy of
the Malaca Conquiftada, I am indebted to the very liberal politenefs of
the Chevalier de Pinto, the Ambaffador of Portugal.

NOTE XII. VERSE 287.

Where Eulogy, with one eternal fmile.] Though a vain infipidity may
be confidered as the general charaƈteriftic of the French *Eloges*, it is but
juft to remark, that feveral of thefe performances are an honour to the
country which produced them; and particularly the little volume of
Eloges lately publifhed by Mr. D'Alembert. This agreeable Encomiaft
has

has varied and enlivened the tone of panegyric by the moſt happy mixture of amuſing anecdote, judicious criticiſm, and philoſophical precept:
we may juſtly ſay of him, what he himſelf has ſaid of his predeceſſor Fon-
tenelle : Il a ſolidement aſſuré ſa gloire .... par ces Eloges ſi intereſſans,
pleins d'une raiſon ſi fine et ſi profonde, qui font aimer et reſpecter les
lettres, qui inſpirent aux génies naiſſans la plus noble emulation, et qui
feront paſſer le nom de l'auteur à la poſterité, avec celui de la compagnie
célebre dont il a été le digne organe, et des grands hommes dont il s'eſt
rendu l'egal en devenant leur panégyriſte.

D'Alembert, Eloge de la Motte, p. 279.

NOTE XIII. VERSE 302.

No great Examples riſe, but many a Rule.] Before the appearance of
Boſſu's celebrated treatiſe on Epic poetry, the French had a ſimilar work
written in Latin. The learned Jeſuit Mambrun publiſhed, in 1652, a
quarto volume, entitled, Diſſertatio Peripatetica de Epico Carmine. His
Diſſertation is founded on the principles of Ariſtotle, whom he conſiders
as infallible authority ; and he introduces the Greek Philoſopher to decide the following very curious queſtion, which he argues with becoming gravity, Whether the action of a woman can be ſufficiently ſplendid
to prove a proper ſubject for an Epic poem.—Having reaſoned on this
delicate point, with more learning than gallantry, he thus concludes the
debate : Congruenter magis finem huic quæſtioni ponere non licet, quam
verbis Ariſtotelis capite 15 Poeticæ, ubi de moribus diſputat, Δεύτερον δε,
τα αρμοττοντα. Εστι γαρ ανδρειον μεν το νοος, αλλ' εκ' αρμοττον γυναικι, το αν-
δρειαν η δεινην ειναι—id eſt, ſecunda proprietas morum eſt, ut ſint congruen-
tes, ut eſſe fortem mos eſt aliquis ; at non congruit mulieri fortem eſſe aut
terribilem ut vertit Riccobonus, vel *prudentem* ut Pacius. The latter
interpretation of the word δεινην would render the deciſion of theſe Phi-
loſophers very ſevere indeed on the Female character, by ſuppoſing it in-
capable of diſplaying both fortitude and prudence.—The Fair Sex have
found an advocate, on this occaſion, in a French Epic Poet. The famous
Chapelain, in the preface to his unfortunate Pucelle, has very warmly
attacked theſe ungallant maxims of Mambrun and Ariſtotle. In ſpeak-
ing of certain critics, who had cenſured the choice of his ſubject, before
the publication of his poem, he ſays, Ceux-cy, jurant ſur le texte d'A-

riſtote,

riſtote, maintiennent que la femme eſt une erreur de la nature, qui ayant toujours intention de faire un homme, s'arreſte ſouvent en chemin, et ſe voit contrainte, par la reſiſtance de la matiere, de laiſſer ſon deſſein imparfait. Ils tiennent la force corporelle tellement neceſſaire, dans la compoſition d'un heros, que quand il n'y auroit autre defaut à reprocher à la femme, ils luy en refuſeroient le nom, pour cela ſeulement, qu'elle n'a pas la vigueur d'un Athlete, et que la molleſſe de ſa complexion l'empeſche de pouvoir durer au travail. Ils n'eſtiment ce Sexe capable d'aucune penſée heroique, dans la creance que l'eſprit ſuit le temperament du corps, et que, dans le corps de la femme, l'eſprit ne peut rien concevoir, qui ne ſe ſente de ſa foibleſſe. — — — Ces Meſſieurs me pardonneront, toutefois, ſi je leur dis qu'ils ne conſiderent pas trop bien quelle eſt la nature de la vertu heroique, qu'ils en definiſſent l'eſſence, par un de ſes moindres accidens, et qu'ils en font plutoſt une vertu brutale, qu'une vertu divine. — — — Ils ſe devroient ſouvenir que cette vertu n'a preſque rien à faire avec le corps, et qu'elle conſiſte, non dans les efforts d'un Milon de Crotone, où l'eſprit n'a aucune part, mais en ceux des ames nées pour les grandes choſes ; quand par une ardeur pluſqu' humaine, elles s'elevent audeſſus d'elles-meſmes ; qu'elles forment quelque deſſein, dont l'utilité eſt auſſi grande que la difficulté, et qu'elles choiſiſſent les moyens de l'executer avec conſtance et hauteur de courage. Pour prevenus qu'ils ſoient en faveurs des hommes, je ne penſe pas qu'ils vouluſſent attribuer à leur ame un ſeul avantage, auquel l'ame de la femme ne puſt aſpirer, ni faire deux eſpeces des deux ſexes, deſquels la raiſon de tous les ſages n'a fait qu'une juſqu'icy—je ne croy pas non plus qu'ils imaginent que les vertus morales ayent leur ſiege ailleurs, que dans la volonté, ou dans l'entendement. Mais ſi elles y ont leur ſiege, et ſi l'on ne peut dire que ces deux facultés ſoient autres, dans l'ame de la femme que dans l'ame de l'homme, ils ne peuvent, ſans abſurdité, accorder une de ces vertus à l'homme, et ne l'accorder pas à la femme. En effet, cette belle penſée d'Ariſtote qui a donné occaſion à leur erreur, eſt ſi peu phyſique, qu'elle fait plus de tort à la philoſophie du Lycée, qu'elle n'appuye l'opinion de ceux que nous combattons." Chapelain then enters into an hiſtorical defence of Female dignity, and oppoſes the authority of Plato to that of Ariſtotle, concerning the propriety of woman's ever appearing on the great theatre of active life. Happy had he ſup-

ported

2

ported the Female caufe as forcibly, in the execution of his poem, as in the arguments of his preface: but Chapelain was unfortunately one of the many examples, which every country affords, that the moft perfect union of virtue and erudition is utterly infufficient to form a Poet; and, as he had the ill fate to be perfecuted by the pitilefs rigour of Boileau, his inharmonious poem can never fink into a defirable oblivion. The treatife of Mambrun feems to have excited, among the French, an eager-nefs to diftinguifh themfelves in the field of Epic poetry; for feveral Epic poems were publifhed in France in a few years after that work appeared; but moft of them, and particularly thofe on fcriptural fub-jects, were hardly ever known to exift.

> Le Jonas inconnu feche dans la pouffiere,
> Le David imprimé n'a point vu la lumiere,
> Le Moïfe commence à moifir par les bords.
>
> BOILEAU, Sat. ix.

The Alaric of Scudery, and the Clovis of Defmarefts, can fcarce be reckoned more fortunate; but in this band of unfuccefsful Epic writers, there was one Poet, of whom even the fevere Boileau could not allow himfelf to fpeak ill; this was Le Moine, the author of St. Louis. The Satirift being afked, why he had never mentioned the poetry of Le Moine? replied with the two following verfes, parodied from Corneille,

> Il s'eft trop élevé pour en dire du mal,
> Il s'eft trop égaré pour en dire du bien.

The judicious and candid Heyne has beftowed confiderable applaufe on Le Moine, in one of his notes to the 6th book of Virgil, where he examines the different methods by which the Epic Poets have introduced their various pictures of futurity. From his account, Le Moine excels in this article. I can fpeak only from the opinion of this learned Critic, for the neglected French Poet is become fo rare, that I have fought in vain for a copy of his work.——The number of obfcure Epic writers in France is very trifling, compared to thofe which Italy has produced; the Italians have been indefatigable in this fpecies of compofition, and, as if they had refolved to leave no Hero unfung, their celebrated Novelift, Giraldi

5   Cinthio,

Cinthio has written an Epic poem, in twenty-six cantos, on the exploits of Hercules.

NOTE XIV. VERSE 304.

Keen Boileau shall not want his proper praise.] Nicolas Boileau Despreaux was born *in* or *near* Paris, for it is a contested point, on the first of November 1636, and died in March 1711 of a dropsy, the very disease which terminated the life of his English rival. The Lutrin of Boileau, still considered by some French Critics of the present time as the best poem to which France has given birth, was first published in 1674. It is with great reason and justice that Voltaire confesses the Lutrin inferior to the Rape of the Lock. Few Poets can be so properly compared as Pope and Boileau; and, wherever their writings will admit of comparison, we may, without any national partiality, adjudge the superiority to the English Bard. These two great authors resembled each other as much in the integrity of their lives, as in the subjects and execution of their several compositions. There are two actions recorded of Boileau, which sufficiently prove that the inexorable Satirist had a most generous and friendly heart; when Patru, the celebrated Advocate, who was ruined by his passion for literature, found himself under the painful necessity of selling his expensive library, and had almost agreed to part with it for a moderate sum, Boileau gave him a much superior price; and, after paying the money, added this condition to the purchase, that Patru should retain, during his life, the possession of the books. The succeeding instance of the Poet's generosity is yet nobler:—when it was rumoured at court that the King intended to retrench the pension of Corneille, Boileau hastened to Madame de Montespan, and said, that his Sovereign, equitable as he was, could not, without injustice, grant a pension to an author like himself, just ascending Parnassus, and take it from Corneille, who had so long been seated on the summit; that he entreated her, for the honour of the King, to prevail on his Majesty rather to strike off *his* pension, than to withdraw that reward from a man whose title to it was incomparably greater; and that he should more easily console himself under the loss of that distinction, than under the affliction of seeing it taken away from such a Poet as Corneille. This magnanimous application had the success which it deserved, and it

O o

appears the more noble, when we recollect that the rival of **Corneille** was the intimate friend of Boileau.

The long and unreserved intercourse which subsisted between our Poet and Racine was highly beneficial and honourable to both. The dying farewell of the latter is the most expressive eulogy on the private character of Boileau : Je regarde comme un bonheur pour moi de mourir avant vous, said the tender Racine, in taking a final leave of his faithful and generous friend.

N O T E XV.   VERSE 313.

Nor, gentle Greffet, shall thy sprightly rhyme.] This elegant and amiable writer was born at Amiens, and educated in the society of the Jesuits, to whom he has paid a grateful compliment in bidding them adieu. At the age of twenty-six he published his Ver-vert, a poem in four cantos, which commemorates

La cause infortunée
D'un Perroquet non moins brillant qu' Enée :
Non moins dévot, plus malheureux que lui.

Voltaire has spoken invidiously of this delightful performance ; but a spirited French Critic has very justly vindicated the merits of Greffet in the following remark :——Le Ver-vert sera toujours un poeme charmant et inimitable, sans souiller sa plume par l'impiété et la licence qui deshonorent celle de l'auteur de *La Pucelle,* le Poete a su y répandre un agrément, une fraîcheur et une vivacité de coloris, qui le rendent aussi piquant dans les détails, qu'il est riche et ingénieux dans la fiction. On placera toujours cet agreable badinage parmi les productions originales, propres à faire aimer des etrangers la gaieté Françoise en écartant toute mauvaise idée de nos mœurs.

N O T E XVI.   VERSE 325.

See lovely Boccage, in ambition strong.] Madame du Boccage is known to the English reader as the correspondent of Lord Chesterfield. This ingenious and spirited Lady has written three poems of the Epic kind—Le Paradis Terrestre, in six cantos, from Milton ; La Mort d'Abel, in five

cantos,

cantos, from Gesner; and a more original composition, in ten cantos, on the exploits of Columbus. I have alluded to a passage in the last poem, where Zama, the daughter of an Indian Chief, is thus described:

Comme Eve, elle etoit nue ; une egale innocence
L'offre aux regards sans honte, et voile ses appas ;
Les Graces qu'elle ignore accompagnent ses pas,
Et pour tout vêtement, en formant sa parure,
D'un plumage azuré couvrirent sa ceinture.

The works of this elegant female Poet contain an animated version of Pope's Temple of Fame. And she has added to her poetry an account of her travels through England, Holland, and Italy, in a series of entertaining letters, addressed to Madame du Perron, her sister.

NOTE XVII. VERSE 344.

To swell the glory of her great Voltaire.] Though the Henriade has been frequently reprinted, and the partizans of Voltaire have endeavoured to make it a national point of honour to support its reputation, it seems at length to be sinking under that neglect and oblivion, which never fail to overtake every feeble offspring of the Epic Muse. Several of our most eminent Critics have attacked this performance with peculiar severity, and some have condemned it on the most opposite principles, merely because it does not coincide with their respective systems. Their sentence has been passed only in short and incidental remarks ; but a French writer, inflamed by personal animosity against Voltaire, has raised three octavo volumes on the defects of this single poem. Mr. Clement, in his " *Entretiens sur le Poeme Epique relativement à la Henriade,*" has endeavoured to prove it utterly deficient in all the essential points of Epic poetry;—in the structure of its general plan, in the conduct of its various parts, in sentiment, in character, in style. His work indeed displays an acrimonious detestation of the Poet whom he examines ; and perhaps there is hardly any human composition which could support the scrutiny of so rigid an inquisitor : the Henriade is utterly unequal to it ; for in many articles we are obliged to confess, that the justice of the Critic is not inferior to his severity. He discovers, in his dissection of the

O o 2   Poem,

Poem, the skill of an anatomist, with the malignity of an assassin. If any thing can deserve such rigorous treatment, it is certainly the artifice of Voltaire, who, in his Essay on Epic Poetry, has attempted, with much ingenuity, to sink the reputation of all the great Epic Writers, that he might raise himself to their level; an attempt in which no author can ultimately succeed; for, as D'Alembert has admirably remarked on a different occasion, Le public laissera l'amour propre de chaque ecrivain faire son plaidoyer, rira de leurs efforts, non de genie, mais de raisonnement, pour hausser leur place, et finira par mettre chacun à la sienne.

NOTE XVIII. VERSE 475.

And, shrouded in a mist of moral spleen.] It seems to be the peculiar infelicity of Pope, that his moral virtues have had a tendency to diminish his poetical reputation. Possessing a benevolent spirit, and wishing to make the art, to which he devoted his life, as serviceable as he could to the great interests of mankind, he soon quitted the higher regions of poetry, for the more level, and more frequented field of Ethics and of Satire. He declares, with a noble pride arising from the probity of his intention,

> That not in Fancy's maze he wander'd long,
> But stoop'd to truth, and moraliz'd his song.

The severity of Criticism has from hence inferred, that his imagination was inferior to the other faculties of his mind, and that he possessed not that vigour of genius which might enable him to rank with our more sublime and pathetic Bards. This inference appears to me extremely defective both in candour and in reason; it would surely be more generous, and I will venture to add, more just, to assign very different causes for his having latterly applied himself to moral and satyric composition. If his preceding poems displayed only a moderate portion of fancy and of tenderness, we might indeed very fairly conjecture, that he quitted the kind of poetry, where these qualities are particularly required, because Nature directed him to shine only as the Poet of reason.—But his earlier productions will authorize an opposite conclusion. At an age when few authors have produced any capital work, Pope gave the world two poems,

one

one the offspring of imagination, and the other of sensibility, which will ever stand at the head of the two poetical classes to which they belong : his Rape of the Lock, and his Eloise, have nothing to fear from any rivals, either of past or of future time. When a writer has displayed such early proofs of exquisite fancy, and of tender enthusiasm, those great constituents of the real Poet, ought we not to regret that he did not give a greater scope and freer exercise to these qualities, rather than to assert that he did not possess them in a superlative degree ? Why then, it may be asked, did he confine himself to compositions in which these have little share ? The life and character of Pope will perfectly explain the reasons, why he did not always follow the higher suggestions of his own natural genius. He had entertained an opinion, that by stooping to truth, and employing his talents on the vices and follies of the passing time, he should be most able to benefit mankind. The idea was perhaps ill-founded, but his conduct in consequence of it was certainly noble. Its effects however were most unhappy ; for it took from him all his enjoyment of life, and may injure, in some degree, his immortal reputation : by suffering his thoughts to dwell too much on knaves and fools, he fell into the splenetic delusion, that the world is nothing but a compound of vice and folly ; and from hence he has been reproached for supposing that all human merit was confined to himself, and to a few of his most intimate correspondents.

There was an amiable peculiarity in the character of Pope, which had great influence both on his conduct and composition—he embraced the sentiments of those he loved with a kind of superstitious regard ; his imagination and his judgment were perpetually the dupes of an affectionate heart : it was this which led him, at the request of his idol Bolingbroke, to write a sublime poem on metaphysical ideas which he did not perfectly comprehend ; it was this which urged him almost to quarrel with Mr. Allen, in compliance with the caprices of a female friend ; it was this which induced him, in the warmth of gratitude, to follow the absurd hints of Warburton with all the blindness of infatuated affection. Whoever examines the life and writings of Pope with a minute and unprejudiced attention, will find that his excellencies, both as a Poet and a Man, were peculiarly his own ; and that his failings were chiefly owing to the ill judgment, or the artifice, of his real and pre-

tended

tended friends. The lavish applause and the advice of his favourite Atterbury, were perhaps the cause of his preserving the famous character of Addison, which, finely written as it is, all the lovers of Pope must wish him to have suppressed. Few of his friends had integrity or frank-nefs sufficient to persuade him, that his satires would destroy the tran-quillity of his life, and cloud the luftre of his fame : yet, to the honour of Lyttelton, be it remembered, that he suggested such ideas to the Poet, in the verfes which he wrote to him from Rome, with all the becoming zeal of enlightened friendfhip:

> No more let meaner Satire dim the rays
> That flow majeftic from thy nobler bays !
> In all the flowery paths of Pindus ftray,
> But fhun that thorny, that unpleafing way !
> Nor, when each foft, engaging Mufe is thine,
> Addrefs the leaft attractive of the Nine !

This generous admonition did not indeed produce its intended effect, for other counfellors had given a different bias to the mind of the Poet, and the malignity of his enemies had exafperated his temper ; yet he af-terwards turned his thoughts towards the compofition of a national-Epic poem, and poflibly in confequence of the hint which this Epiftle of Lyt-telton contains. The intention was formed too late, for it arofe in his decline of life. Had he poffeffed health and leifure to execute fuch a work, I am perfuaded it would have proved a glorious acquifition to the literature of our country : the fubject indeed which he had chofen muft be allowed to have an unpromifing appearance ; but the opinion of Addi-fon concerning his Sylphs, which was furely honeft, and not invidious, may teach us hardly ever to decide againft the intended works of a fu-perior genius. Yet in all the Arts, we are perpetually tempted to pro-nounce fuch decifions. I have frequently condemned fubjects which my friend Romney had felected for the pencil ; but in the fequel, my opinion only proved that I was near-fighted in thofe regions of imagina-tion, where his keener eyes commanded all the profpect.

NOTES

===========

N O T E S

T O T H E

F O U R T H E P I S T L E.

N O T E I. Verse 103.

PROCEED, ye Sifters of the tuneful Shell.] For the advice which I
have thus ventured to give fuch of my fair readers as have a talent for
poetry, I fhall produce them a much higher poetical authority. In the
age of Petrarch, an Italian Lady, named Giuflina Perrot, was defirous
of diftinguifhing herfelf by this pleafing accomplifhment; but the remarks
of the world, which reprefented it as improper for her fex, difcouraged
her fo far, that fhe was almoft tempted to relinquifh her favourite purfuit. In her doubts on this point, fhe confulted the celebrated Poet of
her country in an elegant Sonnet; and received his anfwer on the interefting fubject in the fame poetical form. I fhall add the two Sonnets,
with an imitation of each.

PO

IO vorrei pur drizzar quefte mie piume
    Colà, Signor, dove il defio n'invita,
E dopo morte rimaner' in vita
Col chiaro di virtute inclyto lume:
Ma' volgo inerte, che dal rio coftume
Vinto, ha d'ogni fuo ben la via fmarrita,
Come degna di biafmo ogn' hor m'addita
Ch'ir tenti d'Elicona al facro fiume.
All ago, al fufo, piu ch'al lauro, o al mirto,
Come che qui non fia la gloria mia,
Vuol ch'habbia fempre quefta mente intefa.
Dimmi tu hormai, che per piu dritta via
A Parnaffo t'en vai, nobile fpirto,
Dovrò dunque lafciar fi degna imprefa?

LA gola, e 'l fonno, e l'oziofe piume
    Hanno del mondo ogni virtù fbandita,
Ond' è dal corfo fuo quafi fmarrita
Noftra natura vinta dal coftume:
Ed è fi fpento ogni benigno lume
Del ciel, per cui s'informa umana vita,
Che per cofa mirabile s'addita
Chi vuol far d'Elicona nafcer fiume.
Qual vaghezza di lauro, qual di mirto?
Povera e nuda vai filofofia,
Dice la turba al vil guadagno intefa.
Pochi compagni avrai per l'altra via;
Tanto ti prego più, gentile fpirto,
Non lafciar la magnanima tua imprefa!

THE

THE SONNET OF GIUSTINA TO PETRARCH.

GLADLY would I exchange inglorious eafe
    For future fame, the Poet's fond defire!
And ftill to live, in fpite of death, afpire
By Virtue's light, that darknefs cannot feize:
But, ftupified by Cuftom's blank decrees,
The idle vulgar, void of liberal fire,
Bid me, with fcorn, from Helicon retire,
And rudely blame my generous hope to pleafe.
Diftaffs, not laurels, to your fex belong,
They cry—as honour were beyond our view:
To fuch low cares they wifh my fpirit bent.
Say thou! who marcheft, 'mid the favor'd few,
To high Parnaffus, with triumphant fong,
Should I abandon fuch a fair intent?

THE ANSWER OF PETRARCH.

LUXURIOUS pleafure, and lethargic eafe
    Have deaden'd in the world each bright defire:
Our thoughts no more with Nature's force afpire;
Cuftom's cold powers the drooping fancy feize:
So loft each light that taught the foul to pleafe,
Each heavenly fpark of life-directing fire,
That all, who join the Heliconian choir,
Are frantic deem'd by Folly's dull decrees.
What charms, what worth to Laurel-wreaths belong?
Naked and poor Philofophy we view,
Exclaims the crowd, on fordid gain intent.—
Affociates in thy path thou'lt find but few;
The more, I pray thee, Nymph of graceful fong,
Indulge thy fpirit in its noble bent!

N O T E II. Verse 210.

As wounded Learning blushes to recite!] Milton fold the copy of Paradife Loft for the fum of five pounds, on the condition of receiving fifteen
pounds more at three fubfequent periods, to be regulated by the fale of
the Poem.—For the ceiling at Whitehall, Rubens received three thoufand pounds.

N O T E III. Verse 298.

Receive the Laurel from Imperial Charles!] Ariofto is faid to have been
publicly crowned with laurel at Mantua, by the Emperor Charles the
Vth, towards the end of the year 1532. This fact has been difputed by
various writers, but it feems to be fufficiently eftablifhed by the refearches
of Mazzuchelli.

The cuftom of crowning Poets with laurel is almoft as ancient as poetry
itfelf, fays the Abbé du Refnel, in his Recherches fur les Poetes couron-
nez, a work which contains but fcanty information on this curious topic.
Petrarch is generally fuppofed to have revived this ancient folemnity,
which had been abolifhed as a pagan inftitution in the reign of the Emperor Theodofius. It appears however, from two paffages in the writings
of Boccacio, that Dante had entertained ferious thoughts of this honourable diftinction, which his exile precluded him from receiving, as he
chofe, fays his Biographer, to be crown'd only in his native city.

An amufing volume might be written on the honours which have been
paid to Poets in different ages, and in various parts of the world. It is
remarkable, that the moft unpolifhed nations have been the moft lavifh in
rewarding their Bards. There are two inftances on record, in which poetical talents have raifed their poffeffors even to fovereign dominion. The
Scythians chofe the Poet Thamyris for their king, though he was not a
native of their country, επι τοσετον γαε κιθαρωδιας, ως και βασιλεα σφων, καιπερ
επηλυτον οντα, Σκυθας ποιησασθαι. Hift. Poet. Script. Edit. Gale, p. 250.
Saxo Grammaticus begins the fixth book of his Hiftory by relating, that
the Danes beftowed their vacant diadem on the Poet Hiarnus, as a reward
for his having compofed the beft epitaph on their deceafed fovereign Fro-
the. From the four Latin verfes which the Hiftorian has given us, as a

tranflation

tranflation of this extraordinary epitaph, we may venture to affirm, that the poetical monarch obtain'd his crown on very eafy conditions.

NOTE IV. VERSE 314.

For him her fountains gufh with golden ftreams.] Of the great wealth which flowed into the hands of this extraordinary Poet, his friend and biographer Montalvan has given a particular account. This author concludes that Lope de Vega gained by his dramatic works alone a fum nearly equal to 20,000 pounds fterling; the revenue arifing from the pofts he held, and from his penfion, was very confiderable. His opulence was much encreafed by the moft fplendid inftances of private liberality. He received many coftly prefents from various characters to whom he was perfonally unknown; and he was himfelf heard to fay, in fpeaking of his generous patron, that the Duke of Seffa alone had given him, at different periods of his life, fums almoft amounting to fix thoufand pounds.

It muft be confeffed, that the noble patrons of Englifh poetry have not equalled this example of Spanifh munificence, even if we admit the truth of our traditionary anecdotes concerning the generofity of Lord Southampton to Shakefpeare, and of Sir Philip Sidney to Spenfer. Confidering the liberality for which our nation is fo juftly celebrated, it is remarkable, that not a fingle Englifh Poet appears to have been enriched by our monarchs: yet Spenfer had every claim to the bounty of Elizabeth; he fung her praifes in a ftrain which might gratify her pride; and of all who have flattered the great, he may juftly be confidered as the moft worthy of reward. His fong was the tribute of his heart as well as of his fancy, and the fex of his idol may be faid to purify his incenfe from all the offenfive particles of fervile adulation. The neglect which he experienced from the vain, imperious, and ungrateful Elizabeth, appears the more ftriking, when we recollect, that her lovely rival, the beautiful and unfortunate Queen of Scots, fignalized her fuperior generofity by a magnificent prefent of plate to the French Poet Ronfard. This neglected Bard was once the darling of France, and perhaps equalled Lope de Vega in the honours which he received: his fovereign, Charles the Ninth, compofed fome elegant verfes in his praife, and the city of Touloufe prefented him with a Minerva of maffive filver.

If

If our princes and nobles have not equalled thofe of other kingdoms in liberality to the great Poets of their country, England may yet boaft the name of a private gentleman, who difcovered in this refpect a moft princely fpirit ; no nation, either ancient or modern, can produce an example of munificence more truly noble than the annual gratuity which Akenfide received from Mr. Dyfon ; a tribute of generous and affectionate admiration, endeared to its worthy poffeffor by every confideration which could make it honourable both to himfelf and to his patron !

It has been lately lamented by an elegant and accomplifhed writer, who had too much reafon for the complaint, that " the profeffion " of Literature, by far the moft laborious of any, leads to no real be- " nefit." Experience undoubtedly proves, that it has a general tendency to impoverifh its votaries ; and the legiflators of every country would act perhaps a wife, at all events an honourable part, if they corrected this tendency, by eftablifhing public emoluments for fuch as eminently diftinguifh themfelves in the various branches of fcience. It is furely poffible to form fuch an eftablifhment, which, without proving a national burthen, might aggrandize the literary glory of the nation, by preferving her men of letters from the evils fo frequently connected with their purfuits, by fecuring, to thofe who deferve it, the poffeffion of eafe and honour, without damping their emulation, or deftroying their independence.

N O T E S

N O T E S

TO THE

FIFTH EPISTLE.

NOTE I. VERSE 76.

THE loose Petronius gave the maxim birth.] Ariftotle has faid but little, in his Poetics, concerning that weighty point, which has fo much employed and embarraffed the modern Critics—the machinery of the Epic poem; and the little which he has faid might rather furnifh an argument for its exclufion, than juftify its ufe. But Rome, in her moft degenerate days, produced a writer, to whofe authority, contemptible as it is, moft frequent appeals have been made in this curious literary queftion. In almoft every modern author who has touched, however flightly, on Epic poetry, we may find at leaft fome part of the following fentence from Petronius Arbiter : — Ecce, belli civilis ingens opus quifquis attigerit, nifi plenus litteris, fub onere labetur. Non enim res geftæ verfibus comprehendendæ funt, quod longe melius hiftorici faciunt; fed per ambages, deorumque minifteria, & fabulofum fententiarum tormentum præcipitandus eft liber fpiritus; ut potius furentis animi vaticinatio appareat, quam religiofæ orationis fub teftibus fides.

These remarks on the neceffity of celeftial agents, were evidently made to depreciate the Pharfalia of Lucan; and Petronius may be called a fair Critic, as Pope faid of Milbourne, on his oppofition to Dryden, becaufe he produces his own poetry in contraft to that which he condemns. His fpecimen of the manner in which he thought an Epic poem fhould be conducted, fufficiently proves the abfurdity of his criticifm;

ticifm; for how infipid is the fable in thofe verfes which he has oppofed to the Pharfalia, when compared to the firft book of Lucan! Yet the Epic compofition of Petronius has not wanted admirers: a Dutch Commentator is bold enough to fay, that he prefers this fingle rhapfody to three hundred volumes of fuch poetry as Lucan's: an opinion which can only lead us to exclaim with Boileau,

Un fot trouve toujours un plus fot qui l'admire.

If men of letters, in the age of Lucan, differed in their fentiments concerning machinery, the great changes that have fince happened in the world, and the difquifitions which have appeared on the fubject, are very far from having reconciled the judgment of modern writers on this important article. Two eminent Critics of the prefent time have delivered opinions on this topic fo fingularly oppofite to each other, that I fhall tranfcribe them both.

" In a theatrical entertainment, which employs both the eye and the
" ear, it would be a grofs abfurdity to introduce upon the ftage fuperior
" Beings in a vifible fhape. There is not place for fuch objection in an
" Epic poem; and Boileau, with many other Critics, declares ftrongly
" for that fort of machinery in an Epic poem. But waving authority,
" which is apt to impofe upon the judgment, let us draw what light we
" can from reafon. I begin with a preliminary remark, that this mat-
" ter is but indiftinctly handled by Critics. The poetical privilege of
" animating infenfible objects for enlivening a defcription, is very differ-
" ent from what is termed *machinery*, where deities, angels, devils, or
" other fupernatural powers, are introduced as real perfonages, mixing
" in the action, and contributing to the cataftrophe; and yet thefe two
" things are conftantly jumbled together in the reafoning. The former
" is founded on a natural principle; but can the latter claim the fame
" authority? So far from it, that nothing is more unnatural. Its
" effects at the fame time are deplorable. Firft, it gives an air of
" fiction to the whole, and prevents that impreffion of reality which is
" requifite to intereft our affections, and to move our paffions; which
" of itfelf is fufficient to explode machinery, whatever entertainment it
" may afford to readers of a fantaftic tafte or irregular imagination.
" And

" And next, were it poffible, by difguifing the fiction, to delude us into
" a notion of reality, which I think can hardly be, an infuperable objec-
" tion would ftill remain, which is, that the aim or end of an Epic
" poem can never be attained in any perfection where machinery is in-
" troduced ; for an evident reafon, that virtuous emotions cannot be
" raifed fuccefsfully, but by the actions of thofe who are endued with
" paffions and affections like our own, that is, by human actions : and
" as for moral inftruction, it is clear that none can be drawn from
" Beings who act not upon the fame principles with us. Homer, it is
" true, introduces the Gods into his fable ; but the religion of his coun-
" try authorized that liberty ; it being an article in the Grecian creed,
" that the Gods often interpofe vifibly and bodily in human affairs. I
" muft, however, obferve, that Homer's Deities do no honour to his
" poems. Fictions that tranfgrefs the bounds of nature feldom have a
" good effect ; they may inflame the imagination for a moment, but
" will not be relifhed by any perfon of a correct tafte. They may be of
" fome ufe to the lower rank of writers ; but an author of genius has
" much finer materials of nature's production for elevating his fubject,
" and making it interefting.——Voltaire, in his Effay upon Epic Poetry,
" talking of the Pharfalia, obferves judicioufly, that the proximity of
" time, the notoriety of events, the character of the age, enlightened and
" political, joined with the folidity of Lucan's fubject, deprived him of
" all liberty of poetical fiction. Is it not amazing, that a Critic who
" reafons fo juftly with refpect to others, can be fo blind with refpect to
" himfelf ? Voltaire, not fatisfied to enrich his language with images
" drawn from invifible and fuperior Beings, introduces them into the
" action. In the fixth canto of the Henriade, St. Louis appears in
" perfon, and terrifies the foldiers ; in the feventh canto, St. Louis
" fends the God of Sleep to Henry ; and in the tenth, the demons of
" Difcord, Fanaticifm, War, &c. affift Aumale in a fingle combat with
" Turenne, and are driven away by a good angel brandifhing the fword
" of God. To blend fuch fictitious perfonages in the fame action with
" mortals, makes a bad figure at any rate, and is intolerable in a hiftory
" fo recent as that of Henry IV. This fingly is fufficient to make the
" Henriade a fhort-lived poem, were it otherwife poffeffed of every
" beauty." *Elements of Criticism*, vol. ii. p. 389, 4th edition.

10 " The

" The Pagan Gods and Gothic Fairies were equally out of credit when
" Milton wrote. He did well therefore to fupply their room with An-
" gels and Devils. If thefe too fhould wear out of the popular creed (and
" they feem in a hopeful way, from the liberty fome late Critics have
" taken with them) I know not what other expedients the Epic Poet
" might have recourfe to; but this I know—the pomp of verfe, the
" energy of defcription, and even the fineft moral paintings, would ftand
" him in no ftead. Without *admiration* (which cannot be effected but
" by the marvellous of celeftial intervention, I mean the agency of fu-
" perior natures really exifting, or by the illufion of the fancy taken to
" be fo) no Epic poem can be long-lived. I am not afraid to inftance in
" the Henriade itfelf, which, notwithftanding the elegance of the com-
" pofition, will in a fhort time be no more read than the Gondibert of
" Sir W. Davenant, and for the fame reafon."

Letters on Chivalry and Romance, Letter X.

I have thus ventured to confront thefe eminent critical antagonifts,
that, while they engage and overthrow each other, we may obferve the
injuftice produced by the fpirit of fyftematical criticifm, even in authors
moft refpectable for their talents and erudition.—Here is the unfortunate
Voltaire placed between two critical fires, which equally deftroy him.
The *firft* Critic afferts that the Henriade muft be fhort-lived, becaufe
the Poet *has introduced invifible and fuperior agents* ;—the *fecond* denounces
the fame fate againft it, becaufe *it wants* the *agency of fuperior natures:*
yet furely every reader of poetry, who is not influenced by any particular
fyftem, will readily allow, that if Voltaire had treated his fubject with
true Epic fpirit in all other points, neither the introduction nor the
abfence of St. Louis could be fingly fufficient to plunge the Henriade in
oblivion. Indeed the learned author, who has fpoken in fo peremptory
a manner concerning the neceffity of fupernatural agents to preferve the
exiftence of an Epic poem, appears rather unfortunate in the two examples by which he endeavours to fupport his doctrine; for the Epic
poems both of Davenant and Voltaire have fufficient defects to account
for any neglect which may be their lot, without confidering the article
of Machinery.

If I have warmly oppofed any decifions of this exalted Critic, it is
from

from a perfuafion (in which I may perhaps be miftaken) that *fome* of his maxims have a ftrong tendency to injure an art highly dear to us both ; an art on which his genius and learning have caft *many* rays of pleafing and of ufeful light.

NOTE II. VERSE 166.

But howling dogs the fancied Orpheus tore.] This anecdote of Neanthus, the fon of King Pittacus, is related by Lucian. The curious reader may find it in the fecond volume of Dr. Francklin's fpirited tranflation of that lively author, page 355 of the quarto edition.

NOTE III. VERSE 276.

And fpotlefs Laurels in that field be won.] The Indian mythology, as it has lately been illuftrated in the writings of Mr. Holwell, is finely calculated to anfwer the purpofe of any poetical genius who may wifh to introduce new machinery into the ferious Epic Poem. Befides the powerful charm of novelty, it would have the advantage of not clafhing with our national religion ; for the endeavours of Mr. Holwell to reconcile the ancient and pure doctrine of Bramah with the difpenfation of Chrift, have fo far fuccecded, that if his fyftem does not fatisfy a theologift, it certainly affords a fufficient bafis for the ftructure of a Poet. In perufing his account of the Indian fcripture, every reader of imagination may, I think, perceive, that the Shaftah might fupply a poetical fpirit with as rich a mafs of ideal treafure as fancy could wifh to work upon.—An Epic Poet, defirous of laying the fcene of his action in India, would be more embarraffed to find interefting Heroes than proper Divinities.—Had juftice and generofity infpired and guided that Englifh valour, which has fignalized itfelf on the plains of Indoftan ; had the arms of our country been employed to deliver the native Indians from the oppreffive ufurpation of the Mahometan powers ; fuch exploits would prefent to the Epic Mufe a fubject truly noble, and the mythology of the Eaft might enrich it with the moft fplendid decorations. Whether it be poffible or not to find fuch a fubject in the records of our Indian hiftory, I leave the reader to determine.—Our great Hiftorian of the Roman empire has intimated, in a note to the firft volume of his immortal work, that " the wonderful expedition of Odin, which deduces

" the

" the enmity of the Goths and Romans from fo memorable a caufe, might
" fupply the noble ground-work of an Epic poem."   The idea is certainly both juft and fplendid.   Had Gray been ever tempted to engage
in fuch a work, he would probably have convinced us, that the Northern
mythology has ftill fufficient power to feize and enchant the imagination, as much in Epic as in Lyric compofition.

It may amufe our fpeculative Critics, to confider how far the *religious
Gothic fables* fhould be introduced or rejected, to render fuch a performance moft interefting to a modern reader.   Few judges would agree
in their fentiments on the queftion ; and perhaps the great difpute concerning Machinery cannot be fairly adjufted, till fome happy genius fhall
poffefs ambition and perfeverance enough to execute two Epic poems,
in the one adopting, and in the other rejecting, fupernatural agents ; for
Reafon alone is by no means an infallible conductor in the province of
Fancy ; and in the poetical as well as the philofophical world, experiment is the fureft guide to truth.

F I N I S.

ERRATA.

EPISTLE II.

Ver.   3, for *where* read *whence*
—— 282, for *Critic* read *Critics*

EPISTLE IV.

Ver. 356, for *keep* read *heap.*
Ver. 372, at the end of the line insert a mark of Interrogation.

ERRATA IN THE NOTES.

Page 133, line 3, for *wore* read *bore*
—— 191, — 10, for *Ninus* read *Nisus*
—— 201, — 8, for *neglio* read *meglio* — for *giudicio* read *giudicio*
—— 208, — 28, for *Aranco* read *Arauco*; and line ult. for *Arancunians* read *Araucanian.*
—— 217, &c. for *Lincoxa* read *Linceya*
—— 223, line 20, for *Lantaro* read *Lautaro.*—The Reader is desired to correct this name in
     different pages, as it is repeatedly misprinted.
—— 286, line 2, for *was* read *were*